FRIENDS, BROTHERS, AND INFORMANTS

FRIENDS, BROTHERS, AND INFORMANTS

Fieldwork Memoirs
of Banaras

NITA KUMAR

University of California Press
Berkeley · Los Angeles · Oxford

University of California Press
Berkeley and Los Angeles, California

University of California Press, Ltd.
Oxford, England

©1992 by
The Regents of the University of California

Library of Congress Cataloging-in-Publication Data

Kumar, Nita, 1951–
    Friends, brothers, and informants : fieldwork memoirs of Banaras /
Nita Kumar.
        p.   cm.
    Includes bibliographical references and index.
    ISBN 0–520–07138–7 (alk. paper). — ISBN 0–520–07139–5 (pbk.: alk.
paper)
    1. Kumar, Nita, 1951–   —Diaries. 2. Ethnologists—India—
Vārānasi—Diaries. 3. Ethnology—India—Vārānasi—Fieldwork.
4. Vārānasi (India)—Social life and customs.   I. Title.
GN21.K86A3   1992
305.8′00954′2—dc20   91–33815
                                                                                              CIP

Printed in the United States of America

9   8   7   6   5   4   3   2   1

For
Som
with me every step of the way

Contents

Part Four

Acknowledgments

It is difficult to thank here all those whose influence left a mark on this rather personal book, and I can only mention some of them. I would like to express my gratitude to the following:

First, my teachers, who consistently encouraged me in my writing in school, particularly S. M. Lucy; and those who taught me anthropology much later, chiefly Barny Cohn and Kim Marriott.

My father, Naresh Kumar, who first conveyed to me that there was a viable realm of the imagination; and my mother, Suniti Kumar, for her great faith in me.

My brother, Sunil Kumar, and my husband, Som Majumdar, both of whom declared my private writings of no public interest, twenty and ten years ago respectively, thus presenting the necessary challenge to an essentially lazy person.

My daughters, the two Nandinis, Irfana and Saraswati, so unutterably Mine and yet so Other.

My colleagues who took the trouble to read the manuscript with care: Komilla Raote, Ako Nakano, Ann Gold, Johnny Parry; and especially Eileen and Gaylord Haas, but for both of whom I would not have continued.

Those in Banaras who served so well in various capacities: Lilavati, Shanti, Basmati, Markande, and Nagendra; and the "people of Banaras," my alter ego of sorts.

And finally, recognizing how the spirit must be sustained at the first instance, the American Institute of Indian Studies and the Social Science Research Council, and the wonderful editors at the University of California Press.

Nita Kumar
Banaras

Note on Transliteration

Almost all Hindi, Urdu, and Bhojpuri words are translated when they first appear, unless their meaning is sufficiently clear from the text (e.g., "my brother, Majid *bhai*"). The glossary provides both diacritics and definitions except for those words used only once and adequately explained in the text.

The glossary uses a very simplified form of transliteration: *ā* and *ī* signify the long vowels (as in *far* and *machine*); *ṭ* is the hard *t* (as in *tap*), as distinguished from the soft *t* (as in French *table*); *ḍ* is the hard *d* (as in *dog*), distinct from the soft *d* (as *th* in *father*); *ṛ* is the retroflex *r*, often transliterated by scholars as *d*, but in Indian English as *r*, as in *sari, akhara* (*sārī, akhāṛā*).

Finally, I would like to address two kinds of readers. To those more particular about transliteration, I would explain that because this is not a formal academic work, I felt a simplification appropriate for my purposes. To those who feel overburdened by the use of non-English words, I would offer the reminder that they *are* reading about India. As someone who has confronted not only words but long quotations in European languages when reading Western social science, I felt my use of Indian terms was required to give a flavor of my subject.

The name I use for the city of my research, Banaras, is popular with residents, but is one of at least three frequently used names. Varanasi is the official name of the city, and Kashi the older name, used in a religious and cultural context today.

Introduction

From July 1981 to April 1983, I kept a diary in the field, making entries whenever loneliness and frustration seemed to reach a peak, or I was consumed by self-pity at the hopelessness of my task, or less often, when I simply wanted to express myself about something remarkable, or rarer still, to exult in a special triumph. I should add that scribbling is a habit for me—diary-like, essay-like scribbling—but one which constitutes an end in itself. To make it public needs some justification. I harbor an academic bias against the tendency toward "vulgarization," the notion that a personal experience can be elevated to the status of a universal one. I am usually suspicious of others' impulses to confide, whether as autobiography, as thinly disguised fiction, as sentimental journalism, or as reflections on one's work. Yet what I have produced here are memoirs, and I am not too distressed by them (if they are considered readable, perhaps even amusing) because as I surveyed the diaries from which they were compiled, I realized that they were not so much about "me" as about "fieldwork," that brash, awkward, hit-and-run encounter of one sensibility with others.

The purpose of these memoirs is to describe the process of fieldwork, not as a philosophic experience, with afterthought, but as a practical experience, in all its rawness and candor. There is afterthought, to be sure, in that I have arranged my observations into chapters, provided headings, and peppered them with comments—very few, everything said and done, because I am impressed at how far I have come since then. But I have refrained from rewriting and crafting a fresh narrative that explains in retrospect the complexities of the encounter between Self and Other. My purpose is served by leaving my story as it stands: a narrative that objectifies the fieldworker by focusing on the initial shock of realization that the encounter is a sensitive, creative process calling into play latent, unacknowledged facets of personality as well as more deliberately cultivated professional talents, and that in this difficult process the researcher is surprisingly unprepared.

How much more I would have liked to know on exactly this subject back in 1981: that there was something inevitable about my feelings of intimidation and excitement, ignorance and confidence, and later, alienation and infatuation; that fieldwork is by its very nature an ambitious, optimistic, very personal effort to woo over indifferent strangers through a series of bumbling steps. Like every other graduate student about to hurtle off to the field, I had been educated in many good theories and methodological perspectives and was adept at analyzing the accepted masterpieces. But that primary phase of ethnography called fieldwork had not been part of the curriculum, largely because it was considered something incommunicable. Like others in the same situation, I had a mental image of fieldwork that derived chiefly from half-secret incursions into the prefaces and introductions of contemporary ethnographies; for the rest, my seniors and teachers assured me that "it would work out," as it did for everyone, that I would know magically what to do once I got into the field, that nothing could be fixed or laid down in advance.

They were only partially correct. Now, after ten years of fieldwork, if someone were to ask me exactly how to go about it I would probably give the same answer that my colleagues gave me in 1981, namely, that it depends on who you are, where you go, and how you choose to deal with what you encounter. But I would also recommend that the potential fieldworker read up on the subject and be prepared to be unprepared. Fortunately, there are volumes available now that had not been produced in 1981. I am not referring to fieldwork manuals with chapters on questionnaires, using a recorder, and so forth—though they are valuable as well[1]—but rather to the genre of self-questioning, reflexive anthropology that seeks a better understanding of every step in cultural studies. My memoir joins this genre and attempts to dissect *one* stage of ethnography, fieldwork.

Every experience is unique. Some anthropologists report that their fieldwork has not been difficult at all—or that the difficulties have not been significant enough to remember or comment on. I would say that in most such cases time has erased etchings that were once much sharper. There are three excellent reasons why fieldwork experience is worth sharing.

First, the "person-specific" nature of fieldwork, to use Geertz's phrase, the "highly situated nature of ethnographic description—this ethnographer, in this time, in this place, with these informants, these commitments, and these experiences, a representative of a particular culture, a member of a certain class"—needs as much elaboration as ethnographers have the time, patience, and talent to give.[2] The trend of publishing "reflections on fieldwork" is clearly emerging in anthropology. I am calling for an extension of the genre called by that name.[3] The important books and articles on "reflexive anthropology" published in the past two decades, particularly in the 1980s, are still rare enough to barely cause ripples on a deceptively smooth surface. As these works remind us, anthropologists have always warned about subjectivity and have offered ways to control it, but these reflections are overshadowed by the sheer monumentality of the edifice they have created. My point is simple: the ethnography is the goal, of course, but when so much of what comprises this final product is directly related to the situation of the

1. Bruce Jackson, *Fieldwork* (Champaign: University of Illinois Press, 1987).
2. Clifford Geertz, *Works and Lives: The Anthropologist as Author* (Stanford: Stanford University Press, 1988), p. 6.
3. Paul Rabinow, *Reflections on Fieldwork in Morocco* (Berkeley and Los Angeles: University of California Press, 1977).

investigator, it should no longer be regarded as narcissism or a waste of intellectual and publishing resources (both positions which I have taken in the past), to dwell on that aspect of the discipline more directly. Although sophisticated deconstructions of both the fieldwork and the writing process exist, we lack sufficient *actual records*, the meat to sink our teeth into.

Second, fieldwork memoirs are worth sharing because of the very uniqueness and diversity of researchers, a point not sufficiently acknowledged. Patterns can be identified: the Lone Ethnographer,[4] riding off into the sunset, nostalgic for the pure and unspoiled while himself "innocently" contributing to the despoliation of that which he seeks. I can readily identify another: the Solicitous Indigene, uprooted from her birthplace, yet inevitably and gratefully one with it at various unexpected levels. As long as there is the West on the one hand, and "natives," "ethnics," and "indigenous people" on the other, she is one of the latter, and her developing understanding of her subjects therefore is much more crucial to her self-definition than to that of the Lone Ethnographer, who has his adventure and departs.

All the literature I have perused so far on the question of the anthropological encounter unreservedly portrays it as one culture's clash with another, or by a similar, if less violent, metaphor: one culture, the people's, is translated for, is made comprehensible to, is heard by, another, the scholar's. The notion that the studied culture is static, traditional, homogeneous, and so on—a notion that derives, it seems, from anthropology's unwitting collusion with colonialism—has been quite successfully challenged by the most astute recent writing on the subject. Now that we are clearly in a "post-colonial" world, "it is ever more difficult to predict who will put on the loincloth and who will pick up the pencil and paper."[5]

4. Renato Rosaldo, *Culture and Truth: The Remaking of Social Analysis* (New York: Beacon Press, 1989).
5. Ibid., p. 45.

I would like to make the record clear here: a cultural encounter can and does also take place between *classes*, and the difference making, conflict, domination, and objectification that go on within "a" culture are as resounding as those between "a" culture and "an" other. As an "ethnic," I have long been uncomfortable with "ethno"-sociology and "ethno"-musicology, and all those unreflective linguistic habits that blur spatial and temporal distinctions in the Third World. For example, some refuse to recognize that even in ethnic-land there are classical belief systems as well as popular belief systems. Now that the "Third World" has "imploded into the metropolis,"[6] the West is again adopting a posture of domination through excessive penitence about underrating and underrespecting the dynamics of this Third World. At both moments, the colonized are being treated as *One*.

The issue of colonialism is being simplified and made all-inclusive, because if the problem is or has been colonialism, it is unlikely to disappear through self-reflection or self-flagellation, or anything short of a new world order. But if the problem belongs rather, as I see it, to the terrain of the discipline itself, in its solipsism regarding class, its overdetermined notion of culture, and its ahistorical stance toward everything, including its own past and present, then much can be achieved through self-reflection. These seemingly new writings by Third Worlders need to be incorporated into the body of texts meant to educate students in a universalist mode. And more social scientists like me need to speak about our discomfort regarding this polarization of the world into (ex-) colonizers and colonized, as if these categories always took precedence over all others. We can then look forward to a state of knowledge where every American who read a book like this would not necessarily remark (as did all the American readers of this manuscript): "I didn't know Indians could feel so outside in their own country."

If the equation is simply (Western) anthropologist dominating (Third World) subject, it can be demonstrated as

6. Ibid., p. 44.

faulty in a minute. No one could deny that enough domination, objectification, and simplification can be practiced by an (Eastern) anthropologist studying a (Third World) subject or even a (Western) subject. The weight of historical experience is on the first of these three possible relationships, of course. But having struggled in the field and kept a diary out of frustration and pleasure, I returned to find in the following years that this burgeoning field of reflective, deconstructionist studies excluded me (yet again) by posing West against East. So I naturally ask: What about *within* the East or the Third World, class against class, subculture against subculture, one kind of historical sensibility against another? And what about other equally potent problems of defining subject and method? the personal problems of sheer adjustment? To continue the borrowed image: not only the *ethnographies* but also some of the reflections on them are being produced more and more by those in loincloth. In both genres there are similarities and differences worth noting between the Lone Ethnographer of the West and the Solicitous Indigene of the Third World.

We have to strike a careful balance between these similarities and differences. A native like me, privileged, alien, discovering her other-ness and her one-ness simultaneously, remains nevertheless the anthropologist and scholar, one who inevitably undergoes the usual trials and tribulations of fieldwork. This introduction, on the one hand, will be attractive to those interested in "identity formation," particularly in the Third World as opposed to the postmodern West. The text, on the other hand, is full of the nitty gritty of fieldwork and is likely to seem exceedingly familiar, maybe even repetitive, to anthropologists. But the two aspects, the personal and the professional, have to be seen as coexisting. Fieldwork consists of experiences shared by all anthropologists; the personal and the peculiar are significant as qualities that *always* but *differently* characterize each individual experience. While this introduction discusses what was important in my "identity formation," the book itself, in its preoccupation with getting things done, tells of yet unaccepted facts: that life in India is as full of contradictions, pain, and beauty as elsewhere;

that post-colonial upper classes are, for all their confused sensibilities, the same as other upper classes; that Eastern/Oriental/Asian scholars have most of the same worries as Western ones; that one may forget one's personal and historical identity for certain purposes but must remember it for others. In short, my emphasis on the personal arises from my recognition of its importance in my professional development as a social scientist, not in an awareness of myself as a "Third World scholar."

Last, fieldwork memoirs are worth sharing because for other specialists studying the region they are as accurate as more rigorously planned investigations. A society can never be wrong, and all experiences in the field are to be taken seriously. Given the limitations of any study's perspective, a reflection on one's behind-the-scenes, mundane field experiences allows both researcher and reader to refine their understanding of the way things work. I find my memoirs enlightening, for example, on such subjects as middle-class versus poor Indians' stand on hospitality and servility to office, or on the pragmatic value of hierarchy, reciprocity, and exchange. Such insights comprise an ethnography (albeit incomplete and unpolished) that tells in turn of how a Western-trained Indian intellectual adapted to the field and built relationships with strangers that affected her greatly as an individual but, more important, enabled her to talk expertly about them—and how all such expertise has inbuilt limitations.

SCHOLARLY LOCATIONS

I attended school and college in India; in 1970 I went abroad (Europe and the United States), returning, after an unbroken stay of five years and the formative experience of two graduate degrees. The following three years of trying to discover India through living there and doing a master of philosophy degree in Indian history prepared me to go abroad again.

In 1978, on the eve of my second departure, from Delhi to Chicago to do my Ph.D., I put down Phanishwar Nath Renu's novel about a Bihar village, *Maila Anchal* ("The Soiled

Hinterland").[7] His enticing, remote pictures of rural life left me aching with pleasure and desire. I was acutely conscious of leaving my country in order to return to it with freedom, the freedom that I had found so elusive while living in it. This was only partly the physical freedom to travel to villages and backwaters; it was even more the freedom of being aware and equipped, of having the equivalent of the doctor's training with which the urban protagonist of *Maila Anchal* goes off to the village, as well as the independence of mind to use the training for village work. To go abroad thus was a rash and impulsive step, suddenly to leave my job (I had an excellent appointment in the history department of the best college in Delhi), my husband (though he was to act with equal rashness and follow me shortly after), and a pleasant and quite satisfactorily organized home. I had no physical bars to my freedom, only cultural and psychological ones, or to put it less grandly, those of ignorance and of a restless, awakened imagination that would not be satisfied. I felt bound by my job, my university, the closed intellectual circles of peers, my background, and my prospects. I felt bound by the history I had studied, was teaching, and would do future work in. I needed new dimensions for my interests, new concepts to supplant my well-worn ones, the expanse to set my agenda anew. I needed a freshness of vision, some theories to exercise my mind with—as it turned out, what I largely needed was cultural anthropology.

Once at Chicago, it took me at the most a week to discover my direction and to plunge into coursework, library research, and interaction with colleagues. I was not the average student (whatever that might be) in that I had been out of college for eight years, held three graduate degrees (in Russian language, Russian history, and Indian history), and was too old and too experienced as a teacher to suffer the intellectual strains and psychological terror that confronted many of my classmates. I also had a private agenda. With an eye for the needful uncharacteristic of me, I completed the core require-

7. Phanishwar Nath Renu, *Maila Anchal* (Delhi: Rajkamal, 1954).

ments in history within a year and took my preliminary exams. Then I concentrated on studying anthropology, something I had already started dabbling in, untroubled by the confusion of administrators, teachers, and peers as to whether I was *actually* a historian or an anthropologist. When I got the funding for my field research in 1981, I was satisfied that my quest was headed toward its close: I was going to India to make a historical-ethnographic study of the popular culture of the artisans of Banaras. While each aspect of the proposal had been worked out gradually and painfully over the years in Chicago, the project as a whole aimed to do exactly what had in the vaguest terms always been on my mind: to interact with actual people that I knew nothing about, not merely to engage with them through written documents; to discover, with the heuristic device of a perspective, the world view(s) that lay beneath their actions; and to understand and represent them with theoretical categories chosen self-consciously from among many possible analytical modes.

But, however aspiring and sincere, I was a marginal figure to anthropology, and suffered less from the "faith in Monumentalism," as Rosaldo calls it,[8] than my classmates. That is, I did not take classic ethnographies as models to be emulated nor imagine that, like the father figures of anthropology, I would write a representative account of another culture under certain predictable chapter headings. As Van Maanen puts it, I lacked "the proper respect for our ancestors and the comfort their representational devices might provide."[9] Nor do I think I suffered from the illusion that I was going to capture another culture and objectify it within a communicable structure, since this culture was "my own," and, as individuals know instinctively about their own culture, was too complex, dynamic, and incoherent to allow me to do more than slice out a tiny segment for analysis. Nor was I in grave danger of colluding with colonialism, having been colonialized

8. Rosaldo, *Culture and Truth.*
9. John Van Maanen, *Tales of the Field: On Writing Ethnography* (Chicago: University of Chicago Press, 1988), p. xii.

myself, and having been sensitized to the workings of the colonizer-colonized mentality both from study of an intellectually nationalist Indian history in India and from an academic tenure in Moscow. To be sure, I was bristling with prejudices that belonged to a class closely associated with colonialism, but in India these prejudices are pre-colonial.

Not to overrate the other side, historians usually promised much more than they delivered, and I had problems with the data, the approach, the concepts, the ideology, and the very subject matter of history, the *past*, a construction that I could finally own to having little interest in. I was acutely conscious that archival work left yawning gaps in comprehension: how do you talk about weavers without ever encountering one face to face? How do you effectively describe rituals without witnessing the power of one? Conventional historical research in archives and reading rooms left me clumsy and immature in talking about real people and real events. But most of all I was excited by cultural history, ideas in enactment, so to speak. I felt, along with others, that the discipline of history gave inadequate control over theoretical categories and was guarded in its borrowings from others (I am thinking here particularly of the anthropological "solidarity" and "communitas," as well as "liminality" and "exchange"; what a strain they caused and what a stir they made when finally applied variously by historians).[10] The economic historian, it was coming to be recognized, must know economics. So the cultural historian must learn . . . cultural anthropology, of course.

What pushed me into ethnography as I describe it here was my preference to write about the present—not quite the present of anthropologists, but rather the present as a shifting, forming, changing set of actualities and possibilities—as well as about the agents responsible for all this movement, agents usually located in the (narrative) past. To anticipate the next section and interject a personal comment here, it

10. I allude, for instance, to articles by E. P. Thompson, Keith Thomas, etc., in journals like *Past and Present* in the 1970s.

was partly my Indianness that made the importance of history incontrovertible to me. As many novels, short stories, and lay conversations—but not academic writings—have brought home to me, it is difficult for the South Asian to underestimate the importance of history, so omnipresent is *change* on the subcontinent; if anything, its vehement swirl can be overwhelming. An understanding of self, family, subculture, social phenomena, and naggingly intense contradictions and confusions can be achieved only through reference to history. Intolerant, resentful, and defensive about the present, the educated and self-conscious Indian is, moreover, uniquely aware of its historical dimension. Confronted with "problems"—poverty, disease, communalism, discrimination, and exploitation—the Indian cannot accept a merely cultural explanation: things are that way because they are; we do what we believe and we believe what we believe. Self-love necessitates historical thinking: what are the causes? the agents? the explanations? An indigene studying his or her own society is engaged not only in a more activist project, and in more of a voyage of self-discovery, but also in a more *holistic* project, one that is more generous in its methodological approaches and more liberal in its scope.

PERSONAL LOCATIONS

My own very particular circumstances are often alluded to in the course of the book, and I shall highlight the most important of them here. I am an Indian doing research in India, an Indian—though based abroad and at home abroad—by birth, nationality, and choice ("In spite of all temptation . . . To belong to other nations . . . "). For the West, "Indian" is an oversimplified category: either you fall into certain stereotypical classifications of caste, class, location, and so on, or you are simply "western" or "westernized," that is, not quite Indian. For me, there are worlds and worlds in India, both within and alongside one another, and I have failed to hit on the essence of what makes one "Indian." As Abdul Bismillah puts it in the beginning of his evocative novel about Banaras weavers: "There is a world which is universal. There is a world that is India. There is a world that is Muslim. And there is a world that belongs to the weavers of Banaras."[11] For the last two, I can substitute and append any number of similar discrete worlds, and from the point of view of experience, and equally of scholarship, the distance between any two of these worlds is equal.

I lived in India the first nineteen years of my life, yet I knew almost nothing about it until I left it after college and then returned for various purposes, including the three-year period of teaching and married life in Delhi. Childhood and adolescence left lasting impressions on me. I was in two senses secluded: first, we lived in the Civil Lines or the Cantonments, where the population is two per square mile or thereabouts: these are the extraordinary suburbs created by the British to be interned at a safe distance from the Natives. Second, ours was a small family of four, and my parents preferred me to keep to my own devices. Like any good guardians, they wanted to protect me from the filth, crowds, and disease of the city, and the nature of their work and life-style made this simple. As soon as I started worrying about what I was going to do with my life, I thought of reaching the city, with its filth, crowds, and disease. There may be a discernible cycle to this. My father had grown up next to the bazaars; he escaped the city for the Cantonments. Bred and, as I saw it, suffocated in these remote areas, I plotted to escape them for the crowded city.

A concrete example of seclusion comes to mind. I *had* been to Banaras before 1981, even before my reconnoitering trip to North Indian cities in 1979 to select a suitable research site. My earlier visit had been as a college girl in 1967, with two cousins and my brother Sunil, to spend the summer with my parents, who were "posted" there. We lived of course in the Cantonment, in the gracious and totally isolated bungalow of the Senior Superintendent of Police. Our day went like

11. Abdul Bismillah, *Jhini Jhini Bini Chadariya* (Delhi: Rajkamal, 1986), p. 8.

this: 6 A.M., riding; 7 A.M., when sufficiently sweaty, a swim at Banaras Club; 9 A.M., breakfast, on the coolest foods of May and June; 10 A.M. to noon, arts, crafts (I was experimenting with batik that summer), books and games; noon, a snack and iced Cokes; till lunch, more of the forenoon activities; 2 P.M., lunch, topped with mangoes and ice cream; 3 to 5 P.M., siesta in a dark room kept cool by *khas* curtains; evening, badminton, another swim, cousinly games and conversation . . . The *one* time that Banaras impinged on our consciousness was when, in response to the cavern-dark, gloomy, and eerie Banaras Club swimming pool and our amusement that there were many Shiva (Mahadev) temples in Banaras habitually called Mahesh*war*, Viresh*war*, Kapilesh*war*, and so on, we invented our own god (*Ishwar*) of the haunted swimming pool, Kut-kutesh*war* Mahadev, He who keeps the teeth chattering.

As a child I kept to my own devices, living a progressively rarefied life whose only other denizens were characters from books and whose landscape was created of the black-and-white symbols of letters. The only people I knew in any sense at all were my immediate family and, very unidimensionally, schoolmates and some servants. One person who disclosed a totally different world intersecting with mine in uncertain ways was Shankar. Putting all euphemisms aside, he was our servant. He had been attached to my father from when both of them were nineteen or twenty and had therefore been my nursemaid and surrogate mother from birth. He was as much a part of our home and family as were any of the actual family members; yet, of course, he was an outsider. He had left his village and would go back now and then for visits, from which he would return having forgotten his "clean" Hindi and relapsed into village dialect. The language change—language signaling as it does one-ness or other-ness—left a great impression on my mind. He had a son and daughter, the latter the same age as me, and sometime when I was twelve years old, I discovered that she had been given in marriage. Shortly after, she died in childbirth. Shankar did not hide his tears from me, and the combined impact of seeing an adult mother figure cry and of wrestling with the strange knowledge of the *cause* of the tears opened up another vista to me. As I matured, I came to accept that Shankar had his own home and family, although we mutually pretended that he shared ours, and my first faint stirrings of humanism and egalitarianism were the realization that I must relinquish my earlier possessiveness. I wanted to visit his village and meet his people and know him as a person, not as a role, our servant. Of course I never did; it was all too difficult. But Shankar's existence in my life contributed to making me an anthropologist.

A large part of the pleasure that the reader will detect in my accounts of roaming around in narrow lanes, as well as some part of the difficulties posed by my shyness and ignorance, is a product of my secluded past. Other feelings that surfaced during my fieldwork were also legacies of the past. My persistent love-hate relationship with poverty arises from a familiar middle-class attitude: let them be simple, ignorant, unhappy, in revolt, whatever, but let them be *clean*. I had never found filth or garbage an issue before, but suddenly, overwhelmed with it, I found it repulsive, and by extension, the attitudes of the people who tolerated it equally so. I suffered from the unarticulated expectations of those who grow up with servants waiting on every whim—the expectation of comfort provided by the loyal cooperation of all—and condemned any situation that would make it impossible. My India was one of ease; I had never really accepted that poor communication, inadequate supplies of necessities, the discomforts of dampness or drought, or the unpredictable personalities of others could adversely affect me. Although eleven years of living away from such a life-style, including eight years of economic independence as an academic, had sufficiently declassed me that I felt little but repugnance for the administrators of India, the deeper proclivities that had been cultivated by living in the Cantonments and Civil Lines remained. Yet I continued to strive to understand this instinctive shrinking from the poor, and to understand the poor themselves, in ways that I never strove to understand

anyone with money or power; the latter I mercilessly condemned because they had the stigma of familiarity.

Banaras was such a mystery to me when I arrived there in
1981 ironically *because* I was an Indian and expected to have a
privileged insight into it. In fact, from Banaras I was *thrice* removed: through my education and upbringing, than which
there is no greater molder of attitudes; by language and linguistic culture; and by region and regional culture.

My education, like my mother's, had been conducted
within the four walls of various Catholic convents, the longest stay being in Lucknow, from which there were *never* field
trips to other neighborhoods, other institutions in the city, to
encounter urban life directly. We were fed on the bread and
butter of Shakespeare and Thomas Hardy, and I imagined
myself akin to those who roamed the English countryside
and rhapsodized on "Seasons of mist and yellow fruitful-
ness . . . " This great polarity between internal and external
worlds has been eloquently described by countless ex-
colonials, both at home and expatriated.[12] Talk of it makes me
uncomfortable because it is so much a part of the mental
makeup of us Western-educated Indians that it is *never* discussed by us among ourselves. It is reserved only for a Western audience, and when we attempt to communicate it, it is
ironically oversimplified and problematized by both parties.
Space does not permit me to deal at length with this matter;
even by broaching the subject, by rendering it as a possible
East-West conflict, I feel I am doing it an injustice. Banaras is
not the issue; thanks to my education, I would have been a
stranger—or rather, an observer—anywhere in India, culti-
vating as I did attitudes of pity and distress at the practice of
caste, of disgust at patriarchy, of scorn at ritual, and of noncomprehension (tinged with romanticism) at poverty. None

12. Among recent writings, for example: Upamanyu Chatterjee, *English
August: An Indian Story* (1988); Nirad C. Chaudhuri, *Thy Hand, Great Anarch!:
India 1921–52* (London: The Hogarth Press, 1988); Salman Rushdie, *Satanic
Verses* (New York: Penguin, 1989); Sarah Suleri, *Meatless Days* (Chicago: Uni-
versity of Chicago Press, 1989).

of these observed facts were part of me—necessary to study, impossible to live with—but, as I have since discovered, they do not *have* to be for one to be Indian. How many educated, self-conscious, activist Indians suffer this unnecessary distancing from what they believe must be their "real" culture![13]

I was also an outsider to Banaras because of language and linguistic culture, since Hindi was only my second language and in Banaras, while Hindi and Urdu were known and widely used, especially in my presence, everyone by preference spoke Bhojpuri, which I acquired only gradually and partially. English was my first language—the language of my dreams (as far as one can know) and thoughts, the language I could express myself in, and the language my parents could express themselves in. The standard of Hindi imparted in my school days had been abysmally low—it has risen several notches since—and had left us schoolfellows with an effective language barrier. We could communicate in Hindi with servants and older relatives in a rudimentary way and among ourselves not at all. I improved greatly in Hindi when working in Delhi, but conversational fluency I acquired only in the field in Banaras, sensing that my mere adequacy in simple conversation was not enough, that I should achieve the level necessary to both transmit and understand complex thoughts. My efforts were intense and unflagging, a combination of reading newspapers, journals, and fiction; of conversing whenever possible; of keeping my ears constantly attuned to any nuance of speech; and even of executing laborious exercises in composition. Although progress in a language is difficult to mark, there came a point at which, even if I could not understand every spoken word, I could understand the sense. In my own speech, especially, I could note the change: I could gradually deliver myself of more and more complicated thoughts or propositions and emerge from the trial panting but victorious. For Urdu, which differs from

13. For a statement of this distancing, see Madhu Kishwar's comment, quoted by Julie Stephens, and Stephens's critique in Ranajit Guha, ed., *Subaltern Studies: Writings on South Asian History and Society*, vol. 6 (Delhi: Oxford University Press, 1989).

Hindi in script and partly in vocabulary, the path I followed was the same, although progress was much slower.

Finally, Banaras was unknown to me because of what textbooks call the "regional diversity" of India, eastern Uttar Pradesh being culturally distinct from western or central Uttar Pradesh, whence my ancestors had come. This diversity legitimated my otherness: every Indian grows up with the experience that regions, cultural styles, classes, and intellectual approaches and ideologies have little in common with one another; that "natural" practices and attitudes—child rearing, treatment of elders, behavior toward guests—vary dramatically from subcaste to subcaste, even from family cluster to family cluster; that in meeting a new person seemingly as Indian as you, you may actually confront a culture distant from everything you take for granted.

Even within a family, encounters with "the Other" can be severe. I had never in my various convent situations read any religious text but the New Testament. But I had one grandfather who was steeped in abstract Upanishadic philosophy and another who was a passionate devotee of the incarnation Rama. The former meditated three hours in the dark every morning, sat on the bench of the Uttar Pradesh High Court during the day as M'Lord, and played tennis in the club in the evening. The latter was a specialist on the *Ramcharitmanas* and had published his own version of it. My own father recited English poems as if they were Vedic hymns, that is, with regularity and dignity, and also wrote English poetry in the tradition of the Romantics. Living abroad for five years starting at the formative age of nineteen, I became certain that I would marry a foreigner and I felt my prophesy fulfilled when I chose to marry a Bengali. My first visit to Calcutta as a daughter-in-law was a hybrid of images: unfamiliar humidity; the swollen Hooghly; cone-shaped "Vietnamese" hats on men with strangely Chinese features; odd syncretisms of a suddenly unfamiliar British race working on another unknown race who pointedly (owing to the muddle of their peculiar language) separated themselves from "Hindustanis"—syncretisms that found expression in striking notions of cleanliness and safety, and equally in amusing habits like drinking morning tea only if accompanied by Thin Arrowroot biscuits.

All this was foreign, the Other, yet it was all me, India, *my* history and society. Size, cultural diversity, preference for exclusivity, a colonial experience that made many scratches while leaving many deeper levels untouched, and finally an acceptance of all this untidiness as natural and right make Indians like me very aware of many worlds and the shifting positions of Self/Other. This results not so much in a feeling of uprootedness or homelessness as in a widening of the sphere one can call one's own. When educated South Asians live abroad, they feel not lost or uncertain about identity but rather at home and comfortable (at least if they have a positive outlook as I do) in a progressively greater number of locations. One condition for the making of a good anthropologist is potentially fulfilled here: the creation of a mind attuned to diversity, variation, context, and change. In addition, unlike most U.S. ethnographers whose personal accounts I have read, for me there is finally no "home" and therefore no privileged vantage point.[14] The experience of fieldwork can often be more formative, as Cesara records it to be for related reasons.[15] The culture being discovered has an immediacy and a power to convert that may form new personal locations. Whether this makes for "better" anthropology in any sense depends on other factors that may be quite unrelated to these personal ones.

I did not then discover my "alien-ness" through anthropology; I was overly aware of it already and could "overcome" it through anthropology in favor of a more intellectually satisfying consciousness. I had deliberately discarded the "return of the native" mindset in 1974 when, returning to In-

14. Renato Rosaldo, *Ilongot Headhunting, 1883–1974: A Study in Society and History* (Stanford: Stanford University Press, 1980); James Clifford and G. E. Marcus, eds., *Writing Culture: The Poetics and Politics of Ethnography* (Berkeley and Los Angeles: University of California Press, 1986).

15. Manda Cesara, *No Hiding Place: Reflections of a Woman Anthropologist* (New York: Academic Press, 1982).

dia after a five-year stay abroad, I quickly realized that I would not be satisfied simply to record my impressions of and responses to India as creative literature or as journalism. I wished to do something more directed and precise, more trained and professional, toward understanding my society. The choice of historical anthropology, then, was a first step toward activism of a sort, though anthropology is hardly regarded as such. I did not wish to remain simply a sensitive individual, with luck maybe an eloquent writer. I wanted to have a technique, a theory, a clear-cut method, rigorous ideas.

Foreign as I felt to Banaras, I am very "Indian" in an emotional sense apart from the accident of my birthplace, and, as I grew to discover, "Banarasi." I adore the monsoons and early, early mornings in summer. I empathize with *mauj* and *masti* (the Indian versions of passion, lightheartedness, and *joi de vivre*), although never having discovered myself enough, I have not myself experienced their abandon. I instinctively "think higher of" the person who cares little for tomorrow and can fully participate in something today for its own sake, without worry about the fruits of this action, than I do of those who plot and plan, chart their actions and guard their options. As for the extravagant hospitality which bears no rational relationship to the host's ability to pay, the people of Banaras completely won my heart. Though my mind condemned the waste, and my stomach protested the oppression, and my expression doubtless reflected both, I loved the madness of it. At a more self-conscious level, the dialectician in me rejoices every time a scholar testifies to the wedding of extremes, the union of opposites—that grasping for balance symbolized in the "ascetic erotic" image—that supposedly characterizes Hinduism and that I thought I found in the field.[16]

Because I was identifiable as an Indian, everyone in the field inquired after my caste, class, region, and marital status.

16. For an older representation of this see Wendy O'Flaherty, *Siva: The Erotic Ascetic* (New York: Oxford University Press, 1981); for a newer representation, T. N. Madan, *Non-Renunciation* (Delhi: Oxford University Press, 1987).

Regarding my social status, many quickly discovered that my father was a person of some eminence, then Inspector General and Director General of the Uttar Pradesh Police, that is, the head of the police force in the largest state of India. I was often reduced to "his daughter." Among my artisans, this categorization did not hinder me; my father's position was immeasurably remote for those to whom the local head constable was the lord of the land. What mattered more for them was that I was obviously well off, well educated, well traveled, a metropolitan person who could presumably not understand their jokes (this always irks, because it is what you wish to understand first). The fact that I had a child made me easier to approach and to empathize with; that the child was a daughter almost compensated for the wealth and good fortune I otherwise had. Then there was this husband who was obviously not a native; he lapsed into Bengali and referred to things far away. That I was "given in marriage" to him indicated customs in my family so different from local ones as to be almost foreign. This was all relatively predictable and simple to deal with. What I had not quite expected was the existence of a vocabulary that "explained" strangers like me so efficiently, with no room for disagreement or amendment. At the first mention of writing, for example, there would be knowledgeable nods: *"Shayara hai. Lekhika hai"* ("She's a poet. She's a writer"). At any allusion to handicrafts or artisans, the looks would be even more knowing: they recognized the "type"—the arty lady of means who took a fancy to collecting bric-a-brac and even did something helpful for the manufacturers in the bargain. Most sweeping but least troublesome was the response to all my other meetings and wanderings that they found difficult to categorize: *"Shauk hai"* ("It's her hobby, her fancy").

What did I actually go to research? It would be appropriate to append a copy of my research proposal here, because I stuck closely to it, considering it a strong anchor in my turbulent sea. In my worst moments I could look at it and remember, "Ah yes! *That's* what I'm supposed to do." My topic was "popular culture," that is, "leisure" and "entertainment" activities, whatever people claimed was their "fun" and "pleasure," all terms that I was awkward with, while perfectly confident of the method of discovering the proper terms upon questioning informants. My subjects were the artisans of Banaras, about whose existence and numbers I knew a fair amount from census reports. Of Banaras itself, particularly its history and geography, I felt that I had read everything available when I was in Chicago, but this knowledge receded rapidly as I stepped into the field. My approach was to combine history and cultural anthropology, which in my mind meant, pragmatically speaking, two things: work in the archives until your eyes fall out and hang around with the subjects of your study until you know everything there is to be known about them.

I remember pausing with dismay on the very eve of departure for Banaras—a village ethnography in my hand, no doubt—and asking uncertainly of my husband, "I haven't made a good choice, have I, planning to study Banaras? I should have chosen to do villagers, *that's* what would have been a challenge." And my husband, dependable crutch and tonic as always, stated what may be regarded as the enterprise's epigraph: "Your artisans will be sufficiently like villagers. Challenge enough."

PART ONE

In which we learn of the difficulties of liking anything about a new place, from possible living quarters to its naturally enigmatic nature. In which we also learn how shyness and a respect for others' privacy have to be overcome to do field-work but that when you do get close to people you cannot help but recognize their inviolability. In which finally we hear of problematic guides and methods, of fruitless searches, and of the vast challenge of interpreting anything at all.

1

Physical and Cultural Shocks

Our introduction to Banaras was not a happy one. The drive we undertook from Lucknow—some 180 miles of technically metalled road—was deadening. Because it was monsoon season, I had voted for going by car, thinking that the long drive in the rains would be beautiful. But we had a spell of dry weather at exactly that time, and dust poured into our speeding car. The road, already broken up by the rains (which happens with annual regularity and arouses speculations about dishonest contractors), was full of potholes. What with the bumps and the dust, life did not seem worth living over the eight or so hours that constituted the journey.

Our baby, Irfana, then two-and-a-half months old, was the most cheerful passenger for a long time. Then she got upset as well and would not nurse. We stopped, and I walked her up and down, cooing and singing by the Lucknow-Banaras road for much of an hour. We then gritted our teeth and covered the last lap of the journey. The Banaras we entered seemed part of the general misery we had experienced the whole day. There was not a lonely temple spire or sign of a mighty river to be seen, only more dusty roads and the typical low-lying vista of an unambitious North Indian city.

We stopped at the guest house of the Varanasi Development Authority, a well-equipped, empty, and apparently little-used place. I collapsed with a fever. Sombabu got busy, as he especially does in crises, bathing the baby, washing dozens of diapers, festooning them on our mosquito net poles. The room was air-conditioned, and all slept peacefully except feverish me. I remember the dignified look of my daughter as she lay on her side, wrapped in a white sheet, her fists curled into balls, not budging an inch all night. And such a nice rest did she have, so much had she needed it, that upon awakening the next morning she spent the first hour lying on her back, exercising her limbs up in the air, chirruping and singing with the birds outside. It was the happiest and most vocal that she had been since birth. And so in the months to come: whatever misgivings we harbored about Banaras, she was always sure that she loved it. This was significant for young, first-time parents: a sure test for the acceptability of surroundings is whether the baby responds favorably to them.

As for me, I remember burning with a fever, then swallowing some pills that miraculously cooled me down, so that when the doctor came he didn't have much to check. He prescribed bananas, yogurt, dry biscuits, and a pale lemon compound called Electral (to become a household word for us, as it was for every other family in the city). A little later marched in a procession: the driver, the guest house watchman, the police sub-inspector who had shown us the place, and an unknown recruit, each carrying one of the prescribed foods. The driver, as befit the head of a procession, looked the most solemn, swinging on a knotted string a clay cup containing a half-pound of yogurt covered with a leaf. I looked at the cup, leaf, and string with aesthetic appreciation, and noted, "This is how they do it in Banaras!"

Our initial trip to Banaras was for the single purpose of finding a place to live. Friends in Chicago who were in different degrees alumnae of Banaras research had given us three names in a city of approximately one million. One of the three contacts was a drugstore owner who directed us to a bank manager who, it was rumored, was having a house built. Our urgency then, and always, was awkward to people in Banaras. They would, one and all, respond to a request with, *"Ho jayega"* ("It shall be done"). We would counter with an impolitic "When?" or, worse, "How about now?" The bank manager had many visitors, many cups of tea, and many flies in his office. I sat with my permanent little bundle of baby on the only seat available, and Sombabu stood next to me. We looked and felt uncomfortable, out of place, and desperate. The bank manager abandoned his crowded office to show us his house. It struck us as highly desirable judging by its design and its convenient location in the central ward of Bhelupura, on the grounds of the old Vijaynagram estate, which was being partitioned and sold off for commercial development. But the house had many months of work to go, and the owner was not even sure that he didn't want to live in it himself. Goaded on by our interest, however, he not only promised it to us but assured us that it would be ready by the end of the month. We pretended to believe him; we needed to.

Our initial impression of the city did not change on that visit: dusty, dirty, architecturally unremarkable. One could not readily feel any interest in it, leave aside love for it. Perhaps the only remarkable thing in that trip was that the manager of our guest house turned out to be a Sanskrit scholar whose speech was peppered with syllogisms. He also stands out in my memory because of the prolonged stare he gave us as one of our party (my cousin Manoj from Chicago) asked him for a fresh roll of toilet paper. "Has it all been consumed?" he asked, disturbed. The stress was not on *all* but on *consumed*. What disturbed him was the same realization reported by the famed vocalist Subbalakshami, who in the middle of a performance abroad found herself unable to continue singing because the thought suddenly came to her that "all these people in the audience use not water but *toilet paper.*"

Trivial enough at the time, this exchange was an effective forewarning of two things: one, the cultural importance of water in general and of cleansing in particular; and two, my ambiguous position between two sides, the toilet-paper-using and the water-using sides as it were, which was *seen* as such. Clear as I had been until then that both sides were valid and that I could empathize with each, I realized then that I did not have the ingenuity to express this position and could only seek to avoid any controversial issue, itself a limitation in inquiry.

When we showed up in Banaras two weeks later, we were no closer to finding a place. More people knew of our search, so we were taken around more regularly to a greater number of progressively unacceptable places. This time we stayed in the guest house of the American Institute of Indian Studies, which had many advantages compared to our first stopping place. Food was cooked on the premises and had a homey flavor. In our previous lodging it had been brought over from the neighboring Ashoka Hotel in covered china bowls, every dish the same and garnished similarly, everything outrageously expensive. But this guest house was in the south of the city, off the main thoroughfare and unconnected to it by a proper road or lane. The monsoon season was much advanced, and instead of dust we had floods. Sombabu took a rickshaw out one day and it promptly overturned in a ditch. I desisted from going out with Irfana for a long time, but when we were loaned a jeep, I began to risk it. I remember the wettest of such trips. It rained continuously and the whole vehicle dripped and leaked. We were looking for a neighborhood called Navapura, but since we did not even reach the ward it was in, we did not find (on that trip) a single person who had ever heard of it. I punched the canvas roof of the jeep to push away the store of water that regularly collected directly over my head. Passionate self-declared lover of the monsoons as I was, I decided, "This is the worst."

Diapers would not dry in the humidity. We were marooned in the guest house. We had been invaded by monsoon insects and other creatures. All of this made us look harder for a place of our own, but the prospects of finding something remained as distant as ever. We had exhausted our two or three acquaintances (in both senses of the word), the bank manager's house was of course no closer to completion, and with self-sufficient smugness, Banaras nowhere displayed advertisements or notices for apartments to let.

At this point in the story we have to learn of the mechanisms of the state and local police.

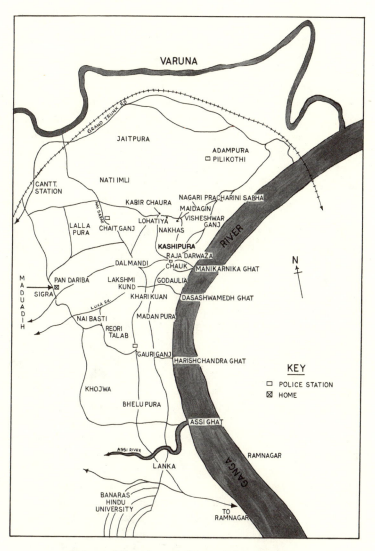

VARUNA

JAITPURA

ADAMPURA
□ PILIKOTHI

NATI IMLI

CANTT.
STATION

KABIR CHAURA

NAGARI PRACHARINI SABHA

MAIDAGIN

LALLA
PURA

CHAIT GANJ

LOHATIYA

VISHESHWAR
GANJ

NAKHAS

KASHIPURA

RAJA DARWAZA

DALMANDI

CHAUK

MANIKARNIKA GHAT

PAN DARIBA

LAKSHMI
KUND

GODAULIA

M
A
D
U
A
D
I
H

SIGRA

KHARI KUAN

DASASHWAMEDH GHAT

NAI BASTI

LUKA RD.

MADAN PURA

REORI
TALAB

GAURI GANJ

HARISHCHANDRA GHAT

KHOJWA

KEY

□ POLICE STATION
⊠ HOME

BHELU PURA

ASSI GHAT

ASSI RIVER

RAMNAGAR

LANKA

BANARAS
HINDU
UNIVERSITY

GANGA

TO
RAMNAGAR

RIVER

GRAND TRUNK

N

A map of the places I discovered in Banaras.
(Compiled with the help of Mr. N. Ravi of the American
Institute of Indian Studies in Varanasi.)

Banaras had eight police stations, or *thanas*. We were currently staying in the territory of one, Bhelupura, and had earlier been in that of another, Maduadih. Over the inspectors, or station officers (S.O.'s), of these *thanas* was the Deputy Superintendent of Police, of which there were actually two in the city: Circle Officer (C.O.) I and II. The senior C.O. was more popularly known as the Kotwal, a position that dates from Mughal times or such and one that I instinctively treat with respect (these persons shall figure in our story later). Over them was the Superintendent of Police, and over him the Senior Superintendent, known to all as the Ess Ess Pee (S.S.P.) and equally as the Supri Tandon Sahab, who was the powerful executive and de facto head of the police in the district. He was the man who had arranged for our stay in the first guest house, and Maduadih's inspector had arranged for the doctor and the unpalatable, expensive food. Over all these officers sat the Deputy Inspector General, the head of the police in the range (there are ten or twelve ranges in Uttar Pradesh). He was the man supplying us with the dripping jeeps.

We had never met nor did we know by name any of these personages. Why were they going out of their way to befriend and assist us? Because we were distinguished scholars from Chicago? No. My father was at that time Inspector General of Police, the head of police in the entire state of Uttar Pradesh. He had one daughter and that was me. We never did figure out to what extent our status as distinguished visitors was due to his *explicit* directions and to what extent to inherent ideas of service in the different echelons of a government bureaucracy. But judging from the inconsistency and spontaneous nature of the service and from my father's general ignorance and indifference regarding our activities, I would say the explanation was largely the latter. My father's mind worked on a grander scale anyway. When I was stuck in Lucknow a year later because of a thirty-hour train delay and was ready to explode with vexation at missing a crucial event in Banaras called Ghazi Mian ka Mela, he calmed me: "Just *tell* me what you wanted to go and see. *I'll* have the event organized for you here."

We quickly learned of the police hierarchy in Banaras, and responded appreciatively to offers of help. However, all the attentions of all the police officers of Banaras could not alter our basic circumstances: we had no place to live and no idea how to find one; we were isolated by the lack of a telephone in the guest house and physically stranded by the monsoons; and the discomfort of our own damp clothes and lack of clean, dry clothing was only slightly less than the inconvenience of our dozens of permanently wet diapers.

After looking at scores of houses, parts of houses, rooms partitioned and sub-partitioned, we understood a few things about Banaras. One realization was that the taste of the local population—I mean here the middle class—and especially of those who showed us around was appalling. Without batting an eyelid, they would point out impossible bathrooms and kitchens created out of the dirty undersides of staircases, leaving us speechless with agony. The other realization was that my dream of living somewhere on the banks of the river, looking down at its lapping waves and smelling its sweet, rotten smell, had been unrealistic. Somewhere in this dream had been the old narrow *galis*, the congested lanes, of the city, within which I would do my research all day, even as I shopped for vegetables or turned to go upstairs to our apartment by the riverside. The *galis* were there, as were houses by the river, together with congestion and age. But living in those parts was a decision I referred to in those days as "fatal." The ground there was thick with steaming turbans of cow dung, the leaves of plates and shards of clay cups used for fast food, the filthiest and smelliest of domestic refuse, and even, I believe, human excreta. The air was equally thick with flies and those unidentifiable particles occasionally visible in a lone shaft of sunlight, but, deep in the Banaras *galis*, visible all the time, looking not mysterious and graceful as they can at other times, but positively threatening. To share one's living space with flies that bred on the refuse littering the streets was a possibility soon rejected, though for months afterwards I continued to feel betrayed by Banaras's filth.

I had mentally admitted defeat regarding my vague dreams of where to live before we ever found the place we did: the first floor (in Indian parlance) of a solid cement fortress in a nondescript part of the city called Sigra. It was solid because its owner was an engineer in a government concern from which he had diverted all the cement possible; that it was a fortress we discovered as we tried to hammer some nails into the walls for pictures and whatnot. It was painted in one hue and trimmed in a grotesquely contrasting one. With its two dying palm trees, it looked ugly and inhospitable from the outside. Inside it was a daily reminder of the tastelessness of a certain class of Banarasis. Each room had three large wall cupboards with polished wooden doors mounted on the walls, all protruding outward. Two rooms were connected to bathrooms and might have served as bedrooms, except that one also contained the entrance way. What was perhaps the living room had five massive cupboards and could be reached only by going past the kitchen and the other bedroom. The sole explanation for the floor plan was that the owner had intended to rent each room out separately, an explanation confirmed when he showed surprise that we wanted the entire five rooms.

Our main worry was how, particularly with its collection of cupboards taking up all the wall space, to make the place livable for the next eighteen months. The crowning touch was that the central corridor was doorless; if we wished to secure the house, we would have to lock up each room separately. On a practical daily basis, this meant that certain creatures like monkeys had access to every room. We eventually got used to coming upon them, about once a week, cleaning up the food on the dining table, ransacking the fruit basket, sneaking into the kitchen, even playing with toys, as well as destroying whatever was left on the front porch and the back roof, of course. What was unforgivable was that they regularly depleted our water supply by taking elaborate drinks from the tap on the roof and then royally *leaving it open*. We tried securing the tap by every means short of ball and chain, but their godlike agility (the Bengali part of my family actually called them, to my consternation, Hanumans, or monkey-gods) outmatched our merely human striving. I never even forgave them for their more general sin: to make it impossible for us to have a civilized cup of tea in our own outdoors, to grow plants there, or arrange a sitting space; in short, together with the landlord, to conspire to prevent us from living the way we preferred.

We were perhaps choosy regarding our domestic conditions. We did not care for wet bathrooms or for visitors—of whom we had an unusual assortment—strolling through our bedrooms; we liked to maintain a constant temperature as far as possible through the extremes of the seasons and to keep bugs out. In retrospect, our stay seems to have been a constant fight to achieve all this. At the time, every effort seemed absolutely indispensable, particularly with an infant. When our truckload of possessions arrived and we set up our curtains, stove, refrigerator, desks, and bookshelves, we began a virtual odyssey of experimentation with the rooms. One room was too hot for a study in summer, another too noisy for a bedroom in the monsoons; a third got the wrong winds (which carried the fumes of a neighboring carpet-dyeing yard) in the morning, and so on. The cupboards turned out to be an unexpected boon: they came to be used as dust shields for books, stereo, musical instruments, and toys.

We looked, perhaps unconsciously, for like-minded people to share our feelings of discomfort and injury. But no local visitor, from the poorest of weavers to the S.S.P. himself (he happened to be from eastern U.P.), ever voiced anything but deep appreciation for this crazily designed ugly fortress of a house. It was a matter, then, of both class and culture. I may have thought that charpoys were more Indian than sofa sets or that open windows were essential for some kind of oneness with nature (an idea our landlord also tried to conjure up when we requested a back door for the central corridor). But the issue, I realized once in Banaras, was not an authentic versus an imitative life-style at all, but mosquito screens, hygienic toilets, and proper places for things (our preference) versus disease, discomfort, and lack of control over space and time (the eastern U.P. version). My mind was effectively cleared of all mists regarding Indianness and non-Indianness, and I had no desire to compromise my instincts regarding how to live nor any qualms in characterizing them as being as Indian as any rival instincts.

I also began reflecting on the anthropologist's "urge to merge" with the native. Many academic friends patronized lodges and guest houses of dubious comfort, studding deep *galis* never free of garbage. Why did they have such a double standard? Daily they looked upon, and lived surrounded by, refuse they would never tolerate as individuals. Did it not give them a skewed vision of India? One did not have to re-create the Mughal Gardens, but certainly, given the royal stipends of U.S. researchers (mine was being liberally taxed by the Indian government), they could choose a more comfortable life-style than most did. They could afford good Indian cottons for the summer, a refrigerator, a cooler, a servant or two, proper furniture, and space. I saw very few scholars in Banaras who were giving India a fair chance by accepting the adaptations to climate and urban living that were available.

I remember my anger at visiting an American friend in the heat of July. He was clad in his synthetic U.S. clothes, sitting on a string cot and eating warm watermelon; the approach to his guest house stank with the garbage of the whole neighborhood, and he was without a properly cooled room, chilled drinks, suitable utensils, or anything he would undoubtedly consider necessary back home. Well, I thought, they were necessary in India too—if you could afford them. I felt resentful that he was returning to the United States with the notion that filth, discomfort, heat, and sweat were *inevitable* in India when these things were at worst problematical, and I suppose I resented also that in the process of harboring and then projecting this prejudiced image of India he was also saving so much money.

I perceive my distance from Gandhi, close as I have always felt to his philosophy of service and indigenization. You do not have to *live* poorly in order to understand or to work for the poor, with a vengeance that implicitly claims that the poor prefer to live that way. From our search for a house, and thanks to our baby, who necessitated direct confrontation with these issues, I realized that I could not choose to live in dirt and discomfort at the expense of productive work and mental peace.

2

The City as Object

Even while all this was being worried over and accomplished, we turned our attention to discovering Banaras. I had started going to the archives within a day of our arrival, a modest and certain project. What was needed now was a *feel* of the city as a preliminary to fieldwork. We had never seen the river, for example, or any of the ghats, those famous built-up river embankments, indispensable for bathing and rituals. On a cloudy, pleasant monsoon day, we mounted a rickshaw and announced, "Dasashwamedh ghat." That ritual of swinging over the high step of the rickshaw and proclaiming the destination of the day became for me the pistol shot that started off each day's work, and it was important to do it in a proper collected mood, as well as to have something fresh and different planned each day.

The rickshaw unloaded us at an unremarkable v-shaped juncture of two roads with parallel rows of shops. These were the two roads that led to Dasashwamedh ghat. One was lined mostly with shops of cloth, clothes, vegetables, and other products recognized as necessities by the people of Banaras, like perfumes, mats, and baskets; the other with *pan* shops and beggars.

These beggars were different from the ones I was familiar with. They did not crowd you or plead, make you squirm by almost touching you, or sing, or demonstrate sores and amputated limbs. They simply sat in a line all down the steps on one side like normal people going about their jobs. They had their bowls in front of them, which they and donors alike regarded as sufficient declaration of purpose. Some, in fact, were busy cooking, washing, folding clothes, or praying. There are more beggars in Banaras than in any other city its size, and there can be no two ways of thinking about them. It is their lot to beg as it is yours to give. A chance event has placed them there; but for the grace of God, there would be you. There is absolutely no question of brushing them off as undeserving—the common middle-class attitude toward beggars. They do not ingratiate themselves. You can ignore them, as you can ignore an architectural or a natural feature in the landscape, but you do not necessarily feel in the right. They are in the right in being there. It has been sanctioned in the scriptures and confirmed by centuries of social practice.

We were unprepared, however, and dismayed, not merely by the beggars, but even more so by the squalid stalls, by the unlovable cows and bulls ruminating or excreting on the road, and by the whole unexciting, depressed scene and its inhabitants. We walked on to the river, and there it was before us, wide and gray and quite still. And there were the umbrellas on the ghats, a favorite illustration for tourist brochures. Boats lapped at the bank or lazily floated past. All activity was subdued. This was about 11 A.M., the time (I was later to discover) when the riverside takes a break from its early morning and evening peak hours.

As we stood on the top step, clutching our baby in her Snugli, surveying the still water and the umbrellas, I was conscious of not going about this the correct way. Our senses were not alert, our expectations were not readied, our mood was not right. We came perhaps to be wooed, to be surprised and impressed, to be confirmed in our judgment of Banaras as a potentially fascinating place. Instead, here was a scene that didn't reach out and serve up a feast but waited indifferently to be attended to, if we liked, to be understood and interpreted. At the least, we could have come at a time of characteristic activity, perhaps with a local person who would either communicate or casually let slip his own feelings about the place.

We stood and walked around for some time. We didn't go down to the water, not only because we could see everything from the top but also because we *felt* as if we had seen it all.

The most interesting thing for us that day was a hawker with a basket of lentils balanced on a bamboo hourglass stand. They were little colorful hills of parrot-green, mustard, brown, and pepper-red *dals*, and he himself smiled and sang. This active little marionette stood out against the dull, still background as both incongruous and gratifying. We did not note any of the other big or small features that mark Dasash-wamedh and other ghats—the Sitala temple, for example, or the Ganga temple, or even people washing clothes—that I was to rhapsodize about later. We were disappointed and bored, and I could sense why. It was a lesson—not very clear, but quite powerful—in the fallacy of tourism. If you want to know a place, start digging to understand it from the first day. Don't look around as an outsider with the vague notion of "familiarizing" yourself with the surroundings and being charmed by their intrinsic qualities.

We beat a hasty retreat to the covered verandah of the stores, a light drizzle having started. We waited out the driz-zle by looking carefully for a sari for our new *ayah*, or maid-servant: not cheap or coarse, but quiet, modest, clean-looking (preferably white), and of course not too expensive. Having made our purchase, we were a little fortified and de-cided to continue our explorations. We took a rickshaw to Chauk.

The Chauk, or Square, as in every old North Indian city, is the central, crowded, indigenous bazaar area. To me, with the two decades that I have spent in distant Cantonments and Civil Lines, it stands for everything fascinating and glamorous in the Indian city. The Chauk is in fact interesting for everyone, from those seeking bargains and exotic prod-ucts to those curious about social structure, history, and cul-ture. The Banaras Chauk is on a hill, and to reach its nucleus the *rickshawalla* had to pull the two of us with our various bundles up a slope of approximately five hundred yards. Be-ing dragged up the hill by a sweating, undernourished man of unguessable age caught us unprepared and left us with a sense of betrayal and acute discomfort. As with living in filth, it was as if we were suddenly being made to participate in ac-tivities not to our taste.

The uphill of Chauk

I should add that those who live in Cantonments never take rickshaws, and New Delhi does not have them at all. We looked around eagerly, but the tourist's disappointment again awaited us. The shops and signs and people crowded into our vision from all directions but meant absolutely nothing. By the time we reached the top of the hill, the center of Chauk, a drizzle had started again.

That day stands out particularly because we had embarked on two major discoveries: Dasashwamedh ghat, the fabled millennia-old seat of the Ten Horse Sacrifice, and Chauk, nerve center of the city. But most of our early experiences were like that. We had only the vaguest notion of what to expect of places such as, say, Banaras Hindu University. We would pack up baby and baby things and ride away on a rickshaw, falling over ourselves on the way to stare at passing sights. The baby seemed much more in tune with her surroundings, perched high on one of our laps, legs swinging, chortling contentedly. Her world, unlike ours, was limited to warm sun and fresh air and the security of her perch. Ours, or I should say mine, was afloat in boundless space as I strove to construct a map: "What kind of place is this? How shall I understand it?" When we reached our destination, there would be a blank, incomprehensible wall. We would go around, poking at this or that, trying to keep up our enthusiasm. But the truth was that we did not enjoy those early days of discovery. Each trip was a disappointment. There was nothing to make of whatever we saw, partly because of the very nature of the objects of our attention and partly—to be again unfair to tourists—because of our packaged tour approach. But to be fairer, it was more especially because of my lack of preparation as an ethnographer. I had not trained my senses; I had not prepared my questions. That was the missing vital link, a notion of the appropriate *questions*. I had never read a thick ethnographic account of *any* Indian city. Having chosen Banaras for its hoary, palimpsest-like venerability, I was discovering that its age did give it an inscrutability which confounded my naive expectation that it would prove alluring and irresistible at first sight. I did not have sufficient information about the place. I could not have had: there was nowhere to get it. I was there to piece it together.

When I compare those early days with later ones, it seems incredible that one can look at so much yet see so little, or want to enjoy and appreciate so intensely yet not be able to do so. Had we by some chance been obliged to leave after one or two months, we would have had practically nothing to report of Banaras, except the aridity of our residential area, the difficulties of survival, the lack of company, and the enigmatic and unattractive nature of ghats and streets.

I carried on my archival work steadily through all this. My first target was the Nagari Pracharini Sabha, the Society for the Spread of Nagari. Nagari in this context was a euphemism for Hindi, not in its literal meaning of the Sanskrit-derived script, but as a cultural-political tool. Located in the northeast, across the city from us, the society's archives were a clattering, bone-shaking half-hour rickshaw ride away.

Luckily for me, the route took me through the heart of the city every day, though the virtues of this route were more evident in the beginning than when my senses became dulled by hundreds of trips. Just as there is an uphill and downhill to the Banaras Chauk, there is an uphill and downhill to fieldwork. Climbing up painfully—pulled up manually by informants, analogous to the Chauk *rickshawallas*, you might even say—you reach a height of clarity and perception. At a particular point, inevitably, the decline begins, and as you go downhill things become fuzzy again, escaping you, you are worn out, and your experiences are all anticlimactic.

One of the calculations I always had to make as we approached Chauk was, do I leave my rickshaw, walk uphill, and then take another one for the ride down? For I had to negotiate the center of Chauk, from a major crossing called Godaulia at one end to another called Maidagin at the other, and then go a few yards further east. Or, I debated, do I retain my rickshaw but alight and walk alongside it for the steepest part of the climb? I tried each variation several times but never resolved the dilemma. Walking alongside my rickshaw marked me as a fool and a foreigner long after I stopped being these things. Trying to bargain for a new rickshaw in the middle of Chauk, where the *rickshawallas* were at their most supercilious, was always a doubtful proposition. I would inevitably waste precious minutes, and a trip broken up into two was always more expensive. The days that I refused to make up my mind and sat, dummy-like, on my pathetic little carriage as my man slave inched me up the steep hill were more uncomfortable still. Every moment of the journey was spent in cursing the system, the geography of the place, the quality of the creaking rickshaw, and my own stupid indecision.

Such mental pressures prevented me from thinking positively or imaginatively about the uphill half of Chauk, which was in any case the market for products, such as electrical goods, cloth, timepieces, and eyewear, for which I had no use. I rather despised the large, clean shops and their well-displayed products. The downhill part of Chauk was more subdued and interesting, with a major post office from where you could even make international telephone calls. It ended in the crossing of Maidagin, for which, again, I could not care at all, with its taxi stand, one of the two biggest in the city, displaying rows of, in Banaras, *white* cars. Who took them and where I couldn't imagine, seeing that there was barely space to go on foot or by rickshaw in most parts of Banaras. There was also a "tempo" stand—those three-wheeled auto rickshaws that were designed for two and carried, as a rule, six or seven people. I quickly found out who took *those*. The first time I volunteered to accompany a new informant, Abdul Jabbar and his family on their Thursday trip to the shrine they patronized, we reached the main road and began bargaining with the drivers of different modes of transport. A tempo, at ten rupees, was chosen. Six of us crowded into the vehicle, excluding Abdul Jabbar, who shared the driver's seat in front. We would have needed at least three rickshaws at five rupees each; I thought, "This is how *rickshawallas* will be inched out." At the Maduadih shrine, I had a minor argument with the family when I tried to pay the ten rupees myself. It seemed condescending on my part, but I couldn't imagine how they could afford so much out of their meager earnings. In fact I was surprised that they argued with me. In their situation, I would have immediately let someone vastly better off than me pay the fare. It was just one of those swift and frequent lessons in their different attitudes toward honor, debt, and equality.

There were two other routes by which I typically arrived at this crossing of Maidagin, and they both deserve to be described here. One went through Pan Dariba, the wholesale market for chewing tobacco, betel nuts, and leaves, and all the related condiments that go into the making of the Banarasi *pan*. It was a narrow lane fronted by tall attached buildings; on the ground floor was an open store each few square yards. Hills of tobacco, coated with silver, color, or perfume, and baskets of symmetrically arranged *pans*, accessible only from the central artery, were all displayed to passers-by and were always open to my scrutiny. This extreme openness made for the result that, occasional resolves notwithstanding, I never started a conversation with any of the merchants and never numbered one among my informants. There was not a corner or crevice to take refuge in; to start a conversation there would have meant holding up the traffic and collecting a crowd.

The other route sometimes taken by my *rickshawallas* was through the locality called Lallapura. The very first time we swung into it, I asked the driver, "Who lives here?" He turned back to gaze at me in skeptical amusement, "*Who* lives here?!" I explained, "I mean, Hindus, Muslims, artisans, merchants . . . ?" And the rest of the trip was a nice discourse on the social composition of Lallapura, though I have always felt guilty about making *rickshawallas* talk while pumping. Lallapura had certain features that always struck me as medieval even though I know there is nothing "medieval," "modern," or "ancient" about Banaras. There was a large mansion, for example, in which I believe lived elephants, for a sign hanging outside read, "Elephants can be hired here for marriages, processions, etc." And, true enough, I had seen elephants go to and from that place, clutching large leafy branches in their trunks, grabbing, as it were, a quick snack around the corner. There was no unity to the Lallapura area; sprawling, crisscrossed by lanes, evidently very poor, I could not quite grasp it. I always passed an open workshop where drums of various shapes and of different shades of leather were made and stored. That was medieval.

I was still looking at all this, it might seem, from the vantage point of the tourist. Although I describe my first impressions casually now, even indifferently, I was very serious about everything, and curious to the point of absurdity, though often amused, in spite of my seriousness, not at them but at the confrontation of me and them. I was straining to understand, and I could sense at least how, with every passing day, I had to try less and less hard. One glimpse of something opened up a world of meanings. One comment from a passer-by explained many things. To look into, behind, and under shades and doorways became my second nature. To act swiftly, with question, direction, notebook, or camera became a habit the adeptness of which surprised me.

Both these routes met at Kabir Chaura, a crossing named after the saint Kabir and famous for many reasons. There is something very meaningful about crossings for Banarasis, and they keep referring to their main ones. In a book on Banaras, the old-time resident Vishwanath Mukherjee takes his readers on a trip around the city. All his points of reference are crossings, places where one territory ends and another begins and where cross-movement is possible, a partial reflection of the stable and culturally differentiated constitution of neighborhoods in old cities. Indian crossings are intersections of four roads (*chau*raha, four paths), hence the hubs of commerce and communication where life at its most intense can be observed. The busiest teashop or *pan* shop, for example, will be at the crossing, and, with its crowds, serve in turn to make the crossing more packed, impossible, and wonderful.

Kabir Chaura was distinguished by the main public hospital of the city, called by the same name, and by drugstores and fruit vendors for the patients and their families. It was also a "dangerous" crossing, a thought that came to me each time as an involuntary touché to my anthropologist friends with their harping on symbolic and ritual dangers. Here the threat was from the traffic flowing rapidly in all directions, including jeeps, trucks, and bullock carts. The *rickshawalla* would stick out his arm to signal the direction of his turn and plunge in without further confirmation. Somehow we would always survive, perhaps because everything was proceeding slowly despite the illusion created by the swinging of the rickshaw. I never saw an accident there, although I always clutched my vehicle with all four limbs and noted how I was approximately one inch away from being crushed from the left, the right, and behind.

If Lallapura seemed medieval, then with the next lap of the journey, Lohatiya, we were in the third millennium B.C. of Mohenjo-Daro itself. The road here was of round, polished cobblestones, making rickshaws jerk their passengers roof high. All the stores, again open to the road, sold iron goods, *Lohatiya* meaning, literally, "place for iron." The shops looked dark, heavy, and, with all the fat traders and skinny iron-mongers, in them, very male. Some of the woks displayed in front were six feet in diameter, the pails four feet high. I tried interviewing here the very first or second day, before I had acquired the necessary techniques or confidence, and was too discouraged by the responses to go back again. I had pressed on bravely with a spate of questions addressed to an ironsmith hammering a metal plate, and our conversation had gone like this:

> I: "How [*bang*] many [*bang*] hours [*bang*] . . . [*inaudible*]?"
> HE: "*Yahi* (Just this) . . . [*bang, bang, bang*]"

Some prejudices and mental blocks persist; most, fortunately, are washed away with time. I never made a study of the iron goods industry or of the ironmongers of Lohatiya after my premature and totally unsuccessful initial incursions. But the Lohatiya crossing came to show itself as endlessly fascinating. At the Muslim mourning period of Moharram, the procession called Duldul passed through in its most choking and pushing phase and gave me an intuition about the attractions of crowded places. At Vishwakarma Puja and Durga Puja, and again at Ramlila, there were many stages and canopies for the gods and it was easy to catch the organizers.

To the immediate south of Lohatiya was Nakhas, where carpenters had their workshops. Nakhas led to Kashipura, the locality of the brass workers and coppersmiths. All the neighborhoods bordered on one another, connected by hidden lanes traversable on foot. Every time I was in Lohatiya, the surroundings were less and less opaque. The city was a blank map gradually becoming filled in with lanes, byways, and turnings, dotted with names of localities, individuals, and homes. Because of the proximity of Lohatiya to the archives, it became one of my first exploratory fieldwork sites. On a given day, I would walk hundreds of yards in the *galis*, with stops to visit a dozen people gradually assuming the status of good friends: a carpenter, a coppersmith, a tea seller, a widow with a *pan* shop, a policeman yawning on a bench, and so on.

And whatever doubts I may have entertained about informal conversation as a method of fieldwork, upon engaging in it and seeing the incomparable richness of my results I became a total convert. No conceivable questionnaire could have revealed to me the casual details, the ironies, the supremely confident or the hesitant tone embedded in people's conversations. The pride with which a place was pointed out or an event mentioned, or, on other occasions, the utter indifference, if not downright denigration, of tone and mannerism—these were all prized bits of information to me, and the only way I could have got them was the way I did, by loitering around, adapting to the informant's pace and inimitable style.

The archives of the Nagari Pracharini Sabha in Visheshwarganj were a few hundred yards further east of Lohatiya, beyond a steady row of teashops. Teashops, around which much of my day revolved, came to figure as pivotal elements in my work. I gave them a fair amount of thought. A tree with a hefty trunk would be taken as the starting point for the construction of a teashop. From one side of this trunk a large stove (say, with four burners) of brick, stone, clay, and cow dung would be built. From the sturdier branches of the tree would be suspended wire baskets of eggs, buns, butter, and cakes. The shady leaves would provide shelter for the customers. A few benches here and there would complete the tea stall. This was its infancy, however. I have seen many teashops at this stage, pleasant and popular enough, but the ones in Maidagin were more elaborate. Walls were hung up on three sides: bamboo frames; discarded matting, jute, and gunny bags; tin canisters hammered out into sheets; even newspapers. These walls were serviceable and were patched regularly. The roof had to have strong beams, but, like the walls, anything might cover the surface. Often tin sheets, still showing off the name of the original canistered or canned products, were used. Inside this cozy room, toasted by the sun in all seasons but always airy and shady, were fitted an amazing number of benches and tables. The teashop became a regular restaurant, and you became oblivious to the composition of the roof and the walls and to the tree that had begun it all. Crockery would clink, little boys darted around to serve and mop, omelets and french toast were created, water was served as you sat down, newspapers were provided, and tips were discouraged.

There was one teashop right next to the gate of the Nagari Pracharini Sabha. It had grown, in fact, not from a tree but from one of the pillars of the gate. Because of its location, it had a rather intense intellectual atmosphere, though all teashops tend to be oriented to discussions of philosophy and politics. I was, typically, the only woman present. Everyone ignored me in a masterly manner, but everyone was aware of me. I began to take a certain amount of protectiveness for granted from this teashop. If a serving boy splashed a little water near me, he was reprimanded. The shopkeeper would inquire, "Biscuits? Sweet? Salty? Bread?" as I placed my order for tea. When I arose to leave, knees would be pulled in and backs straightened on the benches I had to pass. If my way was held up by a person not paying attention, there would be coughs and perhaps a warning announcement. As I brushed past someone with his back to me, the shopkeeper twirled around and barked at him, "Ladies!" No one ever, ever, in my one-and-a-half years of patronage, tried to talk to me. Nor did I speak to anyone. After considering it at length, I decided that in this one case the atmosphere and inner harmony of the place had to be preserved from my active interference.

3

The Library and Its Surroundings

Nagari Pracharini Sabha itself was unrecognizable as a library and invisible as a building. Red, symmetrical, gracious, it stood independently in its compound. Recently the decision had been made to use the land in front for commercial purposes. This meant the construction of a row of two-story shops that sold textiles, dry goods, tea leaves, and medicines. All that was knowable of the Sabha from the road was a gate, half-concealed by the teashop, and a front of modern stores whose owners, if asked, would most likely deny that any library existed in the vicinity. If you did go behind the stores, you came to the large red building, impossible to evaluate immediately because it loomed over you and could not be viewed in perspective as planned. The remaining open land on both sides had been ruined, too, as an aftereffect of the construction: piles of bricks, pipes, and broken-up stone lay around. On each brick was inscribed the word *"AGHOR,"* a fact that puzzled me until it was revealed that the kiln from which the bricks came was owned by a devotee of the holy men of the sect of that name, a sect I was to pay a great deal of attention to in my research. These small revelations were like gifts of the gods: after seeing those bricks I needed no more evidence that it *was* a live cult.

Inside the Nagari Pracharini Sabha was a dark hall, fifty yards long, at the center of which stood a massive wooden table for readers. At its head sat five or six officials of the Sabha, some scribbling or turning over pages, most looking out restfully. The whole place was still, uncrowded, unencumbered. On three sides of the hall were verandahs studded with doors to the outside, many of which were open to let in sunlight and air. After you got used to the place, it was pleasant.

The hall was too dark for me, but the verandahs were ideal—cool in summer, sunny in winter, perfect for watching the rains in the monsoons. I would pull a broken chair and table to my desired spot, balance my folio of newspapers—twice the size of the table—on one side, and place my notebook on my knee.

I note the use of "broken" here: most public objects in India strike one as broken or in disarray. Only two exceptions shine out as models of orderliness and a state of perfect maintenance, both of which I grew up with (which might explain my alacrity in noticing the broken): official buildings and possessions at a certain level, such as those owned by the police and military, though not those of civil, representative, or other public organizations; and certain religious institutions, such as *maths* (monasteries), temples, *akharas* (gymnasiums), and Christian missionary schools. Everywhere else the notion seems to be attuned to total recycling: everything is allowed to crumble uninterrupted back into dust, from which it is built up anew.

Where all the Sabha books and papers were stashed was a mystery in the beginning. At the head of the hall, behind the seated officers, was a stone staircase. No one ever used it, or could, since it had books all over it, this being where loose material was deposited until it was gradually catalogued and shelved. Though never used, the stairs implied that there was another floor. Though the hall itself had a ceiling the height of the building, the verandahs had a second story where the stacks were located. Occasionally, a reader asked for a book, and there would be creaks overhead after an interval. The old newspapers and magazines I was interested in were piled high on dusty shelves along the walls of the very verandah I chose to sit in. I mean literally "piled." To see what was in the middle of a pile, a team got to work. One man on a stepladder would pass down the volumes, each of considerable weight, to another man on the ground, who then called out the date on the volume, and thus their search progressed as I stood by and fidgeted. I had nothing against the men who ran the place, or even against their system of working, except that it was very bad for the materials. The dust and accompanying spiders and insects obviously damaged the paper. Most of the volumes had too much weight atop them; I gathered they were too oversized to be shelved upright. But because their spines were not marked, the moving around that was required when a scholar needed a particular volume pulled and pounded at the bindings. There is absolutely no doubt that the materials I used were in a far worse condition after I called them. I couldn't think of a ready reform. I learned gradually of the powerful people of the Sabha, the member of Parliament and the member of the Legislative Assembly who held court in the office and guest rooms in the complex behind the Sabha. I knew they were unconcerned about the condition of old newspapers and could not be motivated to do anything about them unless they became an issue at the level of state or national politics. I don't want to be unjust. Surely there were other, more academic, members of the Nagari Pracharini Sabha Committee. But they were never mentioned; nor did they make themselves known by signing anything, or coming around, or showing themselves in any other way. I knew only of the politicians at the top and then the foot soldiers at the table in the hall.

I began my work there smoothly enough: entered one day, signed some forms, made a deposit, and started looking through lists. On the first day I made a preliminary note of about twenty journals that would be of interest to me. I looked through the issues of only two journals in detail in the next fifteen months. Then, alarmed at the fast-approaching end of my stay, I quickly scanned a dozen more. But I left feeling that I had barely glimpsed the real treasures of Nagari Pracharini Sabha, and though I have gone back since I continue to feel that way.

The men who sat at the head of the table were a little like the three or four vultures in *Jungle Book* (the Walt Disney movie version) who seem to be dozing on a branch with their chins on their chests but shake themselves awake every few minutes to ask, "What do you want to do?" "I dunno, what do *you* want to do?" They did have work—I could see them filing papers, making lists, dealing with readers—but it was probably sufficient work to occupy one person four hours a day. Two of them were young men in pants and shirts, and they were mobile, being the ones who went upstairs. The others never budged, except to go and relieve themselves in the compound. They wore *dhotis*, those elaborate lengths of white cotton wound around and between the legs, and all they had to do was gather up the cloth and squat—something I firmly believed only women did till I saw them. Their *dhotis* made me nervous. One of these men, Chachaji, often sat with one knee folded up on his chair—naturally he got tired of sitting still for so many hours—and I was afraid to look at him, not sure how revealing his posture might be.

No one asked me any questions or took notice of me. Or so I thought. Chachaji had his sources of information, however. About a month after I began work there, he suddenly asked me about a cousin who lived in Banaras. Through that connection he established that my father was well known and that I was a *pakka*, or authentic, U.P. Kayastha, that is, of one of the (ten?) lineages of the Kayastha, or scribe caste, of Northern India (Bengali Kayasthas did not count, though I never gave up trying to include my husband's Kayastha lineage in the ongoing fight to establish my normality). So, it turned out, was he. I cannot pretend I had not been curious, and we both breathed more easily after that. I had been itching to place all my recent acquaintances and daily companions according to caste, class, occupation, family, and area of residence—for my own reasons of course. But just as they made little sense to me, so I made no sense to them without this positioning. I am fundamentally a shy, retiring person, not a journalist or a socialite by nature, and if I could escape having to make conversation with strangers I would. In the early days of my fieldwork, that side of my personality dominated the professional anthropological one. I wonder now why I remained so subdued and inefficient instead of starting natural conversations with people, asking them who they were, and telling them, of course, who *I* was. But at that time the dark hall was a precious retreat from my energy-draining "natural" conversations on the street and my psychologically exhausting curiosity. At Nagari Pracharini Sabha I could be myself, not my self as presented to others; I could think my own thoughts and be *almost* oblivious to the world as I scribbled away.

What did I scribble? The first weeks, as usual, were difficult to comprehend or to justify. I read through the one page on Banaras in every issue of the fortnightly *Bharat Jiwan*, beginning in 1884, and wrote down whatever seemed of interest. Having no immediate intention of changing the research topic outlined in my proposal—though I thought I might in the long run, since everyone seemed to—I took down mention of all festivals, music performances, other public events, the city itself, politics if they were interesting, and social affairs, that is to say, everything but the strictly accidental: the local thefts, fires, and carriage accidents, which seemed to dominate the news. I wish I could say that I found things about, or even casual mention of, lower classes and artisans. But they might as well not have existed. The world of *Bharat Jiwan* was one of middle-class, educated *babus*, interested in world affairs and political analysis, socially competitive and somewhat amused by one another; their city was humming with activity, including the Parsi theater, wrestling matches, balloon-flying demonstrations, the Calcutta circus, in-house parties and receptions at Holi, Diwali, and a dozen other festive occasions of the year. The Banaras of *Bharat Jiwan* was much like the New York of the *New Yorker*. It seemed somewhat irrelevant to me, with my stated interest in the lower classes, but I doggedly kept copying.

Within weeks the picture started changing. I *knew* what the journalists were talking about, not because their reportage changed but because my notions of the city and its life began to fill in and develop. Everything in *Bharat Jiwan*, for example, was always given a *seasonal* reference. "Ah, the month of Sawan!" it would rhapsodize. "Babu so and so and party went on a picnic to Sarnath." Or, "It's the season for *jhulas* (swings); there are dark clouds in the sky, and each temple thronged with visitors." Now I was discovering that my informants, few as they were, would say the same *kinds* of things. They would always give seasonal references, talk of similar activities, such as going outside and making excursions to gardens, assume the centrality of temples, and so on. The importance of the discovery was not that nothing had changed between 1884 and 1981 but that the upper-class world reflected in this journal was much the same as the street-level world I was getting to know in my fieldwork.

Consider this: the elitist *Bharat Jiwan*, like all such periodicals, was packed with advertisements, and among the amusing and distressing items was a recurrent ad for books of songs, *seasonal* songs, accompanied by pronouncements such as "He who has not read this has done nothing in life" or "For the educated, cultivated, and pleasure-loving." These were the same songs my artisan informants sang out in *pan*-red-mouthed abandon. I could not have found more convincing evidence of the oneness of Banaras culture than this unsought coincidence of what was important for both the elite and the masses. It gave me a solid handle for investigating change through the issues of location, patronage, social constitution, ideology, and function of cultural events. Upper-class participation in the past gave me both a record of activities I could not have found otherwise and an interpretive insight (regarding, for example, the crucial nature of seasonality) that would have taken ages of labor to develop from field data alone, and even then without relating it to the past. Such discoveries provided thrills beyond compare. I turned to the *Bharat Jiwan* with fresh interest, taking care not to leave out *anything* on Banaras. I had hit on the relationship of history and anthropology that I had always expected I would hit upon at some point but had not been sure when and how. I combed volume after volume for such treasured statements, and when I would finally leave—my limit was three-and-a-half hours—it was because of sheer hunger.

Lunch was always a problem in Nagari Pracharini Sabha. I tried bringing some sandwiches, but they tasted awful. Then I made the whole family experiment with having our main meal in the morning, before the day's work, and tea and snacks in the afternoon. Unused to this, I would stuff myself in the morning and would feel dull and heavy for the next two hours. And the truth is that no matter what you eat in the morning, you get hungry again in the afternoon. There was little choice but to flee to the teashop again, as I did in mid-morning and mid-afternoon. Sometimes the "egg and toast" concoction produced there was quite delectable. At other times I fortified myself with biscuits and buns. Elsewhere in the city finding something to eat was not such a problem. There were fruits a-plenty, as well as corn, cucumbers, peanuts, and so on, according to season; and there were, as far as I was concerned, excellent sweet shops. But in the street from Maidagin to Nagari Pracharini Sabha there was nothing to eat except at the teashops. Once I found a lone hawker selling third-rate guavas, but he must have realized that he had lost his way, because he never appeared again.

One day, driven by my stomach, I decided to go the other way from Maidagin, that is, eastward, toward totally unknown areas. I had walked but a few yards when I found myself in the midst of what seemed a gradually thickening *mela*, a fair. It must be a special day, I thought greedily, looking left and right for easily collected information. I didn't venture more than a hundred yards or so, walking in a straight, safe line from Nagari Pracharini Sabha. People swarmed over the road and pavement; hawkers occupied the middle of the road, and buyers crowded behind them to approach the pavement stores. Everyone, of course, proceeded on their business without noticing me. The one interaction I could think of was to join in the buying, which was the idea that had brought me there originally.

I bought voraciously, until it struck me that I had no way of getting my purchases home. I didn't carry a shopping bag, and the best the larger shops could offer me was a half-page from an old newspaper. The hawkers had not even that, and gestured toward the end of my sari. I might have guessed where I was by reason of the goods being sold: foodstuffs ranging from commodities I was blind to, such as *ghi*, oil, and jaggery, to fruits, vegetables, and snacks. What particularly attracted me was the range of *batashas*, crisp white sugar confectionery. I had eaten such sweets in childhood, but as balls about one inch in diameter. Here were ovals and spheres up to eight inches wide. My cloth shoulder bag, in which I carried precious notes, was soon crammed with guavas, *batashas*, savory lentils, and other odd delicacies rapidly turning to crumbs and pulp. I hastily took a rickshaw and withdrew. The *rickshawalla* had to walk till he came out of the glutinous mass of human beings.

A simple measure of my ignorance about Banaras, and about Indian city life in general, was the fact that I had thought this was a *mela*, a special fair, and had failed to recognize it as the city's main wholesale center for food: the market of Visheshwarganj. Once the northeastern side of the city had been incorporated into my range of activity, I went through Visheshwarganj frequently. Curiously enough, the crowd was never again so overwhelming, nor did the *rickshawallas* have to disembark to take me across. The products on sale never again seemed so exotic or desirable. I came to see Visheshwarganj as a dirty, chaotic, difficult place with too much hay strewn around and, as a consequence, too many wandering cows and far too much cow dung. There came a time when it was conquered as well, a time when I would go to a house asking for old residents and argue confidently with the neighbors about who had *actually* lived there; or late at night would turn briskly into a two-foot-wide lane unmarked by any road sign to go to the house of my friend, Pandit Baikunthanath Upadhyaya, to record his singing group; or would crisscross the maze of lanes that lay between Visheshwarganj and Chauk in the early morning or late night—and, better sign of conquest still, would do this in the company of Hindu informants leading me to temples and Muslim companions showing me to mosques.

During these days of refuge in the Nagari Pracharini Sabha, my earliest days in Banaras, I was gathering courage to begin fieldwork in earnest. My first attempts, to approach an impoverished family of brass workers in Luxa and the arrogant ironsmiths in Lohatiya, had proved total failures. The brass workers had in effect requested that I kindly get off their premises and never return, and the ironsmiths had communicated the same invitation by continuing to hammer at their iron sheets while I questioned them. I have one weak genealogy and one page of disconnected notes for each. But those meetings had indeed been undertaken in a tentative way. As with the first visit to the river, I had simply not been ready. All this bungling in the first month of my stay was, upon reflection, partly deliberate. I was not anxious to proceed with a strict professionalism that obtained immediate results at the expense of insights into the complexities of the world I was setting out to construct.

The method of acting like a child in another culture in order to learn its "grammar" suited my predilections. In those first days I was slightly too naive, overly careful to assume I knew nothing and had to learn all. I was scared to impose by mistake my crippled, obnoxious middle-class/upper-class presuppositions on these robust natives. Only *they* knew what they were doing, and I thought I should be prepared to discover it the slow, painful way, without even the guarantee of success that a child has unless I could pass the test of childlike naivete.

By Diwali, at the end of October, I had made a major breakthrough on all fronts, as they say of battles, and I had the same image of conquest in mind. I knew metalworkers and woodworkers and had visited with a weaver. I also had promises of friendship from a potter and a painter. When I think in wonder at how it happened, I can credit it to nothing else but sheer perseverance, the passage of time, and an incidentally growing realization that I did not need to deprecate myself to appreciate others.

4

Unknown Gods and Life-Styles

The story begins with Vishwakarma Puja (the Worship of Vishwakarma), the first signs of which were idols, wheeled to and fro on cycles, rickshaws, and scooters, of a deity seated cross-legged, with a paternal face framed in a mane of flowing white hair. He looked benign, even harmless, and was supposed to be the original creator. Well, I reflected, that was a difficult being to represent, and this approximation, obviously relying on many venerable traditions glimpsed in "mythological" movies and calendar art, was as good as any. The image was reproduced in the thousands, in sizes ranging from that of a thumb to that of a full-grown man. All the Vishwakarmas looked identical. They were made by the potters of Banaras, who could not face up to my unsubtle inquiry concerning the origin of the iconography, though all agreed that the Vishwakarma icon was not very old. After wandering around their stalls for a while, I wisely decided to avoid them on this, their busiest day. As I discovered slowly, many days were equally busy, and it was impossible to find them in a quiet moment. They were always getting their products ready for the next festival, and they had an unnerving habit of fobbing off the curious intruder with a polite "Do come after Diwali" or whatever the next event on the calendar was. Consequently, the people I got to know on that momentous day, the 17th of September, were not potters at all but a family of copper wiredrawers.

Luxa Road, although close to the center of the city, was a safe place to hang around in, not teeming with objects, people, and impressions like Chauk. It was a modern road, more so than the so-called New Road, crowded enough, but not overwhelming. No one knew where the soapy-sounding name had come from. There was a Theosophical Society office and school within a large, shady enclosed compound, and there was the vast Ramakrishna Mission Hospital, whose name had never suited popular tastes and been replaced by "Kauria Aspatal"—the "Cowries" Hospital, from the age when cowries represented the smallest unit of currency. There were also one or two estates with massive walls and gates, now being subdivided and sold off. Lining the street were new shops—tailors, stores for ready-made clothing and electrical appliances—mostly around the Sikh Gurudwara, the whole compound evocatively called Gurubagh, the Garden of the Guru. At the main crossing on the street were older shops, for sweets, bicycle repairs, baskets, pottery; one had been converted into a video store. Potters obviously lived off the road to the north side; just where the northern lanes joined the main road were little displays of clay toys and other clay products—for sale when painted, for drying in the sun when not. In 1981–1982 Luxa also had a video arcade, and, in the same category as far as I was concerned, two temples, both under spreading banyan trees, that hosted all-night programs once a year. The arcade provided me with one of the most memorable sights I ever encountered in Banaras. One day, on the other side of the road near the arcade, walked a man clearly from another age, with his *dhoti, kurta, gamchha* (native clothes par excellence), thick slippers of recycled tire, all the evidences of poverty, illiteracy, and—well—absence of modernity. Preoccupied and inattentive, he was muttering something to himself that I discovered was a playful repetition of the sound emanating from the arcade, a kind of zingy "Pow! Wow!! P-o-w! W-o-w!!" He was participating in yet another cultural leap, which, like all such, was obvious only to the observer; he himself was not aware of any incongruity in his behavior.

On Vishwakarma Puja day, I was hanging around the old stalls, observing who was buying the images, waiting to trap a likely person in conversation. An unshaven, slightly built man of perhaps twenty started buying at a potter's from a long list that included, it seemed, all the ingredients for the

Vishwakarma being taken out for immersion

devotional ritual of a *puja*. The length of his list gave me time
to think. Probably the best rule in fieldwork is *not* to think too
much, but rather to act spontaneously and unhesitatingly.
But sometimes you absolutely *must* be sure of what you are
going to say, and you should not interrupt someone in the
middle of an activity either. When the young man paused to
consider whether he had got everything and the shopkeeper
tied up his purchases, I approached him with great interest.
That was my line, I had decided—not casualness or indifference, but deep interest. "These are all for Vishwakarma Puja,
aren't they? You celebrate Vishwakarma Puja?"

I am not sure what he answered then or later in the day.
The whole event is rather hazy. I was so preoccupied with my
own questions, planning them in advance, shaping my reac-
tions, considering the impression I was creating, wondering
what on earth I could do next, and so on, that I could hardly
be said to have been concentrating on the other, as one ought
to. He was positive and encouraging, however, and when I

told him I was new in the place and would *love* to watch Vish-wakarma Puja, he led me into a lane south of the road. This, as I was to discover, was the neighborhood of Nai Basti, which also had an instance of every other kind of cultural activity I could want.

It was an exhilarating beginning for fieldwork, though the incident itself did not match the more exciting ones to occur later. The family was "irregular" and difficult for me to figure out. Brothers who lived in a joint family were newly separated, and though I met only one, I became acquainted with the wife and daughter of the other. The brothers lived in rooms opposite each other, shared a common space in between, and pretended not to speak to each other. They referred to each other as *"pattidar,"* a technical term for co-sharers of ancestral property that was unfamiliar to me and perplexed me for a while. On the ground floor there were three vast wiredrawing machines in a partially covered court-yard and a little room with a string cot and some clothes. This was the *kothari*, or storeroom, better described as a "room without windows." Apart from stores, it had the signs of a male using it, but I couldn't guess who. Maybe those working at the machines—in turn? Another three rooms upstairs, as well as a verandah and terrace, were divided between the brothers, as were the machines, but I was to get to know the upstairs and the women only later.

Kishan, the man who had brought me here, was not one of the family but a day worker. It was a holiday for him, and like all those who worked in a factory, he celebrated at his place of work. He set up his purchases, created a typical *puja* scenario, and performed the ritual. He was inexpert but unembarrassed and unfaltering. The *puja* I had sat through at the Vedanta Society in Chicago for a headache-laden two hours, with every flower (or was it every petal?) addressed individually, approached with the ordained twist of the fingers, and moved majestically from place *a* to place *b*, had been one extreme; Kishan's was the other, in its utter simplicity and brevity. I sat on a stool and took photographs. The others stood around and gazed on, not indifferent, but not participating vocally (with *"Vishwakarma ki Jai!"*—"Hail . . . " etc.) or in any other way, not, I concluded, because they didn't know the form of the ritual but because they were not in top spirits. To recite or join in chorus at a celebration specifically *yours*, you have to feel good about yourself and the course of your life.

Everyone ate *prasad*, the food blessed by the deity, and the three silent hunks of machines were garlanded and dabbed with vermilion. It was all over in four or five minutes. Kishan said to a co-worker, "Gauri, let's make a program to go to the cinema." I was almost sure that what I would do next was to become invisible and accompany them to the cinema, spying all the time on their words and thoughts. In fact, all I did was sit around till the mood of the *puja* faded, the brief flicker of something special that had been created died away, all of which happened rather quickly. I sat there till everyone else moved off. I didn't have the heart to pin them down with inquiries about themselves, their work, their lives. It was their holiday after all. I wasn't a friend yet, and I had been admitted because of my professions of curiosity regarding the ceremony. That part being so clearly over, I could only continue with an apology for extending my project, no matter how I defined it. No one in the quickly disintegrating group helped me by supplying a question, comment, or even expressive gesture.

"At least I know the house," I told myself—the ultimate argument I became used to giving when I could not bring myself to force what would not yield.

My first real participation may well be said to have been none too dramatic. There was no sudden shock of discovery, no vision of vistas rolling forth. But I *had* seen Vishwakarma Puja, and if it was brief, trifling, casual—so be it. The informants could not be wrong.

When I came back to this house a month later, package of sweets in hand, seizing upon the occasion of Diwali, none of the people I knew were there, and I met a totally new cast of characters. At a hand pump in the courtyard, right next to the entrance way, a fresh, perky young woman was washing some utensils. "Do you work here?" I asked innocently. "Why, no! This is my house!" she told me. I was not sure whether to believe her, but then she led me upstairs. She was Usha, the older of two daughters of one of the separated brothers. Misjudging her status simply because she had been caught doing domestic chores with her sari tucked up and her hair disheveled gave me such an eloquent example of my narrow, middle-class prejudices that I was almost cured of them. I spent the rest of the day with Usha and Nisha and their mother—enticed across the courtyard in the middle for an hour by their *pattidar*'s family—and I count that as the beginning of Phase II, when you not merely get acquainted, scribble down basics, and walk away thinking, "At least I know the house"; but rather you participate in your hosts' activities, recognize each member of the family, feel comfortable in their home, and depart with their exhortations to come again soon.

Usha had attended school, as Nisha was doing now. They shared one school dress, and both had studio photographs of themselves in it. Their full name for school purposes was Verma. This was, for me, the inside view of the schoolgirls in identical uniforms, each with a placeable name, that I had seen all my life. Neither the uniform nor the name "belonged" to the girl, as I had assumed they did all through my school days! Usha must have been about sixteen and had been married a few months. She was spending her first Diwali after the wedding in her natal home, as was the custom. Her father-in-law was expected any time for a meal.

The meal itself was an eye-opener on many counts. The father and father-in-law sat downstairs in the *kothari*, where they were served; they exchanged not a word with any of the women, including me. The food itself, the flour, *ghi*, vegetables, and fuel for cooking had all been specially bought for the guest and sufficed only for him and his male host, with some leftovers for the womenfolk. The *ghi* was enough, for example, for *puris* for the men; as it got used up, the deep-fried delicacies were replaced by well-greased toasted *par-*

athas, then by dry *rotis* with simply a lingering touch of *ghi* on one side. Only a taste of vegetable was left over, and this was quietly put aside for Usha and Nisha's brother, Bahadur. Apart from the segregation of the sexes and the obviously limited resources, the third eye-opener was the sheer frolicking fun of it all, as we, the girls, kept up a bantering, giggling, carefree exchange all through the cooking, serving, and eating. I suppose I must have expected depressed spirits, some explicit signs of deprivation, scarcity, and oppression, some signs of revolt maybe, of the poor against the privileged, of women against men, as one ate dry and the other rich. But these women were having a wonderful time; and I, as one of them, chattering ceaselessly about Usha's school, their neighbors in Nai Basti, Usha's father-in-law, and their awful *pattidars*, felt, too, that life was fun, but kept wondering how to explain it.

Their exhilaration upon the occasion of the festival and the daughter's return home was matched by mine on the inauguration of Phase II. Having been confined to one small world as a child, I also had a *personal* need to expand my arena of experience into other worlds. Fieldwork—once it succeeds beyond a point—allows you to do that. I had suddenly, rather magically, become a privileged insider, recognized by some hitherto unknown Usha, Nisha, and family, as one of them.

The poverty of the house was brought home to me only on my later visits. There was *never* enough to eat. I made gifts under every pretext I could think of till I didn't need any and developed the technique, later to serve me everywhere, of presenting a box of sweets with the barely audible murmur, *"Prasad hai"* ("God's leavings"). I never saw Usha again, because she departed for her in-laws' home shortly after Diwali. Her father, I discovered, was unemployed, supposed to have gone crazy upon the shock of the partition with his only brother in their hitherto harmonious family. The household was supported by the other male in the family, ten- or twelve-year-old Bahadur, who operated the wiredrawing machine and earned the usual three to four hundred rupees a month. Bahadur looked morose, his father avoided the house altogether, and the mother and daughter took in all kinds of work to keep busy, since there was nothing to do at home in the absence of food to cook and possessions to take care of. They rolled *papars*, dry lentil cakes, at the rate of one rupee per hundred and hooked chains of artificial beads at eight annas per twelve dozen. I watched them endlessly. I realized how much difference an individual personality makes, and indeed a special event like a festival. With Usha gone and the silly abandon of Diwali over, there was not a trace of the gaiety and lightheartedness that had left me wondering. In that sense, I had been right to wonder.

I had always held my own stern views on the preferential treatment of sons over daughters. But seeing in this case how the mother and daughter together earned thirty rupees a month and were incapable of doing anything else, and how the far younger boy earned twelve times as much and supported them, I could understand the logic of treating him as special and superior. He didn't drink, gamble, or keep bad company, they said, in the voice of those who would neither control nor interfere, and I could foresee young Bahadur maturing into a gruff, distant, uncommunicative man around whom the womenfolk of the family would flutter, because, after all, he had sacrificed his childhood to keep everyone alive. As for the female protagonist of the tale, his sister Usha, not only had she had a happy childhood but she was still bubbling over with the joy of a child, untouched by any care.

At Nai Basti I had a glimpse from the very beginning of something that was going to confront me directly only later, with Mohan Lal, Tara Prasad, and such close comrades: the dangers of oversimplification regarding, among other questions, the characterization of the poor, the class-specific nature of pleasures, and the passivity of women.

5

Further Pursuit of Informants: The Metalworkers

As September advanced and the monsoons drew to a close, it suddenly became possible to achieve much more in any given day. Even so, I regretted the end of the monsoons. From the moment we had reached Banaras in July, I had realized that there was a lot of "cultural activity" there. If you took one of the two key roads traversing the city from center to south, you passed Durga temple and Tulsi Manas temple. The area around them always seemed festive, with crowds blocking the roads, hundreds of little stores, flowers, sweets, ribbons and trinkets for women, puddles, and monkeys. It was Sawan, the fifth month of the North Indian Hindu calendar, the time of year for fairs and music and small local celebrations.

When I say "local," I mean it. None of the people we encountered was able to tell me of even two or three of the celebrations, leave aside the whole variety or range of them. I had to discover them for myself over the next few months, fervently hoping that I was searching for, and then looking at, the right thing. It was a depressing, disheartening process. Upon hearing of my research, a police inspector, head of the central, important Chauk *thana* and an experienced officer with many years in the sector, remarked, "Oh! This is Sawan, so you'll find plenty of festivities." I pressed him urgently: "*What* festivities?" He looked at me as confidently as ever: "Oh! Well, this is Sawan, so, let's see . . . in Sawan . . . well, there are lots of festivities. . . . " His name, Chandra Bhushan, was pinned on his shirt, but I remember it with difficulty, for after this inauspicious beginning he never evolved into a friend or an informant.

He did assist me in unforeseen ways though. He had helped us buy a refrigerator in Chauk (and received a cut? I could not help wondering later, as I grew to feel uncharitable toward him), and having made his acquaintance through that transaction, I walked into his police station early in my field-work. He jumped up from his chair, exclaiming, "You here! Is the refrigerator working all right?" I reassured him, made myself humble, and introduced myself properly—not as the I.G.'s daughter but as a researcher—again. He recovered and made an important and mysterious phone call. As a result of this, an old, frail, but straight-backed man in a *dhoti* and *kurta* showed up at the *thana*. This was Govind Ram Kapoor. It took me a few days to place him properly, but I will sum him up here. He was a businessman who imported and sold silk yarn and some silk fabric. More than that, he was a commu-nity leader and the most active member of all the Citizens' Defence Committees in the city, voluntary organizations set up in every neighborhood to help authorities maintain peace and order. More important still, he was sycophant of all of-ficialdom, a middleman between the public and administra-tors, and a general meddler in all public affairs. By virtue of having a shop in Chauk, Govind Ram Kapoor knew all about the sari business; by extension, about weavers and their cul-ture. He and the station officer there and then appointed him my guide and mentor.

Wiser after my "What happens in Sawan?" experience, I pinned him down to a time and place. Two days later I was winding my way with him through the cobbled *galis* of Madanpura, known as the central weaving district of Ba-naras. The lanes were wonderful—endless and confusing, a traveler's dream. On all sides rose tall buildings joined by common walls, trapping the sun. From the ground floor win-dows of these came the sound of handlooms clapping, but the windows were too small to permit hurried observations. It was not a poor locality at all. Roads and houses looked clean and well maintained. Children ran around, and though they were eating the usual two-paisa and one-anna things from hawkers, they were combed and fully clothed.

Two or three less innocent months later I was to discover the reason for this obvious prosperity. Madanpura was not the central weaving district at all but the center of Banarasi sari export, where the Muslim traders had their business establishments (the Hindu businesses were located in Chauk). Govind Ram Kapoor naturally knew them because he had dealt with them for decades, but he knew no weavers whatsoever. Nor did he seem to know that the weavers of Banaras were concentrated in two areas, Adampura and Jaitpura, quite distant from where he had taken me. When I made this discovery and realized how far away these two wards were, I felt such a setback that I didn't venture back to Madanpura for another few months.

That day we went to Banaras Silk Corporation, or "BSC" as its owners called it. We sat in a comfortable office-cum-showroom on white sheets spread wall to wall, backs resting on bolsters, everyone relaxed but me. Once again my mind was on what the most appropriate questions would be. I interviewed them at top speed, scribbled down whatever they said, and understood almost nothing. I gathered that a huge family ran the BSC, with a dozen brothers and sons either introduced to me or alluded to. Both because the BSC ran powerlooms and hired semiskilled labor from villages outside Banaras and because those I was speaking with were obviously not weavers, I quickly relegated the encounter to the back of my memory, to be resurrected only when I had to formulate an opinion about sari businessmen. Govind Ram knew what he was doing, but his choices in social interaction were different from mine: he liked to mix exclusively with better-off people. A second foray into the *galis* with him proved equally frustrating. This time he took me to a "museum" of the metal products of Banaras that also served as a clubhouse, meeting hall, and display room for a society of traders in metal goods. It was in the control of one Babu Sharad Kumar Rastogi, head of one of the biggest such trading houses, who had his business downstairs in the adjoining building and his home upstairs. For my enlightenment he had called in two of his craftsmen, who mostly smiled and said "yes" to everything I asked. The other activities that afternoon consisted of feasting on greasy sweets and savories and touring the ceiling-high glass closets stuffed with rather ugly brass, copper, silver, and German silver artifacts. I took down the addresses of the two artisans with adeptness, and as I thanked Govind Ram upon leaving, told him, "Well, now I can go to their homes and see how they live." He was distraught. "No, no! You should not go to these people's neighborhoods. It isn't seemly!" That's when I realized, belatedly, that his ideas of appropriateness were different from mine, and that I could dispense with his help. As I shook off his offers of further assistance, he gave an engaging smile that left me speechless: "Then you are determined to get rid of me?"

In a day or two, I set off on the trail of the first of the two metalworkers, Master Sita Ram, *nakkas* (repoussé worker). Raja Darwaza, the area where he had told me he lived, is a legendary place. Whenever old *mohallas* (neighborhoods) or *galis* of Banaras are mentioned, Raja Darwaza is included. Of course, the truth is that as soon as you acquaint yourself with a place in your fieldwork, you forget the legend. As I stepped into Raja Darwaza, I was afraid. It seemed only about six feet wide, though rickshaws are able to traverse it and I once even saw an automobile parked in a makeshift garage. Both sides of this narrow street are lined with attached shops, all elevated about two feet and accessible by steps or a jump. Most of the shops are tiny, and their floors are spread with white sheets on mattresses. The first shops in the market sell jewelry, which is mostly kept out of sight, so you don't see anything inside but one or two owner-salesmen. They seem to fill the tiny shops till you see one with a dozen customers squatting inside and wonder where all the space has come from.

Now the shopkeepers do not have business all the time. Whereas some look down at newspapers, many sit languorously, facing the road and staring at the passers-by, so when you step into Raja Darwaza, it is immediately an unequal battle. You are longing to enquire into the place, the people, and the activities, but dozens of pairs of eyes are already probing you to discover your activity and your purpose. I could not stand the onslaught that first day and hastily withdrew my inquisitive gaze. I looked down and proceeded straight ahead as if I knew exactly where my potential purchase was located.

After a few yards Raja Darwaza becomes a market for other things besides jewelry, primarily jute products and cheap cloth. Then it becomes Kashipura, largely a market for machine parts, and looks grimy, oil-drenched, and heavy with the weight of iron and steel. I had heard from many sources that Kashipura was the home of the braziers and coppersmiths of Banaras, as I knew it to be the home of the one artisan I had met. He had given me his *mohalla* and had assured me that to find him I need only ask for Master Sita Ram, *nakkas*, in Kashipura. I asked dozens of people, and no one could tell me where he lived. There are, apparently, plenty of "masters" and plenty of *nakkases*, and, seemingly, no Sita Rams. So it has been throughout my research. I began to regard with bitterness the myth of personalized, face-to-face contact in the traditional city, where everyone knows everyone else in a *mohalla*. After my first few weeks in Banaras, I strongly resisted residents' efforts to present their address as "X, of *mohalla* Y, ask anyone," and would insist on having their house number, which every building in Banaras possesses, and a graphic description of how to reach it.

The whole day I searched for Master Sita Ram, my lone contact among metalworkers. Walking back and forth on the road with his vague address in hand, being gazed at speculatively by idle shopkeepers, I felt a trifle more kindly toward Govind Ram Kapoor and a little more tolerant of his protective "It isn't seemly!" Equally tiresome, I couldn't fathom the place, with all those machine parts shops lining the streets. Where *did* all those brass workers and coppersmiths hang out? When I finally saw a shop with metal products prominently displayed, I stopped at it, determined to make this my compensation for the other disappointment.

At the shop sat a beautifully aged man who could neither see nor hear well. For all that, he had time and warmth, and

welcomed me. That first day I didn't care what I asked or
what he said, as long as I could get acquainted—or, less eu-
phemistically, ingratiate myself with him. Of course, it was
rather easy not to care about what he said, because all he said
that first day related to himself as he saw his needs, not to
himself as I saw my need of him. He kept repeating, "Babu,
if you can get a job for any of my sons . . . I have four, and
there is not enough work for them . . . Babu, we can make
anything, whatever you want to get made . . . There are
twenty-five people in this house, and what else is there to
say . . . poverty, Babu, poverty . . . There is no market now,
no work for us . . . " And on and on. It was not a beginning
full of pleasure and satisfaction, as I had unconsciously an-
ticipated when we started talking. But here was a metalworker at last, an ancient one at that, and here was I, firmly
lodged, determined never to relinquish him, and all that he
was saying—however limited in scope—was necessarily
True and Real. Even if his complaints of poverty had never
figured in my calculations as the refrain I would repeatedly
be subjected to, I thrilled at the situation itself while feeling
abjectly helpless about the content of the conversation.

Mohan Lal, the old man, sat in the shop to occupy his
time. He almost never sold anything. He and his four brothers had been legally separated for about twenty years and
had divided the ancestral home along with the business.
Each house, sharing a wall with its neighbor, was only about
ten feet in width but ten times as deep and five stories high,
like a tall chimney. The staircase along one side was extremely narrow and steep. The front room on the ground
floor in each house was the workshop, or *karkhana*, in Mohan
Lal's case with a little shop in front. The workroom had a
mud floor, a hearth and fire, a lathe, metals, and tools. The
shop had a wall-to-wall dirty white sheet on the floor, a cash
box from which coins were always being handed out to the
children of the house, a *Ramayana* that Mohan Lal peered at
with his thick glasses when he had no one to talk with, and
miscellaneous merchandise. A heavy pair of scales hung
from the ceiling because everything was sold by weight.

Mohan Lal

My first impression of life in the place as a hopeless, dismal drudgery rapidly expanded and elaborated in ways that added myriads of dimensions. I confirmed that Mohan Lal was indeed poor and wanted a better life for his family but discovered that that was not all—or even the most important thing—to be said about him. I was put in a quandary regarding the interaction of economic and other controlling conditions of life till I could not in all honesty separate them from each other at all. After I became a regular visitor, had met Mohan Lal at different times of the day, on different days of the year, had eaten with him, laughed with him, heard the story of his life, told him my own, and simply had sat with him for many, many hours—I began to feel that life was a matter of moods and flavors and textures. How and why one did things was as important as what one did. One's actions were always affected by strong principles and philosophies, not merely by sheer "need" and "necessity." With Mohan Lal I fully and finally lost my assumptions of determinism. Soon after getting to know him, I was asked by an intelligent woman comrade also working with "people": "So, what is the basic motivating factor for these poor artisans?" I could sense the range of answers her mind would accept—economic necessity, rest as a compensation for heavy manual labor, caste, religion—and felt a sudden gap open between us as I heard myself express an unpremeditated thought for the first time: "Why, they're just like us. They'll go for a walk if they feel like it, chat with friends . . . take up theater . . ."

Mohan Lal had taken the seemingly extraordinary step of launching a theatrical group that rehearsed every evening after work. He loved to talk of it, to describe its productions, boast of its repertoire and quality, and particularly of the accolades received in various competitions. Somewhere in the back of my mind lurked disbelief, not full and total, but sufficient to demand some proof. Accordingly I pestered him to let me take photographs of the stage curtains they had used, which (he claimed) were now rolled up and stored near the ceiling of the Kasera (the metalworker caste) community center and clubhouse. I knew the building and its halls, and when I was shown giant rolls of dusty canvas suspended up high, I agreed that it was hardly practical to bring them down. I was accumulating evidence aplenty from other sources meanwhile that Mohan Lal's toothless chatter was more than the transformed memories of an aged man. Girja Devi, the respected vocalist of all-India fame, mentioned suddenly in the middle of an interview: "The Kaseras of Banaras, they are the best singers of all." A sophisticated theater group in the city referred respectfully to their productions of past decades. All testified to their amateur talent in Ramlila staging, and it was written of as well in old issues of the *Bharat Jiwan*.

One can explain certain things as "respected traditional activities that they believe in." But to say about Mohan Lal's theater group that "artisans work hard; they like their leisure; they have diverse interests and a love of life," as I finally did (at greater length, of course, and more analytically), misses the actual flavor of Mohan Lal's world. As a statement derived from this desperately overworked, underpaid, but independent-minded, passionate old man with his zest for living, it is simplistic and therefore incorrect and objectionable.

Mohan Lal was the first informant to whom I unqualifiedly gave the title "friend," not only because we became close but also because he lacked certain ideal qualities of an informant. He consistently refused to objectify his values and experiences and to present them coherently for my inspection. His descriptions were always somewhat muddled and incomplete, not because he was incapable of clarity but because he assumed a right to feign fatigue, ignorance, or lapse of memory, to change the subject and inquire about me instead, or to cackle and convert a serious topic into a ludicrous one. The more he did this, the closer we became, for I sensed immediately that he resented being studied, just as any self-respecting person would, just as *I* would. He had tremendous stores of dignity and taught me the precious lesson that simply because I was the observer and he the object did not mean that he was simpler, easier, more static, more accessible than me. Of course we were miles apart, but it was not age, gender, education, or culture that separated us; our difference could perhaps be summed up in the cliché regarding the rich having more money.

Mohan Lal began a phase of my fieldwork in which, thanks to his complex personality and our strong relationship, I learned to shed the inner lens forever refracting the outer world. I left behind forever most of my comrades and all those eloquent observers of the same confusing world that I was studying, all the Naipauls, Ved Mehtas, Nirad Chaudhuries, and Upamanyu Chatterjees. They were all, it seemed to me, preoccupied with their own feelings about the objects of their gaze, not with the objects themselves. I found it more difficult at that point to talk with someone from my own class and educational background than with my "people" such as Mohan Lal.

PART TWO

In which there is great progress in finding informants, in getting closer to them, and most of all in understanding them through the use of indigenous categories. In which also there are many dead ends, as in trying to find weavers; and distractions, as in trying to keep the household running efficiently, dealing with the death of a family member, and using police contacts to advantage.

6

A Shift in Technique

During my first months in Banaras my problems, however, were less of interpretation than of getting to know people. I became panicky as Sawan passed me by, followed by the next monsoon month of Bhadon, and still I had located almost no "cultural activities." I went to talk to my local guide and everybody's mentor, Dr. Suryanath Gupta. Dr. Gupta always had a mysterious, satisfied expression implying a knowledge of many things that would never get shared simply because you couldn't ask him about them since you didn't know what things they were. You could guess at random, as I did, and sometimes hit the mark. When I asked about the Ramlila, Dr. Gupta became suffused with excitement and talked rapidly for hours. Or, when you missed, as when I asked about the indigenous system of wrestling in *akharas*, he could look as grumpy as a child and say something like, "Oh, a lot has been written on that already," or, regarding the culture of a particular community, simply, "No such thing exists." But all these idiosyncrasies aside, Dr. Gupta was one of the most knowledgeable people in Banaras on the subject of the city's social and cultural life.

He told me that at that very time an important *mela*, or fair, called Sohariya Mela was in progress, so called because it lasted sixteen (*solah*) days. It was based at Lakshmi Kund (one of the many artificial tanks, or water reservoirs, in Banaras), centered on the worship of Lakshmi, and was the occasion for the display of handicrafts by the potters of Banaras, who rivaled one another in their production of toys and especially of images of Lakshmi for the *mela*. It sounded fascinating. But the third general rule I discovered about fieldwork (after the ones about legendary places losing their

charm and people in the same *mohalla* being unknown to one
another) was that the description of an event is very different
from the direct experience.

To begin with, I had no idea what a *mela* was, apart from
the expectation of dust and cheap stalls where everything
could be bought for a few pice—both ideas derived from a
short story by Premchand read in my school days. I had been
to the Nauchandi *mela* in Meerut as a child, but all I remember is grown-ups around me saying, "Let's go to Cozy Corner!" My imagination had soared, and I had expected scones
for tea, perhaps cakes and macaroons. I was reading Enid
Blyton's school adventures at the time and relished words
like "marmalade," "fruitcake," and "pie." Cozy Corner
turned out to be the exact opposite of all its name suggested,
a completely *desi*, or indigenous (in the worst sense), place,
almost dirty to my anglophile eyes. The grown-ups ate hot,
greasy *pakora*-fritters.

There is an easy way to find out where something is, and
accordingly I took a rickshaw and directed, "Lakshmi Kund!"
As soon as vendors and balloon sellers appeared, I hopped
off. Again, my timing was wrong. It was the middle of the
day and the magic was gone. I was to find it very different
when I came again the next year with three women all bear-
ing trays to worship Lakshmi, arriving in the evening and
staying on as darkness fell. But this first time, because I was
keyed up with expectation, because I was still so ignorant,
and because it was the middle of the day, I found nothing.

There were stalls on either side of the lane from about a
furlong before the tank to the tank with its neighboring temple. Most of these were manned by children, their parents
being busy with more productive work. Children take over
many stalls around mid-day as mothers wash and cook, fa-
thers bathe and eat, and youngsters are made to sit still after
school. The stalls all sold clay products, mostly images of
Lakshmi and a variety of toys, with some toys like the Ramlila
bow and arrow already making an appearance, Ramlila being
next on the festival calendar. The variety was not as great as
it seemed at first sight. After I had exclaimed over a little clay

T.V. set and bought a few other charming oddities, there was no attraction in the stalls. I made some effort to find out from the children where they lived, who made the toys, how, and so on, but they were really not the people to ask and did not relish being interrogated. I have found it awkward to approach children as informants on the whole because it is difficult for me to weigh their interest against their indifference and to talk on their level. My worst moment was when I started having a good time with a group of five or six dusty little boys on a street near Lohatiya, beginning to understand their game, their fun, and their personalities. Before departing I wanted to write down their names and where their homes were, driven by my familiar greed to know one more person that I could come back to later. Then I made the gigantic blunder of presenting each with a coin for a treat. Like wildfire the word spread over rooftops and through dusty *galis*, "Get your name written and receive a coin! Come and get paid for your name!" I have never made a less dignified retreat.

After plodding through all the lanes of the Lakshmi *mela*, I thought that I should at least *enter* the temple at the center of it all. There were a few worshipers here, along with bathers at the tank, and a little more to observe. But once inside, I could feel everything floating away from me. The old uneasiness I feel in temples came back, along with questions not to be resolved by mythology: "What is this? Who is this? What do I do? Why is everyone doing what they do?" I also never know what to focus on as observer in a temple and try to take in everything at once: the architecture, the sculpture, the ritual, the social drama . . . After this experience of my first *mela*, I was truly at a loss and in need of conversation. I had heard of Vishwanath Mukherjee for some time; an amateur author, historian, and ethnographer, he seemed to vie with Suryanath Gupta for the position of greatest expert on Banaras. I sought him out at his place of work, the Indian Medical Association, where he was on the editorial board of *Apana Swasthya* (*Our Health*). I prepared a list of questions for him, of which one was, "What is a *mela*?"

Vishwanath Mukherjee was confused by my topic, popular culture. Like most people I talked to in the beginning, "culture" meant for him the great musicians and writers of Banaras, and "popular culture" was a contradiction in terms. He kept listing for me all the "great" people I should speak with, and they still weigh on my conscience as a task never accomplished. I kept trying to elucidate my purpose to him. When I told him that I had been to a *mela* but could not comprehend it, and that I had heard of others like the Nakkatayya but couldn't guess the sense of them, he seemed to perceive a logic. He never did tell me about *melas*, but we came to another milestone in my research.

"You know the most special thing in Banaras?" he said that first day. "People like to go on picnics."

"Picnics?" I asked incredulously.

"Yes, they go outside, cook, and eat."

"Since when has this been going on?" I questioned, convinced that it was a thoroughly middle-class activity, at best learned downward through "trickling" or "seepage."

"Since always. Banarasis have always loved to do this," he answered complacently.

"And does it continue?" I persisted, wondering why, if he was correct, I had come across no sight or mention of this activity.

"It was popular till 1947." I discovered later that most people used 1947 as a landmark in their memories to denote some major change during their lives. Or they would say, "twenty-five to thirty years," implying 1947, or simply, "*Azadi ke samay se*" ("Since Independence"). They meant, as it would turn out after further questioning, within one generation, or within their living memory, that they had been familiar with something in their youth but that their children were not.

The lead that Mukherjee gave me was confirmed in the most direct way possible less than a week later. I was talking to Ramji Sahgal, owner of Khatri Medical Hall in the heart of Chauk, as well as a textile store across the street and a store of dried fruits and fruit drinks. When he had a visitor, instead of regaling the person with the usual tea, he would offer, say, a glass of apple juice—but unlike the customary tea offered at each visit, his refreshment was limited to the first visit because it was so much more exotic, special, and expensive, or so it was in my case. Ramji Sahgal is a scion of one of the old, established families of Banaras, not one of the *rais*, or aristocracy, but on the fringe. He is active in his community and is founder-member or secretary of assorted cultural organizations such as Nagari Natak Mandali (Association for Nagari Theater), Ved Vidyalaya (School for Vedas), Sangeet Parishad (Music Club), and so on. He speaks in a reserved, somewhat pompous way, as befits his position—which I have always found best defined by his location, that is, sitting in his open-fronted shop, exactly where the *galis* turn for the famed Manikarnika cremation ghat, governing the vista of what is therefore the most crowded, interesting, and important part of Chauk. I made friends with him because of his location.

On that day, after a great deal of interesting talk, I put the question to him, "What are the leisure activities of the people of Banaras?"

He replied promptly without a moment's thought: *"Bhang chhanana* (straining *bhang*, the local narcotic), washing your clothes with soap, and *bahri alang jana* (going outdoors)." Amazingly, he managed to look pompous and dignified even as he said this.

I was somewhat alarmed to feel reality slip away from me so swiftly, and to gain time I asked my formulaic question: "Has it changed? How is it changing?"

He said, Yes indeed it had changed. The first, *bhang*, was now too expensive; for the third, *bahri alang*, there was now less time and money; but the second continued to be the "hobby" (his term) of the people of Banaras.

I left, still in a daze, trying to picture Ramji Sahgal doubled over, scrubbing the shirt from his back with soap.

He was dead on the mark: soap was a valued object and a precious symbol of luxury and good living, but no amount of observation could probably have brought the fact home to me, with my preconceptions on the subject, had it not been stated to me so blandly. Many disconnected pictures fell in place: families gathered at public taps working up a joyous lather of cleansing; a Hindi movie I had recently seen where the middle-class couple comes to the verge of breaking up because the soap of the otherwise docile husband is used by the wife; the powerful advertising industry's explicit focus on soap.

Thus I entered yet another phase of my fieldwork, in which I started what may be called a systematic search, asking everyone I met about "indigenous categories," in this case *bahri alang*, soap, *bhang*, and water. For the uninitiated reader, *bahri alang* is best explained by its literal translation, "the outer side," and refers to the activity of going outside and away. When I thought about it, "picnicking" was quite an acceptable way of putting it, though in my mind I forced an "indigenous" to prefix the "picnic."

The next time I visited Mohan Lal, I put to him the question, "What is the *manoranjan* (entertainment) of you people?" His answer: "Bathing in the Ganga . . . exercise in the *akhara* . . . *bahri alang* . . . *nahana-nipatana* (defecation and bathing) . . . " He was one of those old men who, partly because they have been extremely energetic their whole lives and feel incapacitated with old age, develop a habit of claiming for everything that it is now finished. So Mohan Lal added, "Now everything is forgotten. Ten people would get together, go out, have *bhang*. Now there is no money, no interest. It's also a lot of trouble. Liquor is quicker."

But by that time, I had stopped taking everything informants said at face value. I could dig beneath the surface of their speech quite effectively to uncover the latent preferences and prejudices. I also learned to change my style of questioning from the innocuous, "What is ——?" or "Tell me about ——," which failed as surely as asking a preschooler (I was to learn), "How was school? What happened today?" With indigenous categories, I had possession of a key, I felt, with which to unlock people's minds and mouths, one which never failed at its task. The element of surprise was essential in its deployment the first time. With a new woodworker friend, for example, I turned suddenly in the middle of a conversation about something else to ask, "*How many times* a year exactly did you go to *bahri alang*?" And Tara Prasad looked at me happily and chortled, "Well, we have to go to Sarnath and Ramnagar, as you know. And then in the Navratras . . . It adds up to quite a lot." With my new metalworker families I would smoothly interject into a discussion of, say, poverty, "Then there's the going out, the bathing . . . soap . . . that must cost quite a lot." They would express appreciation of my perspicacity and proceed to elaborate in gratifying ways. By then also, if further documentation was needed, I had my first photographs of *bahri alang* revelers, on their way with *bhang* and *lota* (water pot) to the other bank of the river.

7

Woodworkers

In the first weeks of my progress with "the people of Banaras" I also met Tara Prasad, who eventually became the closest friend I made among the artisans, and again I use "friend" advisedly. One fine October morning, feeling it was getting "too late"—a feeling that began coming to me more and more often—I decided to explore Khojwa. An excellent article in *Aj*, the local Hindi daily, had informed me that Khojwa was where the wooden toymakers lived. I had with me that day my sister-in-law, Bandana, a serious young woman doing her Ph.D. in industrial sociology at Kashi Vidyapith. With a good idea of "what sociologists do," I did not wish to bore her, so I didn't loiter as I would have if alone. (I expected her to tire very quickly and to ask me pointedly, "What are you searching for?" She had already put me on guard by asking innocently, "What is your universe?") I put on an appearance of knowing my mind, alighted from the rickshaw at the first sight of wooden toys, and started talking to a young man tending a shop. It turned out to be an elaborate introduction to the industry and the people, far better than I would have had by wandering around.

The shop was called Arya Kashtha Kala Mandir, the Aryan Temple of Wooden Art, and the young man was Ram Chandra Singh. He was reading, had no customers, and was more than happy to show off his expertise and knowledge. With pity for my ignorance, which I was at pains to emphasize through word, gesture, and facial expression, he recounted the history of woodwork in Khojwa, the caste and social composition of the workers, and the nature of production. Everything was very clear except, as usual, his own family and social background. He was one of ten sons—could I have got

that right?—whose names went thus: Rameshwar, Parmesh-
war, Chandreshwar, Muneshwar, Gyaneshwar, Amiteshwar,
Gopeshwar, Shrimanteshwar, and then, for some inexplicable reason, Raj Kumar. There was also one sister, Mina Ku-
mari. Of course! The two glittering stars of the Bombay
screen! For reasons of my own—personality, family background, academic training—I always felt awkward and unsure in probing family relationships and processes, considered the subject irrelevant, and tried to relegate it to later
meetings. An hour with him felt otherwise like time well
spent. The only other discomfort I experienced was in pre-
tending I shared his taste when he began showing me the
choicest examples of Banaras woodwork. Only the hand-
made wooden idols struck me as wonderful, utterly lifelike
and charming. Who made those? Where did the ideas come
from? Usually from calendars, I was informed, and my heart
sank. I had expected something more "artistic" and creative.
Ram Chandra then unrolled some calendars for my benefit
and boasted particularly about one that he was going to order
the craftsman to make next: the Panchmukhi (Five-Faced) Hanuman. I seized on the mention of the craftsman: where was
he, how could I meet him? And immediately another young
man, Kailash Kumar, who had meanwhile wandered in, volunteered to take me around to the craftsmen's homes the
next day.

That was how I was introduced to Tara Prasad, though I
had to keep him too for another day because of Kailash Kumar's priorities. Kailash's uncle had a factory of stone goods
in Khojwa, and, as often happened, Kailash saw me as over-
impressed by Ram Chandra's products and wanted to over-
whelm me with his own. He was also educated, and doubtless full of vague ambitions, some of which I vaguely seemed
to touch, being from some vague faraway place in his vague
mind. I inspected the stone products: a seemingly unvarying
array of candlestands, incense holders, ashtrays, oblong and
round boxes for unnamed things. I tried to reason that this
apparent sameness was explained by the lathe they depended on, which could only whirl the stone around rapidly

Tara Prasad (right) performing a *pinda* ritual

like a potter's wheel while the workers scooped with different files to mold the stone. But inwardly I accepted that it was for sheer lack of imagination. I saw some more "factories" according to Kailash's taste, had tea and *pan* repeatedly, and extracted promises from everyone for hosting my further visits, all necessarily after Diwali. Most people offered to tell me the *whole history* of carpenters, toymakers, and stoneworkers in Banaras when I was ready (that is, after Diwali), and one grand man, Ram Khilawan, father of the ten sons, directed me to a publication, *Singh Garjana*, for enlightenment. This, as I immediately guessed, was the laudatory mythological history of his caste.

I went to Khojwa again the next day, though I almost never went to the same place two, leave aside three, days consecutively. Feeling like a thief, I took a different route, afraid to bump into those who had already assured me my work was over. Of course I lost my way and found myself returning to Ram Khilawan. It turned out to be no problem at all to meet him again, and I took one unplanned step forward in overcoming my diffidence and tendency to shy away from sudden familiarity and contact. During a brief chat he told me of what local people had drunk in the past, something called *madag*, made out of opium, but I felt utterly ignorant of the realm of drugs and intoxication conjured up by his talk and intuitively wished to ignore the whole subject.

When I knocked at Tara Prasad's door, hungry and despondent, I discovered that he wasn't in. His wife was illiterate and spoke only Bhojpuri. I for my part spoke "pure" Hindi and had always assumed that I would be able to follow Bhojpuri—or for that matter any "dialect" of Hindi—when the necessity arose. But this particular speaker showed me the fallacy of my simplistic and arrogant beliefs. Lilavati was crusading in her own way for the cause of those who resisted the categorization of Bhojpuri as a mere dialect and had plastered Banaras with posters, usually erasing notices in Hindi, urging, *"Kewal Bhojpuri!"* ("Only Bhojpuri!"). She spoke fast, with the unconcern for listeners that those little experienced in public life particularly have. Every time I tried to slow her down or to translate her words into mine, she either froze into uncomprehending silence or steamrollered right over me with her own thoughts. I had to admit to myself that I could not follow her and that she had no idea what I wanted, but I was determined to make it work. I sat ensconced on the wooden seat, she before me on the floor, and we talked to and fro for an hour, repeating much, and mostly at cross-purposes. A few things became clear, however. Tara Prasad was very sick. There was no money in the house. It was near Diwali and the wages for past work had yet to be collected. But how? Tara was too ill to go anywhere. His wife never stepped out, she did not like to meddle in all this. Why was he not resting then, where was he? He had decided to make his way to the doctor, resting and going, stopping and walking, as she put it, which I thought was wonderfully descriptive.

Very soon I was on my old track again, pleading with her to let me somehow help them. She resolutely warded off my offers, vague as they were. I'm not sure what I had in mind— perhaps finding out which route Tara Prasad had taken, following him, and helping him by the elbow to the doctor's. I knew I didn't have the courage or the confidence to take out some money and hand it to her. Thinking over the scenario many times in my mind, I concluded that giving her money would seem the height of insult, sitting there as I was, an uninvited and uncomprehended guest.

Even as my heart grew heavy at the hopelessness of poverty, and no less at the physical seclusion and resignation of this woman, as an anthropologist I was mentally noting "useful" facts, such as the name of the doctor patronized, one could say, by the woodworkers of Khojwa, or the economic, educational, and gender divisions that characterized Bhojpuri and non-Bhojpuri speakers. To file away information thus, even while expressing and indeed experiencing sympathy for a plight, always aroused in me the anxiety that I was reducing the situation to a drama, even a farce. *Can* one be detached and concerned at the same time?

Empirically speaking: yes. I was often both. I realized, however, which attitude had precedence for me. I obviously had a proclivity for detached observation: I was making a profession out of it. It took me a few more years and some well-intentioned but misguided efforts to grasp how I could also mark a well-defined space for acting on my other proclivity: to interfere in areas I designated as problematic.

My next visit to their house witnessed Tara Prasad properly medicated and restored. Displaying his unlabeled bottle of violet mixture to me like a trophy, he greeted me hospitably and in the right state of mind to take time off for conversation. As all further visits revealed, he was as busy as only the grossly underpaid piecework wage earner can be: he had to get through the first stage of carving at least ten statues every day. I could only sit by him and watch, calculating that one question per five minutes was all I should subject him to.

Tara Prasad's home was approached by a narrow *gali*—six feet across—that branched off the main road of Khojwa about two or three hundred yards after the bazaar began. I could take a rickshaw till the *gali*; indeed I felt it was essential. The main road itself was not too broad, and walking on it could be positively dangerous, with its bullock carts, hand-pulled carts, and speeding rickshaws, all piled high with heavy sacks, heading toward the grain market of Khojwa. For Khojwa's importance did not lie in its being the residence of woodworkers; it was known and feted as the second most important wholesale market for grain in the city, after Visheshwarganj.

The market was in South Khojwa, and I kept a distance from it for the longest time—traders and so on, after all, with their Vaishya (trading caste) values and brazenly economic motivations—until I realized what a unity a *mohalla* constitutes. Most of the points of interest that Tara eventually led me to, such as *akharas*, wrestling matches, Ramlila stages, temples, and meeting places for late night music, were located in the market, as were scores of articulate and culturally active men, all traders. I confronted yet another prejudice I had grown up with: a trader, I suppose I had imagined, was only half a real person, being engrossed in profit maximization; I discovered rather swiftly that traders were, in spite of their profession, as impressive as my artisans in their preference for living well.

No rickshaws entered Tara Prasad's *gali*, nor could I bring myself to stay on my bicycle in such a narrow space—even after I started riding a bike everywhere—though everyone else in Banaras could do it to perfection. I always walked, which itself needed the elaboration of certain techniques. If a bell-ringing bike announced itself as you were walking along, you had to turn to the wall quickly and hug it, hoping that the pedals wouldn't scratch you or the bike squish some fresh cow dung on you. Or, if you were near a step, you simply ascended it and waited at the front of a house for the bike to pass. As in Chauk, every house was raised a few steps, which helped when the place was full of rainwater, slime, mud, and washed-up garbage, but what other purpose this feature served I could not discover. A few Banarasi informants told me that it was the "seat" of the house, that houses were always built with "chairs" to sit on.

As I approached Tara Prasad's house, I always had moments of trepidation, for just there were three or four viewing galleries: a woman selling cheap packaged foods on a little platform, a man carving in a windowless room open to the street, and a housewife and mother inevitably massaging her children out on her verandah. These would all inspect me thoroughly and, seeing me often, must have felt they had a certain responsibility toward me, for as I appeared they would announce, "Go on, they're at home" or "Tara's out, but Mangra's mother is in." If I, whose job was to meet strangers, felt the neighbors' inquisitiveness so keenly, what did my hosts themselves feel? I sometimes wondered. Were they subjected to taunts, cross-questioning, accusations of accepting money, of being in league with the government, or simply of being made fools? All these were problems mentioned obliquely by less-willing informants; of my closer ones, none ever complained that my frequent visits caused them any trouble.

The neighbors, in any case, were clearly not malicious, simply torn by curiosity. Why did I not incorporate them into my widening net of informants and settle the matter once and for all? Even if I had done so, there would still have been "neighbors": for every person you get to know, there are a dozen to watch you. You also have limited resources; if you concentrate on one person or family, you cannot make an equal effort to become intimate with others simply because they appear along the way, so to speak; it is a draining proposition. Most of all, I would say, I could not summon up sufficient intensity to overcome the hurdles their different personalities and situations threw up. To make one conquest itself produced a certain relaxation of tension ("Ha! I am moving to Phase II") and weakening of effort. Then there was the element of chance—Tara Prasad had drifted into my orbit quite without planning—and the still-larger element of compatibility. Mohan Lal, Tara Prasad, and all those I got to know equally well were ordinary people in most respects but different from others in one: they had the imagination and the generosity to extend to me their friendship. By some trifling mannerism or characteristic, they had stuck out in an anonymous crowd in the first place; through some further qualities they made it possible for me to get to know them well. I did not feel the same way about most of their immediate neighbors.

I did make a conscientious effort to keep up the momentum, pushing my courage and aggressiveness to their limits. At Mohan Lal's, my earliest visits were enough to make passers-by pause, stare, and try to overhear what this short-haired, smartly dressed young woman and the blind and deaf old man in tatters could have to say to each other. The shop itself, with its front overhanging the lane, was almost part of the public space. As for neighboring shopkeepers, it always seemed to me that they had far more leisure than was normal, and they inevitably assumed various poses in their shops that gave them the maximum view of me. Mohan Lal minded none of this, and, adding to my embarrassment, we both had to shout because of his partial deafness.

The next family I tried to get to know in Kashipura took much longer to accept me. I turned into a little lane—three feet wide—at random, and there before me in a cobbled square was a well and a *chabutara* (brick platform), that excellent device for outdoor recreation. All around were houses opening to the square. The one directly in front of me was the largest, and in its front room, the workshop, squatted half a dozen men working on silver, an earthy sight, if there ever was one. Their smooth-chested, muscular bodies glowing in the embers of their own fire, which rose and fell with the bellows, their bare-floored workshop with tools of all sizes on the walls, and nothing but metal in different degrees of readiness all around—no matter how I have tried to squash this crude association, the memory has always left me with the aesthetic satisfaction of having seen something totally picturesque.

I was in the uncomfortable position of standing on the ground a few feet beneath them, trying to interrupt five or six working men with no very precise query. They played deaf and dumb for a while, then I think asked each other, "Who is she? What does she want?" I was totally intimidated and would have run away if I could have, but it was easier to hold my ground. Finally, I said, "May I come in?" I was given a folded sackcloth to sit on, but work continued on all sides as usual. That first day I got little information from them, but I was content simply to sit and watch them while they decided whether it made any sense to take a few minutes off to talk to me. Meanwhile, a crowd of children repeatedly gathered at the doors and were shooed off incessantly for blocking the light and wasting the men's time. That the males in the family were less irritated by my disturbance of their work than simply shy and distrustful of me became clearer when I started photographing the children. My camera worked as a wonderful icebreaker. The men began to laugh, joke, and talk, and though they did not look at me directly, they made me feel welcome.

It was even more difficult to get to know woodworkers because the lathe operators worked in groups in shops that were open to the street and were busy, crowded, dusty, and noisy with whirring lathes. It was always more difficult to approach a group of men than an individual, and it was nearly impossible to interrupt a group at work, especially with the deafening machines nearby. I began seeking introductions. For every person I knew, I would ask to be introduced to one more. Tara Prasad became my assistant as well as my informant. Not only did I peep into all the processes of his and his family's life but also I could come to him with any question and, for all his resistance, pester him for an answer. Often I would simply show up and say, "Take me to so-and-so." He would hem and haw but was irretrievably amicable enough to do it.

To the end he was uncomfortable at my "interviews." When I requested, "Take me to your *sardar,* the head of the Vishwakarmas," he literally jumped. "What do you want to ask him? What are you trying to find *out*?" On another occasion I asked him if he could take me to the widow of a man mentioned in my records as an important cultural patron. His dismayed, by then familiar, reaction: "What shall we tell her? What will you say?" It was useless to remind him of my project or to explain that I needed to know others as I knew his family, because he thought of me as nothing but a friend. My project had never been that clear to him to begin with, and he had relegated all knowledge of it to oblivion. Once, telling him that I simply must speak to more woodworkers but was unable to do so, I asked, Would he *please* introduce me to four friends? There followed an old-style anthropological encounter. I sat on the single wooden seat in Tara Prasad's house, his friends squatted on the floor, and I asked them questions as everyone else listened in. I have never used the information I gathered there. It was a silly tactic that turned out all wrong, nor did it make Tara Prasad understand that part of me better.

It must be said that Tara was a wonderful person whom I grew to love, but he was too stubborn and taciturn and, as I was always aware, far too busy to be a good informant and assistant. The lesson I was learning with Mohan Lal was reinforced: the reluctance of people to talk, to be interviewed, to be pinned down, was really their reluctance to be objectified. I measure my growth by my increasing ability to see the validity of their side of it, to drop the effort at outright objectification, to think of my informants as friends, and to accept that most of the time my information gathering had to be indirect. Tara Prasad revealed his specialness in wandering around the city, attending music programs and such events, pursuing his own activities with me in attendance. With him I came closest to fulfilling my somewhat neurotic and perverse dream of simply following an informant around everywhere without being seen or heard.

Tara had two rooms in his house, apart from the covered nook where he carved, the little bit of space that was the kitchen, and the tin shed with swinging door that must have been the toilet. In one room lived the family: the craftsman, in his sixties, perhaps; his Bhojpuri-saber-rattling wife; and the ten-year-old daughter, at the peak of pre-adolescent shyness. The second room was *kachcha*, of clay and thatch, and was rented out to a young migrant latheworker from the village, together with his family. The great thing for me was that this couple had an infant daughter exactly the same age as mine, giving me an honest, un-self-conscious topic of conversation right from the beginning. I could even bring my offspring along with me, and with these credentials in my hand, they had so much less distance to cover in formulating an image of me that they could accept.

Tara worked at home except for the necessary trips to the potters-painters who garnished his toys with paint and varnish and to the shopkeepers to barter for a few pennies his strenuously crafted, magically lifelike things of pleasure and worship. His home, accordingly, became one of my "centers," to which I could head from any place in the city, to breathe easily, talk slowly and at leisure, enjoy the restfulness of knowing that the family accepted me and had ceased questioning my purposes. My daughter took some of her first steps there and visited them at all times of the day and night, eating every kind of meal and grabbing her compulsory naps. Something about the clean-wiped, bare floor, the emptiness of the room, and the fact that everyone there did what children find preferable anyway, that is, conducted all activities on the ground, made Irfana feel in harmony with Tara Prasad's home. I remember her sitting crosslegged on the floor, around the age of one-and-a-half, being directed by her hosts to eat from a plate in front of her. She addressed the rice and was told, "Eat the vegetables! The vegetables! They're on top." And little Irfana dutifully looked up at the ceiling, wondering what other surprises her mother's friends had for her. It was only just and fitting that she should have returned to Chicago, at the age of two, fluent not in English, Bengali, or Hindi, the languages of her parents, but in Bhojpuri.

8

Weavers

My success with woodworkers and metalworkers was not easy to match with weavers, and I made four abortive attempts to enter their world before I finally succeeded.

First attempt: I had decided to eschew the deceptive *mohalla* of Madanpura, which people in their ignorance insisted on calling the center of silk weaving, but I was not sure where to go instead. Meanwhile I was broadening my circle of archival investigation. One October morning I visited Bhelupura Police Station to track down the police festival records I knew existed. The station officer was not in and others were not in a mood to be obliging, so I started my customary stroll in a randomly chosen direction. Immediately I saw a painter painting signs in his wooden stall, getting all the spellings wrong, with some finished portraits of local politicians and grandees standing behind him. "A painter!" My brain, as Sombabu claims it does on such occasions, started whirring. I ordered a nameplate from him and began talking to him about his work and his family. My purpose had to be explained, and as soon as I did so, he introduced me to a stout old man with a Muslim goatee in the shop of Diwali firecrackers next door. Clearly "hanging out," this man was sitting on a wooden ledge in the sun and swinging his legs; he was exactly the kind of man I wanted to meet. He took me to his home in nearby Gauriganj, where his sons and grandson wove saris. On the way I noted other weaving establishments, including a barely visible sign deep inside a lane that would be my next stop: Hai Silk House.

With the friendly Muslim, Kamruddin Ansari, I had the old problem of not knowing where to begin. Now I asked the family about their work, how long they wove, how much they earned, and so on. Now I asked them about their family life and what it had been like in Kamruddin's youth. "We exercised a lot in those days, daily, and ate raw *chanas* [chickpeas, lentils] soaked overnight after we worked out," he said, looking at his sons. "These youngsters don't do anything. Look at their health!" Now I asked about their festivals and was informed that Hazrat Shish Paigambar (whoever *that* might be) had started the craft of weaving. The most titillating information was that they were, all weavers were, Ansari. They were *not* Julaha (the caste name for weavers, both Hindu and Muslim, in written sources and popular usage); Julahas did "coarse work." Some days previously Mohan Lal had told me confidentially that they, the metalworkers, were Kasera, *not* Thatera, as some people believed. Thateras only did "coarse work," he had whispered in my ear.

The sons at first largely ignored me as a friend of their father's; Kamruddin, it was clear by their demeanor, they barely tolerated, thinking him old-fashioned and simply old. After a good hour of eavesdropping on our conversation and placing me in some way, they aroused themselves from their indifference and brought me their "family" albums to survey. It turned out that they had arrangements with *rickshawallas* and taxi drivers, who brought loads of tourists to their doorstep to be given an inside look at silk weaving and almost certainly to make some purchases. Kamruddin's sons had fat packets of photographs sent them by their foreign friends and a diary crammed with addresses from Japan to Hawaii, traveling westward. It was Kamruddin's turn to look amused and indifferent.

I did not stay long after that. I didn't fancy having my name added to the crowded rostrum of foreigners, which would probably soon have happened. As I walked away, I heard a shout, and Kamruddin caught up with me. "Don't forget," he panted. "Don't forget to write in your book that I used to eat raw *chanas* every day in my youth!"

Second attempt: Hai Silk House was a complex of three or four houses joined together, one used for dyeing, one for weaving, and so on. Mr. Abdul Hai sat in his *baithaka*, literally "sitting room," on his *gaddi,* literally "seat," the term used for all those white sheets and bolster pillows set out in every place of sale and reception. Mr. Hai was a middle-level businessman, not important enough to dismiss me offhand but hopeful that there might lurk a possible business deal in our exchange. He had a Hindu accountant whom I was itching to question about what it was like to work in a Muslim establishment, but I could only get enough of his name to gather it was Hindu and could come up with no ready excuse to include him in the conversation.

Mr. Hai claimed that thirty years back he had been an ordinary weaver and by the sheer skill of his hands he had risen to his present position of owning fifteen to twenty looms. He could describe the looms and the composition of the raw material in accurate detail. Then we came to "society and culture." "Our work was started by . . . " he began; "Hazrat Shish Paigambar," I finished, peeping at my previous page of notes and thinking again, whoever *he* might be. Abdul Hai did not take kindly to this display of knowledge on my part. "*You* seem to know all about us!" he exclaimed, not amused, scrutinizing me closely. "Hey, *munshi!*" he brought the accountant into the conversation; "How does she know *everything?*" Like me, he had been aware that the *munshi* and I formed some kind of a twosome, both being Hindus.

I was startled, to say the least. What did he think I was? A Muslim from a weaver family, disguised as a Hindu? A government agent? A foreign spy? I couldn't guess, but the interview was over.

Third attempt: I made at least two other misdirected attempts to penetrate the weavers' world. The first was through the agency of a sari businessman called Seth Govind Ram (different from Govind Ram Kapoor), who invited me to the *satti,* the wholesale market for saris, between 4:30 and 6:30 in the evening, when dozens of weavers would come to him, as to other middlemen in the *satti,* to sell their wares. I went, and sat on his *gaddi,* and saw the weavers come. He would recall my presence occasionally and jovially announce, "And here's a *bahanji* (respected sister) from Chicago

who wants to find out about weaver society! Tell her something!" And a few weavers would be directed to me. Red and
hot and in deep pain at the whole proceeding, I would mum-
ble, "Where do you live? What do you celebrate? How long
have you been doing this?"

Fourth and penultimate attempt: My last unsuccessful
foray followed a disappointing encounter with some potters
at Reori Talab. It was the eve of Diwali and the wrong time to
speak to them, as I should have known. So I breezed into a
shop of firecrackers on the other side of the street which had
a good display and where a team of three brothers and their
uncle were putting the final touches on more explosives. I
thought I was collecting data on the firecracker industry until
I discovered that the work was seasonal. Two of the brothers
did weaving; the third carried on a trade in mutton. The
youngest, as I guessed him to be by his looks and energy, escorted me inside to see his loom. None of them seemed to be
married, nor did they have a mother or sisters or any kind of
a "proper" family or home, but all were exceedingly extro-
verted. I was uncomfortable with all the obvious evidence of
bachelor existence and their readiness to welcome me into it,
but in those days the last thing I could do was voice my
thoughts or clarify a doubt plaguing me. I just went away
and never came back.

In fact, both Gauriganj and Reori Talab are weaving areas,
as is Madanpura, but the real centers are in the north of the
city, the wards of Adampura and Jaitpura. I finally reached
Jaitpura with the help of the "contact" of a "contact." Like
Govind Ram Kapoor, he was a silk yarn dealer, but one who
actually knew weavers. He himself lived in Nati Imli, and
next to his house, conveniently, was located the Bunkar Colony, or Weavers' Colony, a government-subsidized housing
scheme that had made about fifty homes available to poor
weavers through lottery. We went to the house of Shaukatullah, a heavy, balding man, with thick-rimmed glasses
through which he peered shortsightedly, a light-hearted,
amused man, and a true patriarch. He himself had retired
from weaving, though he was perfectly fit as far as I could

make out and evidently seemed to prefer sitting in the sun, shouting at his grandchildren, and going to the market for every little thing. The weaving was done by his two sons and a hired hand, and after a cursory look at the workshop I was handed over to "the family."

This was no small challenge for me to face. There were at least a dozen small children, half a dozen bigger ones, and as many adults. I settled down for the morning; in those days, so aware was I of my own limitations, I saw it as essential to give four hours where one was needed, recognizing that it was not only my informants' natural reticence that had to be overcome but my own shyness and ignorance as well. In a household setting, I was particularly lost. As soon as I had an answer to one question, I would simply nod and look sympathetic, not quite sure how to follow up. Matters of child rearing and child care? No, that subject did not quite appeal to me. How did they cook and what did they eat? Mildly interesting, but not terribly so. What work did the women do? That was clear enough: every stage of nursing, feeding, teaching, cleaning up, getting bobbins ready, and sewing and embroidery besides was before me to observe. They, in fact, asked me more direct, meaningful questions. "Where is our brother-in-law? How many nieces and nephews do we have? What do they do when you go out to work?" I am ashamed now to report that I could not even *understand* in the beginning that they were asking about *my* family, having accepted me as a sister, so unversed was I in Banarasi, and Indian, conversational rules, but as their meaning dawned on me I rushed to take advantage of the opportunity to establish rapport. They had me all figured out by the end of the morning, whereas I needed another four visits to have *their* "case history." In the process, through the familiar anthropological situation of role reversal, where they were the inquirers, I the object, they guided me in necessary ways. I paid close attention to their style of conversation, their Bhojpuri-Hindi lingo, topics that startled them and those they assumed to be natural, and I assimilated and adapted rapidly.

Three things dominated my impressions on that first visit. One was the fact of overpopulation and the related fact of filth. We sat in the courtyard, a cemented ten-foot-square space between the workroom, two family rooms, and the outer wall. All around it was a narrow open drain where the children were encouraged to pee, and at least one small child to defecate. Where the older ones relieved themselves I did not discover, then or ever. The rest of the courtyard was littered with spilled food, garbage, and what must have been urine. There were flies everywhere, and I was the only one conscious of them. I was determined not to let one alight on me, seeing as I could where it must have visited the minute before. When sweets were ordered and set before me on a freshly washed platter, I became engaged in a battle with the flies to keep them away and with myself to decide what best to do with these greasy sweets. Should I gobble them up before they could be further contaminated; refuse them with the excuse that I was unwell—"But these are made of *chhena* (cottage cheese); they're good for you," was the response I had learned to expect—; or distribute them among the children in a swift, decisive move. Incapable of the last, I nibbled and suffered, eating far more than I need have because I chose the disastrous course of saying that I could not tolerate much sugar and that tea and *pan* instead would be "just fine." So, I ended up being plied with the sweets *and* deep-fried salty snacks—since tea could not be drunk after sweet but only after salt—*and* tea, with an extra layer of cream on top for my special enjoyment. The second impression, then, closely linked to the first, was of overbearing hospitality.

The third, by contrast, was the impression of perfect order, as I saw the rest of the rooms. The floors were bare, without furniture or objects, everything neatly folded and stored up on ledges, grain and other food in huge tin canisters, things of daily use in rows on shelves in the wall. Every woman knew her job, no child could touch or play with anything, and there was an obvious pride in housekeeping. "How beautiful!" I could not help exclaiming.

What kind of space was the courtyard then? It seemed that a bottle of quinine or some other household disinfectant was not beyond their budget but that they simply did not care. When I recollect that I did not mention those terribly unsanitary conditions in the middle of the house when I finally wrote my book, I wonder whether I cared either. Or rather, I forced myself to care less since I was helpless to do anything about it, and maybe that was true for the women as well. Perhaps there is a direct relationship between observation of certain problems and one's ability to do anything about them, including report on them meaningfully. I remember one informant's words, as I stood at the head of a repulsive, stenching lane and exclaimed, "This is impossible; this will have to be cleaned up!" "This will not get cleaned up, sister," he replied mildly; "but your eyes will get used to it." To write on the issues of filth and the indifference to it has been on my agenda from 1981, but I have been attending to easier tasks first.

At Shaukatullah's I was for the very first time in the middle of a huge—blossoming, blooming, they would have said—family, as opposed to being among the men in their workplace or with one or two members in a specific context. I made it very clear that I did not want concrete information on this or that; I just wanted to get to know them, to become intimate with them, to get to understand them. There were three or four girls seated on the ground beside me, the older women moving in and out of the rooms as they minded the cooking and children alongside, the children all surrounding me and staring, being pushed away for touching me or my bag, and the men busy with their jobs. They were the ones I really wanted to catch, but they were too elusive. The oldest son, Majid, had ordered the refreshments and stood by me to supervise their consumption, and the father, who had nothing to do, still preferred to sit apart in the sun rather than to meddle in the women's chatter, directing occasional sallies at me: "You want to know about Ansaris. Well, even among Ansaris there are many castes!" Or: "We start working from the age of ten or twelve. We really get to know life!" All of this was delivered in a teasing, bantering way. To make the most of a situation like this, one needed the skills of a politician, or at least the experience of someone used to addressing and controlling numbers of people together—a police station officer, a school principal, or even my mother on her large estate with her staff of sixteen.

I was acutely conscious of being in a Muslim household—not awkward or nervous but simply extra-sensitive to nuances of word and gesture, again an admission of my own ignorance. I felt I had an "in" on Muslims by virtue of my Lucknow background (distant but useful to evoke), thanks to which I spoke in a way that made all language-conscious Indians exclaim, "Your Urdu is so good!" My father's oldest brother, my *tauji*, who lived in Lucknow, looked in his younger days like a *maulvi*, and he and his brothers had all been educated in Urdu, Arabic, and Persian in *madrasas*. Our Kayastha family was acculturated into "Muslim" ways of speech, dress, and civility from the days when "Hindu" and "Muslim" were not distinct cultural categories at all. In times of diffidence, *tauji*'s image comes to mind and I feel encouraged that I can be trusted to know how to act in Muslim company. I had never actually been put to the test. All these feelings of closeness to Muslims were vague ones. The Muslims I had actually known were either nonpersonalities like government bureaucrats or those otherwise neutralized by education and life-style. As a child, my closest friends were Muslims, Shani and Tashi, whose house I visited frequently. Their food was distinct, but then so was that of every Hindu family I knew. The main difference I remember is that in their home the grandmother used the spittoon, whereas in ours only the males did.

In Shaukatullah's family, there was much to make a Hindu observer feel at ease. The women were dressed in the "rural," or old-fashioned, style of *sidha palla*, the loose end of the sari being draped over their head and right shoulder. Their jewelry was rustic and their speech was predominantly Bhojpuri, the language spoken by every caste and community in Banaras. The terms and phrases I noted down from them and other such informants bore little resemblance to the Urdu originals, and for months I did not discover the precise reference for the less familiar ones. They used Hindu imagery freely, speaking, for example, of "Lakshmi departing from the house" to mean destitution or of "filling the parting with *sindur*" to refer to marriage—none of which was necessarily helpful, since I was not a typical "Hindu." I was not a Hindu observer; I was simply a naive observer. The more closely someone fit a stereotype, the easier it probably would have been for me, but these people fit no stereotypes at all. Yet, upon reflection, the fact that we moved toward mutual acceptance so quickly surely had something to do with Shaukatullah's simple notions of brotherhood and love between all and with my vague identification with Muslims from my family's past.

The question of the "actual" and the "proper" feeling of Hindus and Muslims toward each other continued to haunt me throughout my fieldwork. I wished to discard all idealism or romanticism about this relationship and see it for what it was. Adopting an inductive procedure of the crudest kind, I observed every instance of interaction carefully and asked everyone with whom I had dealings what their reflections on the matter were—which were also then observations to be interpreted. I usually learned more about the person questioned than about Hindu-Muslim relations. One good example of this was the owner of a watch shop whom I happened to be interviewing on the same day I had talked at length with musicians and had realized how irrelevant religious categories were in the realm of music. This timepiece expert was a sort of aristocrat, a patron of the arts, avowedly fond of music, and of course from an old, established, and wealthy family of Banaras. He told me about contemporary organizations and the patronage of music. Toward the end of our conversation, I threw in carelessly, "And how would you describe Hindu-Muslim interaction?" "Sister," said he in his quite memorable way, "as far as I know they are not interacting at all!"

In a matter of weeks I was given the status of a daughter of Shaukatullah. When I finally took my husband to meet my new family, a ripple went through the house: the son-in-law had made his first visit. My "parents" made a ritual farewell (*vidai*) that day, giving me a sari, blouse and petticoat piece, and sweets, and Sombabu a hundred rupees. To cover his embarrassment, he gave what I thought was a good line. "Why me?" he asked. "*She* is your daughter. Give it to *her*."

9

Categories and Units of
Observation

In November I started tabla lessons with Pandit Mahadev Mishra. I had already planned to do so in Chicago, thinking, like Ernie on Sesame Street, that I had rhythm in my bones but that vocal music would not be such a good idea, since I had given it a try for three years with mixed success. The lessons were for fun, of course, though with tabla I had the half-serious notion of giving my sitarist husband accompaniment to practice by. I also imagined that learning something would give me access to a musician, his family, and perhaps the whole community of musicians.

This was also around the time that I became determined to nail down those elusive quarries, *kajli* and *chaiti*. These were buzz words that you heard in all kinds of situations, and I gathered that they were names for two genres of folk music. *Kajli* (or *kajri*, the *l* and *r* being often interchangeable in colloquial Hindi) was the more familiar, being alluded to in sundry written sources as a genre popular with women, a phenomenon of the monsoons, an activity associated with swinging merrily on swings hung from sturdy branches. Only the second characteristic turned out to be relevant to Banaras. I had never actually *heard* either kind of music, nor did I know where I might. By that time, I was spending a fair amount of time in artisans' homes, was very close to some informants and developing other relationships further, increasing my circle of acquaintances steadily. But to know them or to visit their homes was not necessarily to discover their music—as it was also not to discover their gymnasiums, the *akharas,* or their picnics, the going out to *bahri alang.*

My other informants were bad, but Pandit Mahadev Mishra was the very worst informant a researcher could imagine. He was imprecise, did not believe in fact or detail, thought it boring to stick to a subject for more than a minute, let his mind wander where it would, and often stopped talking altogether to reminisce and smile privately to himself. Apart from going to his house thrice a week, I also liked to bring him home on a Saturday, partly to offer him hospitality. That evening in November, as we were sitting at the tea table, the electricity went off for a long time. We sat in the dark and talked. He was relaxed and seemed pleased with the atmosphere. Pressing him *gently,* I asked for the umpteenth time, "Tell me about this Banarasi *kajli* and *chaiti.*" He did not, for once, brush my question aside as irrelevant—either you know it in song or you don't; what is there to *say* about it? In fact, he did, in a way, because instead of saying anything, he sang some examples for me. I couldn't recognize or differentiate them for my life. Then he told me, in one of those rare inspirations of his that always meant a major breakthrough for me, "I'll take you to a disciple of mine. He'll tell you all about *kajli.*" I promptly fixed time and place.

Pandit Mahadev Mishra was old even then, though it was difficult to remember that he was in his mid-seventies. He leaned heavily on his cane and walked slowly, but he was braver than I—as is every Banarasi—in trafficking a *gali* about three yards wide fully occupied by a fierce black buffalo. We reached the long, extended side of a one-storied house with many doors, and he called out for his disciples. There were two brothers, Dadu (Kshamanath) and Santosh Kumar, to whom I was introduced. I promised to return the next day.

Dadu and Santosh were tailors, urbane and mild-mannered young men, reserved and refined. They had both learned a little from Mahadev Mishra and had natural talent. Their father was an amateur poet and composer and so were

Pandit Mahadev Mishra singing the *Ramayana*

they. To my eye they looked westernized, with their bell-bottomed trousers and styled shirts, but then I recalled that so had Gauri and Kishan at Vishwakarma Puja, and every other young man I had met outside his workplace or the courtyard of his home. There was in fact no question about any of these men being westernized. They were quite the opposite. The clothes they wore were part of Banaras and did not signal westernization to local people as they did to me. Dadu and Santosh quizzed me for hours about my purposes, and even then I had not awakened a sympathetic gleam in the eye or earned a nod of the head from them. We sat there cementing our relationship, chatting about Chicago, old and new times, coming back to how great a musician Mahadev Mishra was as a kind of refrain. With the sheer passage of time, I became a familiar sight at least. When they sent out for sweets and persuaded me to eat up, I thought I had become accepted. But I was no closer to discovering the meaning of *chaiti* and *kajli*.

When they did start talking about the music, I realized that there was something wrong with my phrasing of the question. No one can tell you "what" *chaiti* or *kajli* is. They would not even agree that it was "folk music" and complicated the whole issue further by telling me of half a dozen other forms that were "actually" folk music—*chhaparya, purbi, bhojpuri, biraha, qawwali, ghazal*—and labeling them in passing as "uncultured" and "of poor taste." They did tell me of music *akharas* ("clubs"), however, of their famous leaders, and of their father's *akhara*, called Jahangir. And they invited me to their Monday evening get-together in a room opposite the Hanuman temple in Khari Kuan, a few yards from where they lived.

I went the next Monday, entering after the singing had begun, and was mesmerized. It was dramatic, exciting, emotional, and very, very charming. The room, about ten feet square, was bare except for an open *Ramayana*, a garland, and an incense stick next to it. Two main singers faced the book, and the dozen or so other men in the room were divided roughly into two groups, one on either side. Each leader had a harmonium, a lanky and short-cropped fellow had the *dholak*, the two-sided drum, and the rest had cymbals. I entered in the middle of a loud, uncontrolled burst of singing, exposing a dozen *pan*-red mouths.

It was the first time that I had heard live folk music close up and in the very making, and the new experience contributed to the excitement. But far more exciting was the countenance and emotion of the singers themselves, their eyes closed, their bodies swaying, their voices eager to follow the lead pitch. That Monday turned out to be the first stop in a long odyssey which took me to byways and alleys, basements and rooftops, teashops in busy lanes and even temples on hilltops outside the city, all to hear and record this music. I began comprehending what *chaiti* and *kajli* and *holi* were and appreciating the fine distinctions within each. Finally

An informal folk music gathering with Brij Mohan, a wooden
toymaker and *dholak* player on the right

came a time when I felt that I knew what Mahadev Mishra
had been talking about when he had said to me, "*Chaiti*
makes the hearts of Banarasis skip and beat with excitement," but, in all honesty, this understanding came much
later, when I was back in Chicago, my headphones glued to
my ears. I understood *biraha* less, then and now, and certainly enjoy it far less. I discovered, totally out of the blue, the
other genres of *khamsa*, *ghazal*, and *Ramayana* (as they used
the term, to designate both book and genre). The mildest
thing I can say about it all was that it was never boring. Even
when the tunefulness was not impressive, the circumstances
certainly were. On one occasion, piles of little hand-crafted
brass and copper vessels, called *lotas*, were piled against a
wall as the two teams chorused under this gleaming back-
drop. On another, a still summer rooftop was filled with

woodworkers and their families from all the surrounding lanes of Khojwa to hear Mohan the *pan*-seller sing and Brij Mohan, the same close-cropped young latheworker I saw in my first encounter, play the *dholak*. In yet another instance, I was placed on a bench over a drain facing a tea-shop transformed into a clean *baithaka* where *panwallas* and *chaiwallas* (*pan* and tea sellers) congregated. Always at ten or eleven at the earliest, always too late to make my pleasure unadulterated.

I felt little surprise upon discovering how dedicated and talented so many of my brass worker, coppersmith, carpenter, and toymaker informants and their peers were. I was getting used to this cultivation of excellence by seemingly unremarkable people. Strange to say, until this time I had heard the poor spoken of at best with pity and condescension, but never with respect. Their varied interests and their attitude toward life as something to be lived to the full were *my* discoveries in the field. I was perhaps quietly testing to see at which rung of the economic ladder this independence and spirit ended, and beneath which were only helplessness, suffering, and subsistence, where the frail structures built by the mind, so to speak, started relating one-on-one with physical impoverishment. I rested the case (with respect and gratitude) the day I visited a *rickshawalla* through the agency of his artisan son. Expecting a wretched hovel, I was stunned to meet this dignified widower leading a meticulously planned existence, obviously rich in the middle of his absolute poverty, his spare time devoted to musical renditions of the *Ramayana*.

How I organized my late-night trips to musical performances is a matter of wonder to me today, because I don't think I now have the energy, enterprise, and sheer daring to chase things thus to their end. I had to find escorts, of course. Coming back would be no problem, I was always assured; one of the singers could be persuaded to see me home. But to go at ten or eleven, or even at midnight, very likely to cold, dark, sleeping neighborhoods, usually by roads and lanes only halfway decent even by the light of day—all this needed determination. I formed, over the months, a platoon of "brothers," young men like Markande the stoneworker, or Nagendra, clerk in an unknown office, who were themselves totally uninterested in the events I proposed to witness but who, having declared themselves my brothers, could not say no to me. So the person in question would bundle himself up, find me a rickshaw, and then cycle along to the destination. I would not let him go, and he had to sit, or slouch, or sleep, or whatever he could allow himself to do, till I was ready to leave. I should add that I was always conscious of my high-handedness and cut my visits to music gatherings shorter than they would have been had I been on my own.

I was always the only woman on the scene at the regular gatherings; the exceptions were the annual celebrations of shrines, called *sringars,* and special programs, such as the one on the Khojwa rooftop, when women and children formed the outer rings of the audience or made themselves comfortable on adjoining rooftops. I do not remember ever minding my solitude or suffering any discomfort from it. Either people ignored me—though they did not ignore my tape recorder, treating it gently and reverently as it was "filled up"—or they treated me with respect and protectiveness. "A chair, a chair! Get a chair!" was one way of expressing this, though no chair would appear out of the darkness. There was no teasing, bantering, joking, or even questioning. I think the assumption was that *of course* their music was special enough for me to come a great distance, leaving family and home, to hear and record it. I had not known of this great music for many reasons; my informants uniformly put it down to India's regional diversity. Native Banarasis clearly understood that "Indian" is a term needing qualification. They matter-of-factly attributed my ignorance to my origins at variously conceptualized points lying in westerly directions. In their more euphoric moments, I was often flattered by informants: "It's really miraculous, how you can come from outside and understand the music [or whatever other thing at the moment it was] of this city"— where "outside" for them meant not Chicago or New York but Lucknow.

10

Among the Police and
Administration

I have neglected to mention my ethnographic adventures at the beginning of our stay, when we got to meet the high society of Banaras. Within our first week we went for dinner to Mr. Rishi Pratap Singh, a prominent businessman; for dinner to the Senior Superintendent of Police; and for lunch to the Superintendent of Police, Intelligence. The first was a family friend of many years' standing, the second a subordinate of my father's, a lively and likable person who had worked hard to help find us a house, and the third was the husband of an old school friend I had met again after many years. The reason for all these social gatherings was the transfer of the District Magistrate, the kind of event that occasioned farewell parties. The dinners took place after midnight, the lunch at only 4 P. M., all preceded by long hours of formalities, high-flown declarations of friendship, and very poor jokes. The food was the most elaborate conceivable, unbeatably expensive, and lavish, with almost every delicacy that was available in the market served at the meal. There was always soup for starters. Now if I were to serve soup with Indian food, I might hope that it would fill people up a little and make my food go further. But the guests needed no such consideration; there was always one vegetarian and one nonvegetarian table laden with dishes, and the hostess circulating: *"Bhai Sahab! Bhabhiji!* (Brother! Sister-in-law!) You are not eating anything!"

We were alternately revolted and saddened by it all: the poverty of taste, the vacuum of interests and purposes, the wastefulness and underlying degeneration. Yet we went to every one of these functions, without ever feeling kinder toward this society, because I reasoned to myself that my curiosity about it all could be satisfied only by personal participation. We also found it difficult to say no and could never think of satisfactory excuses in time. Yet each degrading experience made us despise ourselves for attending and resolve never to do so again.

I had perhaps an easier time of it than I could have had, because I was not obliged to sit in the drawing room in a row of ladies, enduring the jovial pressure to "finish my drink." With the excuse of a little baby, I could retire to a quieter room to nurse Irfana, put her to sleep, or sit with her. At the Singhs' house, the youngest daughter, Meena, was doing her lessons in the room I retreated to. She was learning by rote answers to certain questions for her General Knowledge test on the morrow. "What are *stockings*?" she kept asking restlessly. The subject, apparently, was festivals, and the question was "What happens at Christmas?" In that warm bedroom draped with mosquito nets, I concluded there was little connection between children's curriculum and the social or historical reality around them. As for the problem of the language itself, Meena did not need to have trouble with "commemorate" for me to feel that there was *no* connection between the medium she was learning in, English, and her consciousness.

At the S.S.P.'s house, our hosts were so thoughtful as to arrange for a woman to watch our baby during the party, the wife of one of the servants, who came in occasionally to massage the mistress, help out with guests, and so on. I was delighted to have a person to talk to. Finding out about her was simple enough, but when I learned that she was a Banarasi, I grew more ambitious. "There was this Burhva Mangal *mela* that was held in Banaras years ago," I told her in a confidential tone. "Tell me about the Burhva Mangal fair." She absolutely denied any knowledge of the fair, as if the confession would jeopardize her in some way, and, shutting up altogether, sat in a bundle, probably tired and dozing. I was nonplused. Everyone else seemed to know of the fair. Was she too young? Had she been too secluded? Was she a moron? The meeting pricked in my mind as an unresolved riddle until I decided, after other similar encounters, that it was impossible to turn servants into informants. Or, for that matter, informants into servants.

I had occasion about a year later to use an informant in a serving capacity, with the idea of helping her out and saving her from worse drudgery in uncaring homes. What I discovered was this: the master-servant relationship could not be reconciled with the empathy and closing of distances aimed at in fieldwork. Once you were familiar with another's values concerning food, spatial and temporal preferences, and devices for maintaining individuality and freedom, you could not, without considerable agonizing, order the person to conform to a different set of values. But you had to do so as a master, and indeed to condemn these very freedom-preserving devices as lazy, dishonest tricks. My quarrels with my informant-turned-servant were about things as petty as teamaking. Being perfectly attuned to the sweet, cooked tea served all over Banaras, I proceeded now to *dictate* the terms under which tea could be made in *our* home: always in a teapot with a tea cozy, leaves steeped in freshly boiling water, milk and sugar on the side, and so on. Nor could I stand it if my new maidservant brought anything preserved on a platter, in ordinary Banaras style. The very same habits I accepted as rational, legitimate features of another life-style were intolerable in my own home: it was oppressive to be made to eat and drink in ways not of my choosing under my own roof.

My poor ex-informant could not fathom the dilemma and proceeded as cheerfully as ever to supply me data regarding Banaras customs through her behavior. For example, she habitually took a couple of days off for any festival, major or minor. I knew perfectly well about the leisurely pace of Banarasis, their lightheartedness and love of holiday celebrations. But when victimized (as I saw it) by these otherwise admired characteristics, I threw a tantrum: "How can another person (me) work if the first doesn't stick to the rules? Don't you have a modicum of *responsibility* toward the task you are committed to?" and so on. Thus addressed, my subject sulked, suffered, and degenerated into a still more imperfect servant *and* informant. This was during my first stay in Banaras; in later visits over the years I had the good fortune (it would seem) to be in close daily contact through domestic service with men and women from weaving, woodworking, stoneworking, carpenter, *biri* (cigarette) making, and *rickshawalla* families. I learned to close my eyes to their occupational backgrounds and cultures and to acknowledge that the roles of servant and informant were *not* complementary. But my first round of fieldwork had such a long-term formative influence on me that I was doomed to have only inefficient control over my servants ever after that.

To return to the high society of Banaras, I was constantly trying to calculate whether the officials we supposedly knew were of any use to us at all or whether they were leading us up blind alleys all the time. They seemed utterly sincere when they promised help, as they did at the drop of a hat. Yet their offers for housing, gas, service people, introductions to informants, and shots for our child had only delayed us, and finally we obtained everything without their help. Sometimes we had actually suffered from their help, as when, through their mediation, we would meet a musician or other important person who would prefer to ignore us, classifying us as members of a despised officialdom. Then we would make an entirely new approach, in our own capacity, and woo the individual back to a neutral stance regarding us. The outstanding case was the tabla player Kishan Maharaj; he became so incensed at what he imagined were arrogant demands on our part to come and play in our house that he threatened to write about it to a local daily. We had a showdown and developed an excellent relationship after that. Most people in India, even when they pretend to be allies of the administration, harbor a deep and just distrust of officials; simple people like my artisans do not even need to pretend. If one appears on the administration's side in class or status then one suffers the same distrust automatically. So, for us the job was clear-cut: disassociate ourselves from the rulers, not only because it made sense culturally but because it was a pragmatic research need.

In some matters, however, our police contacts were fortunate. As soon as I would ask about a particularly crowded *mela* or celebration, a jeep would be offered. Sometimes the offer would materialize and sometimes not. One did appear, at least, to take me to the Ramnagar Ramlila in Sombabu's absence and to show me the Durga Pujas around the city. The immersion of the Durgas in the river the next day, a festival in its own right, was happily planned for me by the S.S.P.'s wife. My name was added to the guest list of a motor launch fitted out for Banaras VIPs, and we chugged up and down the ghats in the dusk for two hours. All the ghats were silent, dark, and primitive, except for Manikarnika, bright with funeral pyres, and Dasashwamedh, a sea of figures, where the Bharat Sewa Sangh *sadhus* (monks) were dancing before radiant images. I would never have guessed what it was like had I not seen it, and seen it from the boat, because I would never have found a place in the dense crowd on the ghat. The following year I used my contacts again. The police had a camp on the highest point of Dasashwamedh ghat, and with little Irfana I sat in the best spot on the promontory the whole evening, both of us soaking up the spectacle of various-sized boats carrying their Durgas out and unloading them into the river. All other immersions—Kali, Vishwakarma, Ganesh, and Moharram—I have witnessed from yet other perspectives, and I readily admit that police help has been unnecessary for them.

The first day that Sombabu was away for a prolonged time, the inspectors (station officers) of Bhelupura and Maduadih *thanas* visited me in quick succession to offer their assistance in my time of solitude. They could not have guessed *how* desirous I was to meet police inspectors in Banaras. An inspector seemed to me, before I learned differently, to hold the key to what goes on in his circle (his *kshetra*) and to be eminently interviewable regarding the crimes, events, persons, and general character of the area he is in charge of—a living doc-

ument, as it were, a nicely detailed administration report of
the present that you could cross-examine. My plans for interviews were never realized. There was always something
more immediate to ask of the inspectors when I *could* meet
them. That in itself was not easy, as my repeated visits to
Bhelupura *thana* proved to me: the man would always be out
on "tour" or unavailable for unspecified reasons. I suspected
that as I grew less novel and more familiar, and also less impressive, perhaps even ludicrous because of my childish interest in ordinary, daily, common things, the inspectors concluded that it was not worthwhile to pay attention to me. On
my part, I came to realize that there were people far more
knowledgeable than police inspectors to interview, even regarding a *kshetra*, and I no longer found time to chase them.
I had made some advances to likely individuals, such as the
Circle Officer II, who sat in the Dasashwamedh *thana*, but
none of them—neither he nor other officers, not even the husband of my old school friend—ever responded to my gestures of friendship. The one exception was Krishna Chandra
Tripathi, but his motives were not above suspicion, as I shall
shortly describe.

I do not recall exactly how I discovered the existence of police station records important for my topic, except that it was
in my early 1979 foray, when I also discovered the Nagari Pracharini Sabha, *pandas'* (pilgrim priests') records, periodicals,
and Dr. Suryanath Gupta. In 1981 I was finding it difficult to
start work on the police registers and was unable to catch the
Bhelupura inspector in his office or to improve my poor relationship with the Chauk inspector. When the latter was trans-
ferred, I thought I could make a fresh start. I entered the inspector's office and, without any allusions to police
connections, introduced myself to the new person, offering
him a copy of the letter from Professor Akira Iriye vouchsaf-
ing that I was a research scholar from Chicago. He was polite
and had me sit—I kept chattering out of nervousness—while
he thought. Before long I saw his eyes widen with recognition and knew that he had guessed my identity. The grape-
vine in Banaras police circles was more efficient than I had

given it credit for. His initial reaction was the closest I came to finding out how he would have reacted to a "mere" research scholar. He was an extremely nice person, one whom I could joke with later about our first meeting, but on this matter he always became serious and claimed that he would have treated me the same no matter who I was.

I have tried the same tactics with other police officers. No one gives you special consideration unless you are in *some* way an important person, though how the importance comes to be understood is, fortunately, flexible and unpredictable. When we had alighted at the Banaras train station the second time around in 1981, still homeless, with nowhere to go, and found all the telephones out of order, I betook myself to the Railway Police Office. "I need to use the telephone," I commanded the armed constable at the gate with what was a superhuman effort for me. "I am the daughter of the I.G." The man was a fresh recruit and didn't grasp the meaning of what I said, but he took me through to the inspector's empty office, nodding at questioning countenances on the way, "She's a big person." In fact, it wasn't the "I.G." that was crucial; any two or three initials would do. As for reaching closed places, if we had a jeep all we needed to do was to put a large plate on the front reading "R.S.C., Varanasi City" (Research Scholars from Chicago) to match such signs as "A.D.M." (Additional District Magistrate), "C.S.C." (Civil-Surgeon City), "C.E.E." (Chief Executive Engineer), "U.P.S.E.B.M.D." and the plates of other VIPs who could reach places.

My Chauk Police Station experience was the most pleasant, although it became progressively awkward. I had to sit in a dignified manner at the chair and table provided for me, could not dream or doze, could not leave for tea at the nearest teashop, and had nothing to eat. The first couple of times Mr. Govind Ram Kapoor wandered in to improve my knowledge of my chosen topic in general; I kept pulling him back to the subject of the Citizens' Committees and his role in them, which he tackled with enthusiasm. The registers more than compensated for all this; they were bursting with information, and I laboriously sifted through them, full of excitement, greed, and jealousy that someone else might discover them at any moment.

The Bhelupura inspector believed that no one on earth was superior to him, a belief that the undiluted despotism in their *kshetra* breeds in many inspectors. To preserve this belief intact, he avoided all contact with me. So difficult was this R. S. P. Srivastava to find, so many unanswered notes and unreturned messages did I leave for him, that he quickly became Mr. R. S. V. P. Srivastava to me. I saw the Bhelupura registers last of all.

In the police registers I noticed references to public meetings of Hindu and Muslim leaders on the subject of possible communal tension during Durga Puja, Moharram, and other festivals. To attend one I had to learn the venue, time, and purpose from a police officer. For months I kept losing this battle to those I talked with; they would simply shrug me off with "It's not for you" or "We're not sure about it yet" or "I'll let you know about the next one." Only when the next round of festivals began around Holi did I know how to insist and get results: humbling myself totally, striding into the inner courtyards of police stations, not merely sitting politely in the inspector's room; waiting on cold benches for him to return, arguing patiently with underlings, knowing it was not their cooperation I sought; and even walking into the shaving session of the Dasashwamedh inspector to ensure his not escaping before he said yes to me.

On balance I would say that involvement with the police taught me a little more about life in the city but slowed me down at times as much as it helped me. After a few months the novelty of my presence had worn off. The police became used to me and were finally convinced that I was more a student than a *memsahib;* I stopped requesting anything from them other than an occasional escort, which could have been wrangled from them by any other researcher given sufficient tact. My father retired within a year, and then there was nothing but mixed memories of when I had been *bahanji* (sister) to the whole police force, and Sombabu the brother-in-law.

11

The Researcher at Home

In November Irfana was going to be six months old, and we had had our share of baby care problems. We had arrived with no knowledge of where to get domestic help and had turned to neighbors for advice on all matters: finding cleaning help, a newspaper man, a supply of milk, and a carpenter, electrician, plumber, and washerman, the last of which curiously was the most difficult for us to get and to keep. A rapidly growing pile of laundry, of all things, makes me exceedingly nervous because I—unlike Banarasis—regard washing clothes as the worst form of drudgery. The neighbors had been pleasant and helpful and always positive. One finally directed an *ayah* toward us to look after the baby. Being an *ayah* meant, in our minds, washing diapers as well as all the other clothes, sweeping and mopping the floors, doing the dishes, and then, after bathing thoroughly and putting on one of the two fresh saris we had supplied, keeping the baby cheerful and occupied.

But looking at our cherubic three-month-old, we hesitated to entrust her to a perfect stranger. Miss Malti, our new find, did not excite our confidence either. Dark, ugly, and pockmarked, she sported what I labeled "a false smile" and walked with an elephantine swaying of the hips. We decided that she was "not too clean" but could not agree on the reasons why. My husband thought it was her half-painted nails, which indicated careless personal hygiene; I always considered her dry, dusty hair suspect. I was biased against her from the beginning because she took every opportunity to reiterate that she was a "Srivastava" from Bihar, implying an originally high status that had now befallen hard times. Instead of sympathizing with her misfortune—and in a remarkable denial of my anthropological role, I never pursued the matter and always changed the subject instead—I was irritated at the sheer ordinariness expressed in this passion for social mobility.

I was out for approximately six or seven hours of the day, the nursing schedule ensuring my presence at home at 10 A.M. and 5 P.M. at the outer limit. I quizzed Sombabu on what went on the rest of the time. Malti was not allowed to hold the child or prepare her bottles. She sat near Irfana while the baby took her naps, rocked her nice cane cradle that we had inherited, and made faces and sounds at her when she awoke—for the five minutes that elapsed before Sombabu came bounding in to her. I might have made a compromise with her "dirtiness," but since Sombabu did not, I couldn't interfere. This was not our only problem. She was sloppy with all the other work entrusted to her as well and would simply not respond when the call went out, "Malti!" —usually for a glass of water or some other simple chore. I confronted her about that. She assumed a tragic expression: "Bahanji, I am not used to being called, and I do not go out in front of men very readily." Given that she and the man of the house had to share the premises most of the day, this was an impasse.

In early October, on the eve of Dassehra, Malti decided she wanted to go on leave for the festival. We were relieved and helped her pack up comfortably with gifts and food. She swayed off and, as we expected, never came back. But she had the last laugh, for one of our neighbors asked us the next day: "Did you give your maidservant a lot of stainless steel to take with her? She had bowls and spoons in her basket when she left."

For a month we had no one. I worked like a slave—at everything except the laundry, at which my husband is fortunately very handy. The morning began with the newspaper, our cups of tea, and a cutting board, knife, and *lauki* or *torai*, the watery monsoon gourds we were fond of eating, partly because they were so easy to chop and cook. Three things would be cooked together in the three compartments of the pressure cooker, and we would feel very heroic. Meanwhile Irfana's orange juice would be squeezed, her bottles sterilized, her bath water heated, the beds made, the apartment swept . . . Within a week the housework had caught up with me and defeated me. I would leave home already exhausted when practically half the day was over (not a great loss in objective terms, for my first destination was usually Nagari Pracharini Sabha, which did not open until 11 A.M. and where work began a little later). I tried different devices to maximize the returns from those days. For my ethnography, I decided to venture only around the route to the archives. In the neighborhood of Sonia near Sigra there were potters and painters galore. I wandered through their lanes and stood and looked at their work; they all wanted me to come back after Diwali. At a *pan* shop nearby, I spent long hours with the *panwalla*, Mahant (Head Priest) Ramdev, so called because there was a small temple nearby and he was its caretaker. The temple also had an *akhara*, a wrestling pit, on its premises. Those were my pre-*akhara* days, when I had not yet realized what an *akhara* was, so I toured it with Ramdev, noted the latrine in a corner—a couple of bricks on the ground, judiciously placed—and filed the information away. At his *pan* shop, too, because I sat around so much, I also overheard a fair amount of seemingly irrelevant talk, thrilling inwardly at certain exchanges, as when two customers could be overheard saying, "What is your mood today? Should we go outside?" "Yes, let's go to the other side."

I had also realized that the U.P. Regional Archives, Banaras, were right next door to Sonia, in the shopping center called Shastrinagar. On most of my visits there, the director, who had complete control over requisitions, was missing. Undaunted, I went through all the indexes and noted the items of interest to me. I was not the least eager for him to be present, for the first time I had met him he had completely wasted my afternoon with insufferable tales of his own heroics in different research contexts. I could wait for these noted items, since they all sounded distant and vague in the context of the Banaras I was getting to know.

Another kind of day would start off like this: "Irfana is almost asleep. Maybe we can *all* go." So we would pack up bags and baby and depart for whichever place one of us had work, say Banaras Hindu University. We bounced around, being pedaled laboriously through the sunshine in a broken rickshaw over a broken road through a broken city. At B.H.U. there was some shade from mango trees, but the pedaling was just as laborious. Even after stopping at two or three buildings, we failed at the first job on our agenda: to get our library cards. The students had closed up the administration building so we couldn't pay our deposit. We clung to our rickshaw as if it were a lifebuoy in the middle of this sea of a campus. The second project was to meet Anand Krishna, professor of art history and a slight acquaintance. This was also accomplished only after two or three stops. He was gratifyingly hospitable and took us home, where we rested, fed Irfana, and packed away snacks and sweets ourselves. He made gracious promises of help, which always cheered us up.

The worst of my domestic experiences promised to begin when Sombabu was suddenly called away to Bombay in early October to clear our shipped goods through customs. Said he as he departed, "Maybe you can take the cradle to Nagari Pracharini Sabha, and push it while you work" (with one toe, I imagine he meant, like the *pankha*-pulling boys of yore). I wondered what my ingenuity would cook up to beat that, and I wasn't disappointed.

First of all, informants came to me instead of my having to go to them. Number one was Sidhnath, whom I had met after a weary walk in Vishwanath *gali*. That particular marketplace is so frequented by tourists that the artisans and vendors seem to have lost their naturalness. After many frustrating attempts I found this man to sit down and talk to. Sidhnath painted the faces and the folds of garments on otherwise blank marble icons. Perhaps I was overenthusiastic, sat too long, and drank too many helpings of tea because no other person I ever talked to reacted the way Sidhnath did after only one meeting. Sidhnath arrived the next day at my place

with a one-year-old child in tow and gifts of grapes and biscuits for my own child (she had not matured enough to appreciate these, needless to say). Whereas I had found it easy
to be friendly and talkative in *his* surroundings, I was awkward and at a loss in my own. But, thought I to myself, this
is excellent, this is how it should be. I should be able to bring
these two facets of my life together. I realized in retrospect
that it had indeed been special to witness a dimension of his
life very important to him, that of father, filed as he was under "painter," cross-referenced "miscellaneous artisans," in
my scheme.

Another visitor was Markande, a stoneworker in the factory of Kailash's uncle in Khojwa. I had met him along with
a dozen other young workers on my visit to the stone factory;
all wore rags over their nose and mouth to keep from breath-
ing in the dust, all were yogi-like in their bare-chested thin-
ness and their white coats of stone dust. They all heard me
announce my name, address, and purpose, but only Markande had decided to follow up on that information, which
definitely marked him in my eyes as more interesting than
the average. He had absolutely nothing to say when he came
over, however, and sat there, shy and dumb, admiring the
odd vase and lamp in the room (both of stone, coincidentally)
and deciding he could copy them if he tried. We then talked
about his job. He was immensely proud to be a craftsman. He
presented me many creations through the rest of my stay,
and I kept packing them away quietly, so heavy, nonutilitar-
ian, and nondecorative were they. His big question that day
was, Would I visit his home? This was truly the water coming
to the thirsty horse.

While I was ruminating on my good fortune with useful
visitors, there came to my doorstep a neighbor whom I was
quick to welcome as a potential informant. Nandlal was the
watchman employed by our landlord, a small, wizened man
of unguessable age, except that he could always be found
resting in the sun and was arguably quite old. He squatted in
front of me and declared that he had a request. I was filled
with a sense of helplessness and pity as I listened to his tale

of land and property being snatched from his family through a trick document signed by one who did not know what it contained. I was both powerless and unwilling to do anything about it. Already in my experience, such vague and hopeless requests poured in at any attempt to get to know anyone. All my acquaintances so far were embroiled in lawsuits or preparing for one. Mohan Lal's brother had lost his house to a scheming tenant; Tara Prasad's old tenant owed him many months' rent and would neither pay up nor respond; Shaukatullah's second plot of land was illegally occupied by some Ahirs . . . and so on. The only thing I could decide in my own naive and anxious mind was that as soon as possible I would study law (it being too farfetched to aim for medicine, the other service everyone seemed to need) so that the next time around I could actually *do* something for my informants.

After a few mildly productive days at home, I decided to be bolder, and I packed up baby and baby things. My destination was Bengali Tola, literally the Bengali locality, the natural center for the celebration of Durga Puja, the Bengali version of the U.P. Dassehra, celebrated with a pageant of the goddess Durga rather than with the theater of the Ramlila. I saw some Durga images right away in a courtyard, entered and met the craftsman, Prafulla Kumar Dutta, originally from Calcutta. His mother and sister worked with him, and the whole visit was quiet, happy, and—productive, I was going to say, but in those early days, I could not even have said what I meant by the word. They took me around the maze of lanes, and I learned to see Bengali Tola as a normal place humming with activity, not as "dirty" and "puzzling"—the simple difference between seeing it from their point of view and seeing it from my own, uneducated, one. Prafulla's family reminded me of Moscow acquaintances in their "socialist" manners, the way they welcomed me, observed no distance, stood on no ceremony, made no speeches about high and low—even though there was no denying their poverty and absolute lack of security. I had been shown their home, whose ceiling had collapsed in the monsoons; they were

Durga image maker in Bengali Tola

being allowed by the kind owner of a vacant house to work and live in its courtyard.

Prafulla's mother had immediately reached out for Irfana as I had come up, before we had even started talking. I was willing enough to part with her, and my daughter, who shines on occasions like this, chirruped and looked laughingly around. Later the thought crossed my mind: this woman touches mud and clay, the ground and dirt, as does her sari, and she does not wash. Although she is far less clean than Malti, I hesitated to give the baby to Malti but not to this woman . . . ? The unalterable difference between servants and informants aside, I was progressively sloughing off my own trappings and entering informants' worlds on their own terms, accepting that to measure others' choices by my standards was both unworkable and undesirable. And while I continued to scheme and plot to ingratiate myself on each occasion, not averse to using even my own baby as a tool, I no longer found this plotting and scheming shocking or guilt-ridden, but a natural, adult way of building relationships, and therefore not scheming at all.

In my remaining days of solitude I did a different kind of fieldwork: I went to see the many pageants of the Durga Pujas and the enactment of the Ramlila at Ramnagar. For all my long residence in India, I still imagine the unseen to be far different from what it turns out to be. I think I expected the Ramlila—never having been to one—to be a feast of color and romance. The Ramlila field at Ramnagar turned out to be a vast, dusty plain, ill-lit with gas lanterns, and dotted with men and women squatting, gathering, waiting. Little trucks of parched rice and *rewri* (a sesame seed candy) stood among them. Other foods consisted of round baskets of peanuts, carts of overripe bananas, and an occasional *chana* seller. Other entertainment consisted of nothing.

Three sparse structures were proudly pointed out to me: one, Chitrakoot, when Rama lives in exile; two, Lanka, Ravana's "castle"; three, a flat stage, on one side of which Rama and Lakshmana were seated on a throne, surrounded by their managers and PR men. As I approached them, someone whispered an introduction of me to them, derived from my policewoman companion, upon which Rama innocently asked, "What is an I.G.?" The priest attending him replied, "Shhh . . . He is a very big man." "Well, isn't she going to give us something?" "Shhh . . . " The drama, when it began, was painfully slow, crude, clumsy. But it sent shivers of excitement down my spine as, after every speech by Rama, the crowd roared, "Bho-o-o Rama!" It was because of the audience that I wanted to keep seeing more, because of the evidence of their acceptance of God on earth. I had bagged a little space on the edge of the stage and sat holding my baby, no doubt making myself as comfortable as I could. A woman constable came up and told me strictly, "Cross your legs please! This is God's play."

The Durga Pujas, by contrast, were clean, bright, well organized—altogether modern. I heard their number was on the increase, and that made sense to me. It seemed more satisfying and more relevant in some sense to decorate a deity according to your taste, as elaborately as you could, have everyone file by for *darshan*, an auspicious sight, and vary your entertainment according to the year's taste, than to stage a complex tale night after night and to arrange for huge crowds to see and hear it well. The Bharat Sewa Sangh monks had a demonstration of *lathi* (pole) wielding at their Puja; the Diesel Locomotive Works, a movie; other places, all-night plays or movies. Deeper observation would have to wait: as I made the rounds to scores of events, I kept taking the addresses of the young men who were apparently the organizers, judging by their busyness in putting last-minute touches on the show.

Sombabu returned in good time, and we could hardly believe our sudden streak of good fortune as we found not only a new *ayah*, but a cook and an odd-job man besides. Our new trio was wonderful, ensuring order and harmony at home but keeping routine resolutely at bay by virtue of their personalities. They were the cook, Lal Mohammad (Dear to the Prophet); the maid, Shyam Dulari (Beloved of Krishna); and jack-of-all-trades, Raja Ram (Rama the King). To prevent little islands of recognizable sound bobbing up on the smooth surface of the otherwise incomprehensible sea of our strange language, English, when we discussed them, we preferred to call them Red Prophet, Christ's Lover, and King Canute.

Lal Mohammad was retired from the police; he had served all his life as a "follower," one of those men in the background who knead, chop, fry, ladle, and maintain. He was a professional cook and baker trained in British times, and the touch was evident. His expertise encompassed the most exotic fare of the British Isles, and he could not be challenged or corrected on any point. Nor, as a true chef, would he deign to touch any work but his immediate specialization, no matter what the emergency—not the dishes, or the kitchen sweeping, or preparation of the baby's juices or formula. We loved the feeling of endless horizons that Lal Mohammad's presence gave us, though we never came close to exploring his potential to its fullest. His presence also ensured that some self-conscious Brahmans could never eat at our place, being prisoners of the coded substance theory that forbade their accepting food from outcastes such as Muslims. We sometimes pretended that what we served was store-bought, arguing to ourselves that such food would have been cooked by people like Lal Mohammad under other roofs in any case. Or we served it anyway when we knew that the guests couldn't say no, and we would enjoy their discomfiture slyly as they sat eating with obvious reluctance. Lal Mohammad, as befitted his Imperial heritage, acknowledged or cared for none of this. The only distinction he knew was between high-brow and low, and his own brows often furrowed as he quizzed himself as to where we belonged. He was old, too, like many of my informants, and he gave me my first nomenclature for them. I had discovered that words like *karigar*, the Hindi equivalent for "artisan," did not work, and when I told our new cook what my subjects were, he said with proper derision, "Oh, the *nich qaum*, the *chhote log* (the lower orders, the smaller people)?" He was himself a Pathan, one of the original Islamic conqueror-invaders from the northwest who had strenuously kept their lineage pure, and made it quite clear that all poor Muslims were not equal.

Shyam Dulari, a modest, unpretentious Harijan, was a breath of fresh air after the upwardly mobile Malti. She was quiet and efficient, so silent in fact as to be unnatural. She had worked for a foreign academic couple before, and we discovered that through her experience of noncommunication there had simply forgotten that she *could* talk and be understood in a work situation. Shyam Dulari came from a community occupied at rolling *biris*, those poisonous pointed cigarettes wrapped in leaves with which *rickshawallas* are always shortening their lives. She smelled of tobacco, the dusty, wholesale kind, and because she chewed it habitually, of the aromatic, masticated kind as well. But she was impeccably clean, and—the highest virtue any child watcher can have— she had boundless energy. Around the time that my husband went to Chicago in March to teach spring quarter classes, I started leaving Irfana, now nine months old, with her for half a day at a time. The two hit it off perfectly. I would return at lunch time to find them rollicking on the carpet, jumping, tossing, rolling, and tickling, always activities that signaled health and good spirits and left me with a twinge of jealousy as I thought of my own relatively barren and lonely work.

Raja Ram, finally, the most solemn of the three, kept us the most amused, as we, in some private recess of his mind, did for him. He frankly found our personalities, life-style, professions, and lists of tasks for him absurd, and he had un- usually expressive ways of showing it. If we suggested that he go to the railway station and buy tickets for the Punjab Mail . . . Before we could quite finish, his mouth would fall open: "The Punjab Mail? Why, it's left already!" He was agape most of the time, not because he was stupid so much as because his mind worked in a precisely different, alterna- tive, parallel way to ours, and there was no possible meeting of the two. He did not care for the vegetables we chose to eat, the spices we preferred, the clothes we fancied, the furniture we owned, the language we spoke, or the people we mixed with. Raja Ram was indispensable for the greater part of our stay, battling his distaste to shop for our groceries, arrange for the services of washerman, tailor, and carpenter as needed, deliver our messages, and fetch, carry, and find whatever it was that we required. He was not particularly knowledgeable about the city, being from a village on the outskirts, but he had a decent bicycle, youthful energy, prac- tical common sense, and plenty of time—all qualities that we felt we would never again possess.

12

Death

We decided to stage a function of our own on the occasion of Irfana's *annaprasana*, her ritual first solid food in the seventh month of her life. On the 26th of November, we planned, there would be a *puja*, accompanied by the singing and drama of a *gaunharin* (folk singer), the way these ceremonies were traditionally done. In the evening we would have an open-air music program with Mahadev Mishra and Kishan Maharaj, followed by a catered dinner. Ravi Shankar was on our guest list, as were some of our informants and new friends, and the grandparents were coming from Lucknow and Calcutta.

I added another interesting activity to my daily rounds, visiting presses, finally choosing the Royal Press in Godaulia to print the invitations. I was aware of the satisfaction I got from merely walking through crowded places, noting the details of shops and billboards, of people's clothes, expressions, and actions, and best of all, exchanging a conversation with someone, anyone. That pleasure never wore off. The whole of Banaras was like a universe, and every person opened the door to yet another world. What I wanted, I suppose, was to understand the lives of *all* the people—of, let us say, one *mohalla*, to be modest. How did the pickle maker's business work? What was the life of the printer and binder? Who comprised the family and what was the family life of the basket maker? What were the "cultural activities" of all those who had little stalls at Dasashwamedh ghat? What went on in their minds? What did they think of when they were silent?

My parents-in-law, whom I called Ma and Baba, arrived three days before the event. I had a particular affinity with Baba, though I had never talked at length with him, because he was a member of the Communist Party of India and treated me with respect for having lived in Moscow. He was also a very *shaukin* person (a person of taste and passion), fond of music, politics, conversation, and food. The journey had not been too comfortable, and his meals had gotten off schedule. He complained of a chest pain, such as he occasionally experienced owing to gas. He took to bed, and we sent for a doctor, who came only the next day.

That same evening our custom-cleared goods arrived from Bombay on a truck. Sombabu got busy having them unloaded, I in making a place for them. We both felt guilty later: if that distraction had not occurred, would we have responded more sensitively to Baba's complaints? He often had gas, however, and we were all used to the routine for treatment. The summons to the doctor was repeated.

At two in the morning, Baba arose to use the bathroom, found himself unable to make it, lay down again, and closed his eyes. We banged on the door of another doctor close by, and he came immediately. He peered at Baba's pupils with a torch and when he looked at us to ask, "How long has he been like this?" I knew it was all over. We rushed the patient to the B.H.U. hospital, but it was too late, "fortunately," as everyone said, because B.H.U. is outside the sacred precincts of Kashi—the original Banaras—and therefore does not guarantee *moksha*, supreme and absolute release from rebirth. This active Communist who cycled miles daily on party work and was admired for his unflagging energy and strong heart had come all the way to sacred Kashi to have a heart attack.

The rest of the night and the next day are a series of impressions. We took the body to Harishchandra ghat, one I had read much about as being the place where Raja Harishchandra had displayed the force of his sacred word and sacrificed both son and self to Truth. The place united ancient centuries with present-day Kashi/Banaras through such tales, which everyone could tell you. Its appearance mirrored this image: it looked like something that had been undisturbed for millennia. Another funeral pyre was being lit, and I saw for the first time how a body could be consumed, the skull crack and the brains ooze out. When it was Baba's turn, I sat a distance away and left Sombabu to do the circumambulation, lighting, and stoking. Suddenly I felt activity near me, and turned to stare at what certainly was a vision.

The Dom Raja, representative of the oldest royal lineage in the region, was sitting on a throne right there in the middle of the sands. How he had arrived there and had arranged the props so efficiently was impossible to say. No doubt it had been reported to him that the D.I.G., S.S.P., and sundry other police officials were all members of a funeral party and had decided to supervise it in person. He was wearing a crisp, freshly gathered *dhoti* and a ceremonial cap cocked on his head, and he carried a scepter. His mouth was red with *pan*, and his eyes were equally bloodshot, all adding to a picture of royal terror.

He signaled to Sombabu to approach him, which Sombabu, surprised, naturally did. What the details of the exchange were I do not know, but he demanded a proper tribute for the honor of using Dom territory and the Dom fire to ignite the pyre. This was a procedure I knew about from previous anthropological work on the subject. Sombabu said something to the effect: "You had better forget it. I have nothing with me, nor do I believe that I owe you anything. Can't you see what this occasion is for me?" The majestic raja looked around at the uniformed police officers and policemen standing at ease, staring straight ahead with severe gazes, and decided to forget it. Whether it was their presence or whether he simply had no way of dealing with a "No, go away" answer, the Dom's stature seemed to shrink visibly. He sat on in a semi-dignified manner and at some point disappeared in the same mysterious way he had arrived.

The Dom Raja is one of the legendary figures of Banaras, but those who know the place know that he has strong competition. His claim to fame is that he is head of the lowly caste of Doms and of the cremation ghats, the unwritten law being that only the Doms may give fire for the pyres, making theirs the second oldest profession for the Hindus; as their leader, he therefore comes of the *oldest* lineage in the district, one far more venerable in age than that of the nouveau royalty across the river in Ramnagar. Moreover, the Doms charge heavily for their services, reducing to penury many villagers who wish to give their deceased the benefits of a Kashi cremation, and he as their king is heir to vaster treasures than the average raja.

The Dom Raja at that time was a fat, greasy, reportedly lecherous personality who sported all the explicit trappings of royalty, such as gargoyles and tiger skins in his home and on his private fleet of boats. He was renowned as intensely Banarasi in his passion for music and boating and simultaneously stigmatized as "Dom" for his pastimes of drinking and patronizing dance. Before and after the Harishchandra ghat encounter, every source in Banaras described him to me in roughly the above terms, but I never spoke with him, preferring to preserve a distant image of him.

This was only one of many ethnographic items that interested me during the death and cremation, and that is a very telling admission. I left the cremation ghat earlier than the men because my mother-in-law was alone at home, but when I arrived I discovered that she had been joined by a Bengali neighbor. "Now that the cremation is over, chew some bitter *nim* (margosa) leaves and spit them out," she told Ma. I immediately became curious about the significance of this practice and restrained my urge to question her with difficulty; it would hardly have been fair to Ma to get engaged in an intellectual discussion. So, throughout, I was sharply aroused by this or that custom that was declared essential, as well as by the overall assumption of an inalterable, accepted discourse of practices that had to be performed. But I kept swallowing my questions, recognizing that the researcher's detachment was inappropriate in the actual family tragedy in which I was participating. I even remember thinking that it was "just as well" that I was not "interested" in death, because I would have made no progress in understanding it anyway. I felt that I was indirectly confirmed in my choice of a topic far from this one, because death did not arouse in me what I was coming to recognize as "ethnographic emotions": indefatigable curiosity, an obsessive greed for explanations, a thick-skinned facility to withstand any discouragement in the quest for information, and the conscienceless ability to disassociate self and family from the object being studied.

What was largely the case was that I felt guilty, such as only the relatively inexperienced can feel, at being emotionally less involved in the tragedy than other family members, rather than accept that as only realistic and proceed to be true to myself. I was tense at the realization that my mind was also working anthropologically when it had no business to do anything but grieve. This, when I was really saddened by the sudden end of a busy and creative life and angered further by the tireless reiterations all around of his *peaceful* look and his *peaceful* end and how *peacefully* he went—because of course Baba did not want to *go;* he was not seeking *peace*. The event of that death brought me to the realization, then in embryo and later in full form, that on some matters I was not going to compromise my autonomous thinking in favor of what informants believed. Let them chorus "peace, peace" as much as they liked, shaking their head in that inimitable way denoting resignation and inner harmony. *I* would continue to carp about the highly unprofessional behavior of the doctor who had disregarded two urgent messages, and I would *continue* moreover to express *regret* at the departed's *untimely* death rather than come to see it as "all for the best."

My feelings, hesitant as they were, were sound ones. By the end of our stay, we had lost two more relatives; within the next couple of years, two more; and then I lost my guiding spirits Tara Prasad and Shankar. All the deaths—Baba's, Virendraji's, Meera chachi's, Nani's, Baldev mausa's, Tara Prasad's, and Shankar's—were, according to me, untimely and avoidable, testaments to the poor training and even the callousness of Indian doctors and the deficiencies of the Indian medical system. If bereavement provided Rosaldo the key to the comprehension of Ilongot rage, the shock of Tara's death in 1985 gave me a clear vision of my distance from the world view of my informants, or, as I called it in my book three years later, of "the limits of ethnosociology."

In a few days we left for Calcutta to complete the *pinda* (death) rituals, for the oldest son was there. The baby was given another occasion for becoming the center of attention when we had her *mundan*, the ritual head shaving, three months later. Some such rituals, including some fasts, I found acceptable for myself, either because they satisfied my curiosity to know them from the inside, or because they had an aesthetic appeal, or because they seemed to have a "scientific" basis. A first food ceremony was colorful and pretty, but a head shaving was absolutely necessary to make sure the child's extra-fine hair was replaced by an invigorated, plentiful crop.

PART THREE

In which paid and unpaid research assistants are happily cultivated; the practicalities of working as a woman are spelled out; and the worst side of people's characters is encountered and overlooked in the interests of research.

13

My Research Assistant

December, after our return from Calcutta, saw a new phase in my fieldwork begin for me, one in which I became progressively immersed in the lives of the people I was working with, or as I saw it, in which I could accomplish thrice as much in a day as I had previously done. Many factors, apart from the length of our stay in Banaras, made this possible. The first was the acquisition of a research assistant. He was in need of work, was well educated, was from Banaras, and was without ideas, opinions, or knowledge that could make him difficult to guide.

Nagendra Sharma was brought to me by the famous Virendra Singh, famous in my mind because he was one of the three names we had when we first reached Banaras. He had taught Hindi to many of the American students who were now valiantly busy with South Asian studies, "future professors at Harvard and Yale," as Sombabu called them, and many regarded him as a good friend. He had offered us his help and friendship as well—once we had found him, that is, because, as in other cases, just to look for "Virendra Singh, Hindi Master, Assi" was not the most efficient way to track him down. But he lived too far away, was too busy, and seemed to specialize in too different a cast of actors for me to take up his offer of help. One day, finally, we made a definite appointment, and he declared he would introduce me to people at Manikarnika, the main burning ghat of the city and apparently the hub of the city's cultural activity, as many (but clearly not I) saw it. I have always been too greedy and acquisitive ever to say "no" to such an offer, even when I faintly thought to myself, "What do I want with Manikarnika?" The prospect of wandering in those mysterious *galis* with a knowledgeable companion was not one to turn down.

Virendra and I set out at dawn, walked a decent distance from ghat to ghat by the riverside, and then started introductions. According to the list I compiled when it was all over, I met some sixteen people, including *pandas* (pilgrim priests), *pandits* (assorted priests), *karmakandis* (ritual specialists), shopkeepers of cremation goods, and the death census taker. They were all exciting in an objective way, but my own project was becoming sufficiently defined in my mind that I felt little excitement. Manikarnika people were, and have remained, a haze of interesting colors, patterns, images, and activities that has become progressively fainter. I was unable to say anything coherent to any of the people I met, apart from answering or occasionally asking basic questions about place and nature of work; I usually stood by awkwardly, laughing at their jokes, playing perhaps more the role of the first part of Virendra's introduction: "This is my sister. She is an anthropologist, too." The "too" further subdued me, made me seek invisibility. I felt trapped by this hint of the numerous other scholars, some quite renowned, whom he had assisted. Their shadows followed us everywhere. I have never been able to function comfortably in a situation where something is expected of me but I do not know *what*, and where my guide has an agenda and understands it much more clearly than I understand mine. That morning, I concluded my brief exchange with each of the sixteen people saying, "I'll be back." As we paused to rest and breakfast on delicious *kachoris*, Virendra turned to me frankly, "It has struck me the whole time that you were more the silent observer than the active participant, that you were simply watching my face." For him, thinking of Manikarnika as the city's high spot, it was an appropriate condemnation; I had little to say in my defense and thought unhappily of my artisans, a vague group of faces, as if they were waiting for me somewhere. I almost believed that Virendra would be disenchanted after this exhibition of my incompetence and not bother with me again, but he subsequently turned up with Nagendra. An air of mourning still pervaded the house, but with distinct ability Virendra put everything in place by voicing my unexpressed thoughts: "The best way to combat tragedy is to get on with your work." Thus I acquired Nagendra and proceeded to train him.

Nagendra had many qualities, foremost of which were a sense of duty, perseverance, and precision in carrying out instructions. What I had to train him in was to use his own brains when complying with the tasks I set, to remain flexible, to imagine that the questions he was asking mattered to *him*. I had a long list of jobs for him, most of which left him agape. In fact, he was always agape in the first few months, and my most lasting legacy to him may be the acceptance of all kinds of projects as possible and worthwhile. Interview the keepers of teashops, the haunters of parks and bazaar crossings, temple goers, cinema fans, bathers at the ponds and tanks, those strolling the streets at certain times of the day and night . . .

I was acutely conscious that my project was becoming a little too well defined and that instead of seeing all the possibilities in "popular culture," I might end up discovering only those that I had already identified, diverse and fascinating as these were. I was also conscious that even with these perceived domains, I was useless for gathering certain kinds of information. I could be sure of the feelings of one family, or two or three or even four, about temples, but what of the hundreds of visitors who thronged the popular temples every day? What made them choose a particular temple, what did it mean to them, what did they think they were accomplishing, what else did they do that could compare with this, and so on. I was positive, as I still am, that the responses to such queries would vary with age, occupation, caste, class, and personality. The only way to deal with this problem was to take a sample. Now this was a sort of "evil" thought that came to me, since I was dedicated wholeheartedly to the notion of intense observation of a few, without questionnaires or even preconceptions about what one would find. Both sampling and questionnaires were outside my methodology, but, in a kind of extension of Hindu methods, I was willing to tolerate them as long as I did not sully my own hands with them. I did modify their impact by making Nagendra memorize the questions, encouraging him to let the interview subject lead him on if so inclined and always commending him for long, rambling interviews.

I further recognized that no matter how skillful I became at approaching and mingling with people, there were certain people and situations beyond me. The dark, cavernous mouths of teashops were among these, no less terrifying than the mouths of wild beasts. They were terribly attractive and Dostoevskian, and occasionally I went to one with an informant, but in such cases the two of us were clearly isolated and may as well have been sitting in the informant's home. Never did I strike up a conversation with a stranger or, as was my biggest dream, with the teashop owner. I suffered from an illogical and inconsistent apprehension. The same men, young and old, whom I considered courteous and "decent" in other contexts and who repeatedly proved themselves to be so, became, I imagined, threatening, perhaps perverse, certainly rude and prying, in these teashops. I am speaking of course about the sooty, solid shops in single rooms in the older parts of the city, not the outdoor extravaganzas in places like Maidagin, although the apprehension I felt was almost the same in both places. Now, since I absolutely had to find out when, how, and why most of these shops were established, who and how many frequented them, what the customers preferred to eat, and what the tenor of discussions in them was, I needed Nagendra.

Anyone who has ever engaged in research knows the luxury of suddenly having an assistant to command. To call it having an extra pair of hands or feet is to idealize the situation too much, because the "command" remains at a somewhat removed level. What happens, or what happened to me at least, was that I could let my imagination loose, think adventurously of all the data I would have liked to collect if I could, formulate strategies, sometimes wild and difficult, for accomplishing this, and unload them all on the assistant—because, simply speaking, he worked for me. I had a wide

My brother Nagendra with my sister-in-law,
mother, nephews, and niece

range of possibilities because it seemed ridiculous to pay
someone less than a certain minimum per month, and in the
Banaras of 1981 a lot of work could be devised for two or
three hundred rupees. I indulged myself, thinking of all I
would like to ask the wanderers, travelers, hangers on, loiter-
ers, and passers-by, in assorted locations, if only I could, and
passing on the tasks to Nagendra. The results were never as
exciting as the formulations themselves, which I believe is a
basic characteristic of this methodology.

Nagendra himself was consistently noncommittal when
asked to respond to the quality of the questions, their appropriateness or their focus. He didn't seem to realize that he
had been born and bred in the city that I—now we, jointly—
were researching. For some time, I suffered from my typical
doubts in thinking that his unresponsiveness reflected a

problem in my project itself: it was wholly off the mark, made no sense to the subjects themselves, addressed no relevant issues, rang no bells. As I received confirmation from many other quarters that this was not so, my confidence increased, but Nagendra's did not. He never had a suggestion for addition or deletion, for place or person, theme or form. He looked the same whether he encountered failure or success. I continued to fantasize about the ideal research assistant and to wonder where such a person could be found, but meanwhile Nagendra won my heart with his conscientiousness and precision. In any case, I could never have been cruel enough to take away employment from anyone once I had given it.

Where he exceeded all expectations was in the archival part of my research. I had long abandoned trying to copy down everything from the newspapers in Nagari Pracharini Sabha and had decorated them all with paper markers instead. I had applied, formally and in triplicate, for permission to photocopy these pages, in the company of Sabha officials, at the nearest photocopying place. The permission came through one year and two months later, and said: "Re: The photocopying of pages of *Aj* and *Bharat Jiwan* by research scholar Nita Kumar. The above-mentioned research scholar is permitted to copy the materials she has requested, provided she does it on the premises of the Nagari Pracharini Sabha."

Since no one within many hundred miles of the place had a portable copying machine, that was that. I got Nagendra to work, and over the next year he produced for me some five hundred pages of notes in a pearl-like, impeccable handwriting. He became a more familiar institution at the Sabha than me, coming and going before or after his office hours, getting through one page here, another there. Yet, at the end of the year, when I surveyed what was left (for I daresay that I was going faster in marking than he was in copying), I panicked. For one week I hired three typists. They came not only with their machines but with one assistant each. The dusky silence of the Nagari Pracharini Sabha was broken with the sounds of three typewriters clacking, three voices reading out passages, and three regular series of grunts, "Uh, what? What?" No one, to give them full credit for their patience and tolerance, minded the disturbance. One or two asked me solicitously, "Too bad! Does this mean you are leaving us soon?" which made me in turn regretful about my imminent departure.

The pages of typed Hindi were beautiful, but there is no match, I still claim, for what Nagendra Sharma could achieve. Whenever I see a page of closely written notes, I feel it must be his. Strange to think of it, all this brought us very close together. I habitually addressed him as "Nagendra *bhai*," a form that came easily to me, and before I knew it I was established as his older sister. This was no mere formality. I was his wife's sister-in-law, his parents' daughter, his children's *bua* (paternal aunt), and many convoluted relationships with the rest of his large extended family. Unhappily, none of the other kin categories came easily to me; I could never address anyone appropriately, nor could I keep up the banter and lighthearted conversation that went with my new position.

14

Inside a Police Station

As days passed, the city shrank in size. Adampura and Jait-pura, particularly, had seemed quite outside the bounds of possibility the first six months, lying as they did at some unspecified distance in the north of the city. By January, with the advent of near-perfect weather, I told myself, "Why not?" and swung onto a rickshaw with the instruction, "Adampura *thana!*"

The journey that followed almost made me change my mind. We covered the greater part of the city, including the uphill and downhill of Chauk, the main crossings of Godaulia and Maidagin, and the grain market of Visheshwar-ganj. More than an hour after starting we stopped at a large, heavy, orange-red brick building, and the *rickshawalla* announced, "Pilikothi!" meaning "the yellow mansion." This was, I discovered, the police station for Adampura ward, after whose hue the whole area was known as Pilikothi. Only outsiders like me called it Adampura; as with most places in Banaras, the area had an alias that its residents preferred, and every little neighborhood in the ward had several names that could be thrown out at you, but not "Adampura."

Having resolved the dilemma of how much to pay a man for a ride that seemed too long for a rickshaw at all, I gingerly stepped into the police station. Not into the inspector's room as was my habit, since he wasn't in and I was prevented from entering by the guard, but into the more public, completely male record room, with railed-in counters at which sat the clerks and record keepers who registered complaints and filed the infamous "first information reports," better known as FIRs. At every door was an armed policeman, and everywhere there were only men. Because policemen both work and live at police stations, they can be glimpsed in various postures of relaxation and various stages of undress, at any time of the day, since they work, as we all know, odd hours. All this is very awkward for a woman, and, as far as I know, no woman enters the record room of a police station. If she urgently needs to file an FIR, she can surely locate a brother, neighbor, or well-wisher to do so for her. There are women constables and sub-inspectors, of course, but so few that they are almost never seen. Nor, I think, does every *thana* have one. Less tangibly than all this, there is an ambience of maleness that pervades the average *thana*. The men develop an old-boy, clubbish mentality that leads them to use language, gestures, greetings, and so on not readily seen in the world of the family. They also leave possessions around such as packets of *biri*, pouches of tobacco, or, in Banaras, a *langot* (the Indian male version of the g-string), which reinforces the effect. Not only are the men none too careful about the finer points of dress, but also most of them are big and solid, a requirement for joining the police force. The inspector is likely to be the biggest and hulkiest of all, the most aggressively male, the most immune to female sensibilities, a regular old-boy club leader. After glimpsing such places, I was quite intrigued. I would have sat for the sub-inspector's exam if I could have, joined the force, and *then* done research with the full freedom to poke around that my uniform gave me.

At Adampura *thana* I almost had a taste of that freedom. When I explained to the crowd of questioning policemen that I was interested in the station's festival registers, they were too startled by the unusualness of my request to have a ready-made reply. They huddled among themselves but ultimately could only respond that the officer in charge was out and that I should sit down and wait. I was put on a chair in the best sunny spot on the verandah. After some time and persuasion, I was given a table and the festival register "just to look at" until the station officer returned.

This eminent personage breezed in one hour later. Remember that I was on a verandah inside, facing the courtyard that lay at the heart of the building, as in every old Indian structure. The inspector stood in the middle of the courtyard and roared for his *lathi* (bamboo pole). I then noticed a thin, ordinary man cringing in the shadows, being pulled out by policemen. The inspector started whacking him with the pole. The man would try to back off from the blows but would be pushed back into the middle of the courtyard to be targeted once again by the *lathi*. As he suffered more and more, he grew progressively desperate and had to be held as he was struck. I noticed then that although the inspector himself was a fat and terrible figure, none of the other policemen were. Most of them were of average size, even small and weak, and some were almost emaciated. They were grinning and enjoying the spectacle as if it were prime entertainment. The inspector made sense, as overblown and suggestive of inhumanity as his personage and position were, but these ordinary, starving policemen—starving, I mean, for good, clean fun, grinning as they were at a fellow man's inflicted suffering—seemed totally pathetic and strange.

I watched the whole drama from my vantage point in the sun, my eyes growing bigger and bigger, my heart thumping harder and harder. No question but that I had reached the inner circles. I had wanted to know what goes on inside the privileged domains where the ordinary female does not peer, and here I was. This was what the menu had to offer! To say I was shocked is not quite sufficient. My eyes were wrenched open by the cruelty, the matter-of-fact brutality, and the mismatched show of physical strength that existed on a day-to-day basis. This was no exceptional day or exceptional situation, but rather as average a day as I, by simply breezing into the police station, could have picked. And the sheer drama of it was something that my timid, humdrum, middle-class background had not prepared me for. It made my nerves tingle and my stomach palpitate.

When Mr. Tripathi, the inspector, was quite done, the prisoner cowering in a corner in near collapse, he brushed the incident off his hands and noticed me for the first time. He walked past me into his office, signaling for me to follow him, saying expressionlessly over his shoulder, "This fellow has set fire to someone's property! I got so angry . . . " In his office was another person who rather resembled the one beaten up and who looked rather scared at what he, like me, had witnessed. This, presumably, was the man whose property had been set afire. He sat in a corner of the room while the inspector dealt with me.

"What do you want?"

I gave the bare essentials of my purpose with a controlled face and voice.

"Do you know that these records are not public property?" thundered the officer.

I cited what is known as the Thirty Years' Rule, by which all official records are open to the scrutiny of researchers after a thirty-year period. The inspector humphed and went away without a word, perhaps to think it over or perhaps to wash the blood off his hands. On his return, he was cooler and stared at me. "So what is the topic that you have been given?" This, I had discovered, was the form of verb always applied in Banaras to my research, not the topic that I had "chosen" or "picked" or "decided upon," but the topic that I "had got" or "had been given." It told me much about Ph.D. research in India.

"Oh, festivals and things," I said hastily, aware that this was the point at which I sometimes went wrong. "Celebrations, processions, the things that people like to do for entertainment."

"Well, you've come to the right place—*everything* happens in Adampura. In fact you may as well do your research only on Adampura. This place has been around, do you know, from Baba Adam's time." My spirits leaped at his words; it was one of the only two responses possible to the statement of my research topic: either "Nope, there's no material at all to be had here" or "*All* the material is here, and only here." But with the close of his sentence, my flight of joy rudely ended. "Now," he stared hard at me again, "our I.G.'s daughter is doing some research here, too."

"Yes," I said miserably. "That's me."

Mr. Tripathi then did an extraordinary thing. He jumped straight out of his chair, joined his palms in reverential greeting, and, bowing and smiling excessively, repeated, *"Namastee! Namastee!!"*

I brought his attention back to the festival registers, which of course were set before me, as, gradually, were platefuls of sweets and snacks. Now Tripathi had good taste in snacks, being basically a villager attuned to corn, orange juice, peas, peanuts, sugar cane, and *chhena* sweets, and he was simple enough to offer this rustic fare even to his most distinguished guest. He was also a large man, and to sustain his size he snacked often. That day, and in the many days to follow, our relationship was partly constructed on our mutual search for something to eat—I, with the miles I covered daily in the city and the mental exercises that accompanied them, and he, with his erratic duties, habits, and sheer appetite. He knew places and had ideas about food that were irresistible to me. So, whenever he was with me, as escort or guide, we spent a necessary part of our time taking breaks for snacks. Of course I justified these breaks on the grounds that they not only satisfied my hunger but also contributed in an essential way to my research, in that I was "discovering the eating places of Banaras."

Mr. Tripathi was a Banarasi also, a different kind from my artisans Tara Prasad and Mohan Lal or the suave poets and writers of Kashipura and Madanpura, but no less typical for all that. His face resembled depictions of the wrestlers and weight lifters of old, as did his body, save for a growing paunch. That is, his face was broad, with a tiny stooping moustache forced up at the ends, his hair was on the long side, and a darkness and languor about it all that suggested nothing to me but I think aroused in traditional Indian (or just eastern U.P.?) minds the idea of beauty. Everything about him—face, girth, movements, laughter—was big, making him as typical a police inspector as a Banarasi.

That first day in his office, I was starving as usual, and after politely declining offers of refreshment at first, savored everything put before me. That gesture of acceptance was the end of any strict speeches I may have been planning on the subject of torture and physical abuse in police stations. I did raise the subject, but he was so unembarrassed about the incident that I decided to wait for a more effective moment, maybe, planned I with some satisfaction, after I had checked up with his I.G. as to the appropriate punishment for him. The punishment, let me tell the readers, never materialized. Not only did my father look bemused at the mention of the incident, but also he as much told me that such things were more the rule than the exception. As with liquor, drugs, prostitution, and violence in general, I had no desire to follow up the matter in any way, and it was slowly pushed to the back of my mind.

Once I had rearranged my perceptions to minimize the impact of this beating scene on me, I had progressively less difficulty in capitalizing on Tripathi's help in discovering Adampura. He had been there long enough to know the place well, and in his own country bumpkinish way, got along well with all levels of people—though not, of course, the ones he beat up. I needed a guide to people and activities, say to the Shobe-raat festivities, an all-night event celebrated variously at tombs and shrines, impossible for me to reach on my own. But with Tripathi in his jeep and Abdul Jabbar guiding us, we covered shrine after shrine; and having spent only half the night, we felt we were doing so well that we ranged outside Adampura and attended shrines in other parts of the city as well. Tripathi's protectiveness, his affectionate respect, indeed reverence, made me feel exceptionally secure by bringing back, I suppose, memories of my childhood.

One must remember that I had been *brought up* by policemen. Because of the way an officer's household is constituted, it was policemen who had cooked for me, served me, taught me to ride a bicycle, accompanied me everywhere, played with me, and communicated to me my first lessons in gentleness, kindness, sweetness. I had never encountered violence or harshness anywhere. The closest I had come was the experience, as a child, of driving through our gates, where the armed guard would point his rifle at the entering car and shout, *"Tham! Kaun ata hai?"* ("Halt! Who comes there?"). I would undergo a few seconds of trepidation; *what if the driver forgot the magic word of reply, *"Dost!"* ("Friend!")?

So over the years I retained a soft spot in my heart for policemen, and they remained—in spite of later wisdom—people I instinctively turned to for help, people I always spotted in a crowd. Even the knock-kneed raw recruits or junior constables in their half-pants aroused my affection and interest, certainly not my mockery or, as I was amused to note Rashdie write in *Satanic Verses,* a desire to escape "India's clutches."

I spent a long time at Adampura *thana* that day and on subsequent days, poring over the festival registers, which were unusually descriptive. I was even supplied a translator, who deciphered the older entries in scrawled Urdu. In one sense the ward did have "everything"—all the usual Hindu celebrations and Muslim ones, and some innovations besides, such as "the marriage of Lat Bhairav" and, thanks to the predominance of weavers, some "deviations" that seemed to belong only to them. I was rather overwhelmed and simply copied down the data; there was no question of anything making much sense at that early stage. No researcher should expect patterns to emerge and meanings to divulge themselves before the first year at least.

The police station also had Registers No. 8, the so-called Village Crime Notebooks, the nomenclature continuing even after areas had been squarely categorized as urban. In these, one register to a *mohalla,* there were actual *statistics* on the number of houses in each *mohalla* and the caste and occupational structure of the neighborhood, as well as comments on the "nature" of the residents: rowdy, cunning, docile, hardworking, and all those other British stereotypes inherited by the Indian administration. Unfortunately, there were too many *mohallas* in any ward, some fifty to a hundred, for me to make the most of such information, except very selectively.

I sometimes wondered if I should circumscribe my topic in some way, restrict it to a group of *mohallas,* or a ward, or in the same vein, to a community, occupation, whatever. But I could not persuade myself to part with all the rest of whatever I would have excluded. With the things I was discovering, expanding my subject in length and breadth gave me in fact greater depth—so I reasoned. But primarily it was greed, possessiveness of the city, and growing pride at a certain mastery over it that made me reluctant to part with any section of it. Whereas in music I liked solos and small ensembles, in my research, I preferred the symphony that the total city produced.

15

Abdul Jabbar

I saw many things in Adampura that first day: the Lat temple and mosque, a space revered by both Hindus and Muslims, high on the list of Banaras tension spots; the renowned "Nagina" *taziya* ("bejeweled" Moharram artifact), kept in storage all year round by its skilled maker; many, many lanes and dusty streets; the famous temple of Hanuman, where Tulsidas had apparently stayed and written part of his epic. I also met many people of importance to me, such as Lallu, *sardar* of one *mohalla*, and two of crucial importance, Maulana Abdus Salam and the dyer Abdul Jabbar.

Abdus Salam was a grand man. The imam of the most important mosque in the city, the Jama Masjid, Gyanvapi, he was one of the foremost religious leaders of the weavers and, apart from his legal status, was truly popular and beloved among them. He was an author in his own right and had published two books on Banaras, at the fine Urdu print of which I could only gaze in dismay. He had a small publishing house as well and wrote and published textbooks for children, uniformly orthodox and paternalistic. That he himself was a man of imagination and cultivation did not show in his life-style because he functioned from one small office spilling over with books and papers, where the once white sheets on the floor were liberally stained with ink and tea. But he wore a grand turban, sported a flowing white beard, spoke slowly and thoughtfully, and was always the scholar. I could discuss with him all my questions and doubts. Where had this name "Ansari" for weaver come from? Where had the weavers themselves come from? What was the status of their beliefs in classical Islam? How should one classify their festivals and rituals? Their language and clothes? They seemed fairly un-

Maulana Abdus Salam Nomani in his study. He died, deeply
regretted, in January 1987.

Islamic and Hinduized in my naive opinion. I had spoken with a few *maulanas* (religious leaders) already and was aware of the mental blocks to be encountered in discussing something of such proximity to them. They had been reformers, critical of existing practices, judgmental and denunciatory. But Abdus Salam did not allow his interpretations to be influenced by his values, at least in his conversations with me; I doubt that he was different in his dealings with weavers, judging from the affection in which they held him. As a *maulana*, he was an official maker and interpreter of social codes, but he did not do his work in a bookish way. His own brother, another *maulana*, whom I met separately as a scholar and religious leader in his own right, was so different as to make me appreciate Abdus Salam all the more. His brother had a small mind, could not see beyond the immediate and obvious, and could locate problems only superficially. Abdus Salam could see the past with a professional historian's vision, could make connections like a sociologist, could analyze with the patience of an intellectual, and in short was much more than a *maulana*.

Abdul Jabbar I met not in his professional capacity as a dyer of silk yarn but as one who hung around the *maulana*. If the *maulana* was my match in his scholarship on Banaras (mine projected, of course), Abdul Jabbar was more than my match in his investigative abilities. He knew all kinds of people, all castes, occupations, classes; all parts of Banaras; all events and activities. He could go anywhere at the merest suggestion, find out anything, make friends and acquaintances, ask difficult questions, sift information, follow it up, close the case as efficiently as the best detective on the loose. I was fascinated by him, I was drawn to him like a magnet, I wanted to hold on tight to him and not lose him. Fortunately he found my company amenable and my notions attractive, and he stuck with me for the rest of my stay. If he had not been unlettered and untaught, in an occupation that he was more or less born into, he would have excelled at something far more intellectually challenging than yarn dyeing.

Abdul Jabbar also had a very clear philosophy of life, one difficult to pin down because it was not so much articulated as lived. He loved, valued, and respected people, all kinds of people, and did not think anyone beneath interest or consideration. That struck a familiar chord in me and, I think, brought us close together. He could be outrageously aggressive in approaching people because he was never shy, timid, or hesitant as I was, but his brashness always worked because his sincerity and single-mindedness shone through. His greatest pride was that he knew more people than anyone else, and that they not only knew but also liked and respected him and, most of all, *came to him for help.* Now here was a slight difficulty. I slowly acknowledged that in poor communities in a less-than-efficiently working preindustrialized or semi-industrialized city, there were a lot of problems, and everyone had one or two at any given moment. Abdul Jabbar was into many at once, handling this or that for one friend, running an errand for another, comforting a neighbor, visiting an acquaintance, unearthing crucial information for yet another. He probably got interested in me because I had this immense problem of research. Here I was, trying to pin down a subject as vast as the cultural activities of Banaras, with such poor equipment as no intimacy with the city, its language of Bhojpuri, its past and traditions, its mental set and moods. I would simply never achieve my objective on my own, as Abdul Jabbar saw it. He rallied to my aid because, as he saw himself, only he could help me achieve it. He stuck with me throughout because he could see what positive results his proximity brought me, how I turned to him for all kinds of succor, and how the actual plot thickened the more we stayed at it. So, while I didn't care for his semi-patronizing relationship with me, in which he already knew everything I had to find out and I should preferably remain the passive recipient of the knowledge, I truly loved him for his selflessness and gregariousness. We could both, without planning or contemplation, get lost in wandering around, meeting and talking at random, and feel exhilarated without ever bothering to calculate why.

I often felt guilty about Abdul Jabbar. He was one of the poorest men I knew, his poverty exacerbated by the fact that, like all artisans, he lived from day to day, earned according to the hours he worked, and had no security whatsoever. His wife, mother, and two daughters lived upstairs in his house in Daranagar, a more mixed *mohalla* than usual, being predominantly Hindu but with many Muslim weavers and *zari* (gold and silver thread) embroiderers. The house was subdivided among brothers, and tiny rooms remained, one on each floor of a three-storied house, each looking more obviously halved because one wall was freshly constructed of raw brick. The frequency of partition within families did not reduce my apprehension that it must be an awkward subject for those involved, and I treated it as if it were taboo. In fact, families remained friendly to each other even after quarrels and legal separations. Abdul Jabbar's immediate neighbors were the members of his brother's family; he himself took me to meet them, referring to them as *garib* (poor, literally) and *bechare* (poor, metaphorically), and the girls of the two houses were the best of friends. They could not visit each other, however, being in total seclusion and also, technically, antagonistic. Taken up to the roof of Jabbar's house by his daughters, I discovered what a perfect vantage point it was for a number of purposes. Best of all, because it overlooked the courtyard of the next house, it brought the girls close enough for long conversations and gossip. I was introduced to the cousins, and there followed some stylized joking on how I had lost my looks and appeared downright "pale" because of my prolonged separation from my husband. The jokes irritated me initially till I remembered the position of my new friends, physically in complete *pardah* (seclusion) and mentally almost so. They were indeed separated from their menfolk for sustained periods, and from the outside world for always, and such jokes were comments on their situation.

Although I spent long hours and the better parts of days in Abdul Jabbar's home and was part of the women's world all that time, I remember the women of the house predominantly as those confined. The image that comes to mind is of their peeping out of the little windows upstairs, revealing the smallest parts of their faces, as I approached the front door and called out. More often than not, Abdul Jabbar, being the busy man he was, would be out. It made more sense to call out "Bilquis!" or "Vakila!" They could not come downstairs to unlatch the front door, but they had a rope connected to the latch which traveled upstairs through many tunnels and pulleys and which they could tug at to open the door. I could enter and grope my way up the stairs in the dark—for, like Tara Prasad, Abdul Jabbar refused to have electricity as an unnecessary expenditure. Bilquis, her sister, mother, and grandmother were thrice confined: out of tradition; out of poverty—the absence of diversions and activities at home; and out of illiteracy and ignorance.

Abdul Jabbar's illiteracy was not something one remembered, because he simply knew too much for it to be important. He was far more educated than the average person, and certainly many times more than I was, on how the city administration functioned, where one went for which purposes, who was who in the place, what people believed, thought, and did. He was not merely functionally adapted to life in Banaras, as many people I got to know were, but he was extremely clever and knowledgeable as well. The problem with him, which might or might not have been reduced by schooling, and which I struggled with continuously, was what may best be described as his "speech impediment." Abdul Jabbar spoke very indistinctly. I lost valuable statements, sometimes whole paragraphs and speeches, because I simply could not decipher his words. In the latter part of my stay, when I was totally comfortable with him, a family member of course, I made him repeat, very slowly, many things that I thought he had been saying which I missed the first time around. But there were too many things I missed.

A speech impediment was a common Banarasi complaint, cross-cutting the population from the top (the maharaja) to the bottom (the average artisan). An impediment could have many causes, but bad teeth, poor training, occasionally old age, and general lack of care were probably important ones. When Tara Prasad told me the name of the wood he used most often for carving, I could not comprehend the word. In my notes I find, in successive places, *"gurukul," "bhulkul," "bhurukul,"* and *"gulkul"* as the best wood. Many things in Banaras had a frustrating array of alternative names: *"chau-muhani"* and *"chauraha"* for crossing; *"kajali"* and *"kajari"* for the music; "Ahir," "Yadav," and *"sardar"* for the milkseller caste—but that is a different problem deriving in large part from the time it naturally takes to get a handle on another culture. When encountering words that I initially misinterpreted, I often thought of our Jewish Community Center experience in Chicago. Passing on to me a job that involved calling up the Center, my husband innocently remarked, "There's a woman called Shalom who always picks up the phone."

Words were extremely important to me, to the extent that I could have claimed that my whole enterprise rested on language: hearing the right words, understanding them, using appropriate ones myself, getting the multidimensional nuances of words. Besides the utter disgust I felt with myself when I let precious sounds pass in noncomprehension, I often felt impatience with my new friends. The inability of some Banarasis to enunciate their words carefully was greatly compounded by their refusal to do so because their mouths were full of *pan*. To eat *pan* in the correct way, you have to stuff it in a corner of your mouth and store the juice in your lower jaw until you deem the juice sufficient to squirt out, which you do in any direction you consider expedient. Having done that, you have a few seconds to make a clear statement to those who may be waiting patiently; then the juice begins to accumulate again, and you had better keep your mouth shut. I ate *pan*, too, and I often practiced this style of juice storing before the mirror. I believe it is better for your innards than swallowing the juice wholesale as I habitually did. Moreover, if I could have mastered the technique, it would have given me a posture, a mannerism to fall back on, that would have exuded both familiarity with and confidence in my surroundings. I think I would also have liked to have a method handy whereby I could, if I so desired, find myself unable to reply or forced to reply inaudibly.

These diversions aside, the fact remains that for many and sundry reasons people in Banaras were difficult to understand. If they were not chewing *pan* and had no speech disability, they might be simply sleepy or bored and refuse to open their mouths wide, as elocution trainers recommend. Many of the informants I picked out were old, with wheezing throats and quivering mouths. Tara and Jabbar were not that old, but their mouths sort of ran away with them. Abdul Jabbar's main obstacle was his beard, I believe. Thick, unkempt, junglelike, it covered most of his mouth, so what actually emerged from his mouth was unknowable and what remained after the passage through the beard was not very helpful.

Abdul Jabbar may have been fifty or sixty; people like him age easily, develop grandfatherly mannerisms, addressing everyone as *"beta"* (child) and coming to be themselves referred to as *"baba"* (old man, father). As I said, his teeth were either bad or gone already; he preferred to eat with his bread soaked well in his curry, but that may have been simply a device to make the food go further. For me he was ageless, and we were more comrades than anything else. Yet he could get tired out from our endless travels. On a few occasions he fell asleep wherever we had stopped. Sometimes he looked exhausted, and he was often, I suspected, hungry like me. But he never admitted to any of this and kept going doggedly, not only serving as guide and companion but also carrying some of my bags and, when it came to the crunch, the baby as well. Irfana was so used to this that the very first name she learned to say was "A-boo-oo-oo-l Ja-bbaa-aa-r!" What he would have *preferred* her to say is "Khan Sahab"; he kept teaching her that alternative, but she stuck to her choice.

Where exactly did we go and what did we do? I had the privilege of making a grandiose plan of my choice. I would propose, for instance, that we go around to all the old mosques of the city. Abdul Jabbar, abandoning work and family, would agree with enthusiasm. We would set out, leaving at dawn because in his calculations we would need those extra hours to cover all the essential places before dark. We would sketch out an itinerary, based on locations and his instinct of who would be available where at what time. Neither of us was interested in looking at buildings. I took pictures like mad, but the structures themselves were meaningless for me and mere artifacts for him. He searched out the imams and the *maulanas*, the old caretakers and the neighbors. Guided tours and rich exegetical narratives followed, better than my fondest hopes could have led me to anticipate. Abdul Jabbar had a way of presenting himself and me, by extension, that removed any doubt about the logic and acceptability of our search. I'm not sure precisely what he said: perhaps "She's writing a book but had no way to meet you"; "She's interested in Islamic society and culture but needs a little help"; "She has come all the way from Chicago, and our *maulana sahab* offered to teach her what she wanted, but we decided to come here first"—a combination, that is, of flattery, deep respect, even reverence for the addressee's knowledge; of our own relative ignorance and frustration; of the *maulana*'s support and goodwill; and of the intrinsic value of looking at mosques and shrines to understand much about anything. In short, he was an eloquent interpreter of my research project and throughout served to make it clearer and clearer, as well as succeeding consistently in having it accepted. No one ever hesitated to trust me, since I was in Abdul Jabbar's company, but they probably would have felt more comfortable if I had not had this unnerving habit of whipping out my notebook and pen. It wasn't so much the person we were talking to who objected—he would appreciate my seriousness—but all the others who passed by, peeped in, or gathered around. They would frown and whisper, "What is she writing? Who is she? Where is all this information going?" Abdul Jabbar would immediately shoulder the whole responsibility and explain me anew, with careful consideration for the social level and assimilative capacity of his audience.

I did not even have to press home the point to Abdul Jabbar that it was not merely formal representatives of authority

Abdul Jabbar (bearded, center) took me to various ceremonies I
would not have otherwise seen, in this case, a goat sacrifice.

and religion that I needed to talk with but some simple folk,
the ones visiting the mosque or shrine or even not visiting in
some cases. Jabbar's repertoire of friends included many
such, and, since all was for him pure pleasure, he as naturally introduced me to impoverished weavers as to powerful
maulanas. On the way to or from somewhere we would pause
at a teashop or someone's home and spend delightful hours
chatting about what we were looking at that day and the
larger phenomenon. The trouble with such a technique was
that *everyone* always offered us refreshments, and as many
times as I tried to decline these and persuade our hosts that
they were unnecessary—conversation alone would be just
fine—Abdul Jabbar insisted that we (I, as he would put it)
must have tea. With my anxiety about feeding off poor people
who were already giving me valuable time, this insistence

was acutely embarrassing for me, but I had to accept it as the Banarasi custom and Abdul Jabbar's way. He patiently explained to me that in Banaras to refuse anyone's hospitality was the worst possible insult and that, no matter what I imagined, my hosts' insistence would have overridden my reservations. I agreed inwardly on the strength of my experience of visiting people in Banaras. But I could not resign myself to it and have not managed to even now, besides which I live in constant dread of otherwise long and productive days of fieldwork, with their dozens of cups of boiled tea, leaving a permanent hole in my stomach. My basically awkward adaptation to Banarasi hospitality continued throughout my stay: as soon as I visited someone, tea and *pan* would be produced, and I would start protesting instead of looking happy and gratified.

It should be clear that, as wonderful as Abdul Jabbar was for me and as well as our personalities suited each other, I did not entertain clear-cut feelings for him, nor he for me. I know, for example, that he found my lack of style demeaning. As someone with wealth, education, family name, and a passion for culture, I should have been more in the school of the old-style *rais* (aristocracy) of Banaras, probably should have spoken less (depended more on him), spent more (taken taxis rather than rickshaws), argued infinitely less, and never, never, never should have appeared intimidated but simply should have *known* that my qualities overrode everything. For me, Abdul Jabbar was not merely a little too pushy, somewhat too quick to take advantage of hospitality and help, and, of course, imperfectly articulate, but also sometimes questionably ambitious. He had met me initially through the *maulana*, who in turn knew that I had a relationship with the police station. So Abdul Jabbar comprehended that I was a special person of some sort. What he couldn't grasp, or maybe wanted to, was why I needed the police in my role as supplicant for their records rather than their needing me, respected sister of the police force as I was. Of the many problems with which ordinary people could be beset, there were those in a category that involved the police. Abdul

Jabbar helped people with these as well as with others and frequently entered or hung around police stations. He must have calculated, perhaps indistinctly, that I was good for him, although repeated efforts should have also convinced him that it *never* helped either to cite my name or even to have me physically present. Policemen could make the distinction between being courteous to me or helping me in harmless ways and allowing me to influence their important decisions.

Abdul Jabbar never gave up trying to get me directly involved in his—sometimes, in our mutual—friends' problems. More often than not, his very introduction of a new person to me would incorporate both sides of the relationship, thus: "This is Shakur, a great merchant. He can tell you all about the Banaras silk trade with Nepal in the fifties. Here, sit, sit . . . make yourself comfortable . . . Some tea for the guest, Shakur? [*Indistinct moans of protest from me.*] And Shakur also has a son in some trouble at the police station . . . " Deciding to educate Abdul Jabbar in the virtues and indeed the necessity of noninterference with the affairs of the administration, I spoke to him at length about the fact that I was finally a layperson, a *helpless woman* to whom no one would pay any attention, and I demonstrated it to him in diverse ways. Most of all, I simply ignored all requests for any kind of intervention. But he educated me instead in the realities of city functioning. People had legitimate problems, and the recognized, legitimate way of dealing with them was through a person who could talk effectively with both parties. All Jabbar and the others were doing was trying to incorporate me into the social structure and, in the absence of any other qualities in me of value to the society, to use the one I had, namely, my family connections, to make me an integral part of society, giving to others as well as taking from them.

The question of how to help others had haunted me from the beginning, as I've had occasion to describe. I never did resolve my dilemma on that visit, but my responses over the course of the twenty-two months can be divided into two phases. In the earlier and more naive phase, when someone

made a request of me, I would conscientiously sift the facts of
the case and judge it on its merits. If obviously impoverished
and oppressed, the person deserved to have a word put in. If
the supplicant cited an outright example of injustice, then it
deserved further action. I must have made a good one- or
two-dozen efforts to help informants before I realized that not
one attempt had been successful. My failure had as much to
do with my conviction that such interference was unethical
as with my lack of talent for the business. To make a sufficiently plausible request to a police or an administrative officer, you have to humble yourself at least subtly. I couldn't do
that, lest I inadvertently become part of the all-India conspiracy, with everyone busy at giving and taking. Somehow I let
this attitude slip in even as I was making my request: "Here
is a deserving case," would go I. "But you will be a better
judge of its validity, and far be it from me to impose . . . "
The officer being approached would guess that the case
didn't matter, that I would not do anything about it. Since he
was involved in a transaction, I needed to make him feel like
an active, voluntary transactor, not a mere cog in the machine
that was being pushed to perform. In other words, I was
inefficient.

My successes were in inverse proportion to the significance of the cases being pleaded. I succeeded in bringing the
S.S.P. here and there or in providing three mounted constab-
ulary for Ram's marriage procession at the Manikarnika
Ramlila; but I couldn't get Mohan Lal's house vacated, or
Shaukatullah's land freed, or Alimuddin's partition settled,
or prevent Bharat from being beaten up by a rival gang. The
truly worthwhile cases, such as the collapse of Markande's
room in the monsoons, for which relief was theoretically
available from the district magistrate's office, were effectively
botched as much by my interference as by anything else.

The second phase was marked by almost total retreat. My
life became so intense and busy that I decided one could be
either a successful activist, a useful member of society in
some way, or a useless and seemingly self-centered anthropologist. At times it broke my heart to say no, which I
learned to do automatically in case I waivered. When the

thin, exhausted-looking policeman who had helped us particularly after Baba's death came over one day and explained,
with defeat already in his eyes, that he was having a house
built in Banaras and if his transfer from the city could be
stayed for only two months . . . I could feel the pity of it, my
unfairness as I told him quietly, "No, I can't help you. I never
do this on principle." He nodded and cycled away without a
word.

Part of my fear was of opening a Pandora's box if I relented
and allowed my sympathy to move me to action. *Everyone*
had problems, from policemen with ailing children to artisans whose houses had been seized by scheming brothers.
Either police officials, it seemed, or some closely related
breed of administrators could solve these problems. I was
supposed to be on close terms with the dozen or so district
and city officials in Banaras; people were always giving me
the impression through mime and suggestion that I had but
to pick up the phone and demand redress, or even more effectively, to pick up the phone, order a jeep, drive to some office, and demand redress. The more modest plaintiffs, such
as my artisans, wished me simply to stop at the local police
station and plead with the inspector on their behalf. In my
first phase, as I said, I responded to both kinds of sugges-
tions, only to realize, to my relief—and, I suppose, to my
chagrin—that the technique didn't work. I tried offering my
own personal services as a member of the public instead:
"No, I can't phone the district magistrate, but I can go with
you to the municipal office and look into your problem." I
don't recall anyone taking up such offers.

Partly as compensation and partly because, unlike other
anthropologists, I had no moral compunctions in the matter,
I made gifts of money or material things, indeed always seeking an excuse to do so. Poverty was such an overwhelming
fact of life for my informants that the money was unarguably
useful, no matter how much, presented under what guise, or
how used. And since such help was not part of people's expectations, or where they directed their efforts, monetary
gifts felt easy and natural.

16

Questions of Gender

The discussion of how to remain myself while interacting meaningfully with my subjects also brings me to the question of what it was like to be a woman wandering in the streets of Banaras. I should say at the outset that my experience as a woman has been unequivocally good wherever I have lived, the result both of fortunate circumstances and, although the realization didn't strike me until rather late, of a low level of sensitivity to harassment and discrimination. When I lived in Lucknow as a college girl, my friends and I experienced our share of "Eve teasing," that wonderful Indian euphemism for publicly making girls' lives miserable. Eve teasing included for us everything from men pinching our bottoms in crowded places to boys on bikes snatching away our *dupattas* (the long scarf worn over the chest as a symbol of modesty). We took this with a mixed attitude of indignation and I-can-be-a-good-sport-too; it was absolutely a part of life. When I worked in Delhi, both as an unmarried and then as a married woman (with no external sign to distinguish the two states), I was free and happy. No one bothered me in any way that I remember, and I had long debates with other women on the safety of the city. I vehemently argued that much depended on the woman, since I went around the whole place on assorted modes of transport, chiefly buses (my research at the time was on Delhi), and was quite comfortable doing so. I had developed a few techniques then—which implies, of course, that I had inferred the existence of hidden dangers, even though I did not experience them directly—which I put to use again in Banaras.

The first was to be totally cool and confident, as if the place belonged to you, which almost no young woman feels about a public place for the obvious reason that a public place is not a woman's domain. As you walk along, you should look this way and that, asserting your right to look where you please. This is dangerous in the Banaras *galis*, however, because men habitually urinate on the sides of the road. You can also keep your eyes thoughtfully to yourself, knowing your purposes, but reveal by an occasional glance here or there that it is because you are lost in thought, not because you are afraid. You are interested, when you do look, at the whole social scene in an adult way, not at any individual in a personal way, and you must accordingly avoid direct eye contact with variously interested men while comfortable enough among them. You should be dressed sensibly, not in this or that fashion, Western or Eastern attire, bright or dull colors, but in a way that shows you to be straightforward and reasonable, someone that people can understand.

The most important moment is when you approach a stranger, or when he approaches you. The crucial step is to look him in the eyes, with no fear, no hesitation, no awkwardness; he's a person, you're a person; he has a job, you have a job; he has a family, you have a family; he's normal, you're normal. Don't wait too long, or speak too soon. You *know* that he's not going to bite you, hurt you, abuse you. You're aware that you may have to explain what you want, so you are, not apologetic—because apology has no place in Indian life—but very, very courteous. The rest is a linguistic trick. You must have enough command over your language not to stutter or stammer, search for words and get trapped in phrases—all of which can create the wrong impression. You speak clearly, to the point, *honestly*. You say what you mean, but say it in good Hindi. The stranger is immediately at ease. He makes the necessary leap, classifying you as one of the figures familiar to him: mother, sister, daughter, depending on how well you have slept the previous night and how recently your hair has been brushed. Before that, of course, you have the choice before you. For me, the choice was clear-cut. No matter how old or young the man, I would inevitably call him, "Bhai sahab," respected brother. This would be automatically appropriate for most males; for those much younger, it would carry the not undesirable connotations of affection and interest.

I developed these techniques to perfection, so crucially did I depend on the ability to be able to talk to absolute strangers comfortably. I became aware, to my lasting surprise, that men could not be judged by their looks either. Some were forbidding because of their sheer size, or their arrogant postures, or by the way their mustaches curled. Most were terrifying because of the way they stared unblinkingly, a simple subject-to-object stare: "How should I judge this specimen now?" But when I drew near a man and began speaking with this "he's a person, I'm a person" approach, these other characteristics retreated into the background and I could read the normality in his face. Some of the most unpromising-looking people, *pan* juice in lower jaw and all, turned out to be the most "normal," even likable.

What about when people try to be smart and approach you? If it is ostensibly a legitimate request, such as for directions to a street, although you may guess that it is really to stop and observe you a little better, it should be taken at face value. Telling a group of smart young men the directions they want in a businesslike fashion is the best way of making them move on. To look abashed, or embarrassed, or at a loss is to invite trouble. Who are they after all? Young men with no girl friends, no jobs, probably no prospects, and lots of vague ideas about talking with females and developing relationships with them. The only device that deters them is to bring them from these abstract heights of fancy back down to earth. Smile at them, there's no harm in that; even enter the conspiracy by adding a question of your own to prolong the conversation they so much desire for another minute.

Occasionally a young man or a group of men care so little for the appearance of sanity that they call out whatever they like to you in passing—usually something on the order of, "Hello darling!" The reaction that came most naturally to me on such occasions was to look up swiftly at the offenders, then shake my head in surprised regret, as if I were disappointed to see that nice, intelligent, proper-looking young men could be responsible for such an old, unimaginative trick. It was too much to hope that they would take this to heart, and they would probably continue in the same vein. But my reaction was the best that could be thought of in such a situation, for condescension is something everyone minds.

I hardly had any such experiences, however. The local wolves of Banaras either haunted other parts of the city than the ones I did or wisely ignored me. I don't think I looked *old*—people tell me I don't—but I did have this aura of being older and wiser than the average girl or young woman who walked around independently with no ostensible purpose. And as soon as I opened my mouth and said "Bhai sahab," the stranger found a mooring. I must say, in certification of my methods, that by using them I met and talked to more people and made more real friends than I could ever have laid down to strict necessity.

Why do women have such a problem in India though? Both my Indian and my foreign friends have told me that it is impossible to do anything as a single, unescorted female on the streets, that the comments and abusive behavior that greet them are intolerable. Sociologically speaking, this problem is due to the widespread loneliness and separation from their often village-based families among males in urban areas and to the fact that any woman who is found outside the defining sphere of home and family is seen as a target, like a prostitute or a film star, for one's frustrations. As long as these conditions exist, there is no escape from the problem. You can try all kinds of devices, such as the ones I have suggested, but as long as you have to stay constantly alert, you have far from solved anything. But there is, I believe, that middle zone, where what happens to women depends on their own actions. If you wear *sindur* (powder) in the part in your hair, bangles and a bright sari, and look and act like the typical married woman, you are definitely of little interest to men. If you appear the unprotected little "college girl" in *salwar kamiz* suit of latest cut, shy and scared of men, you will draw trouble like a magnet. If you are sensible, as I have suggested, expect and look as if you expect civility, with none but intelligent brothers all around, very likely the desired behavior will follow. For me it did.

Another consideration is where you are. Delhi, the present version of which dates from post-Mughal times, and Lucknow, circa eighteenth century, are relatively *new* urban cultures, with all the awkwardnesses of new, growing cities. Banaras, by contrast, with its millennia of tradition, has a smoothness of social relations; considerable provocation would be required to disturb them. Of course, some things can strain these traditions, such as lighting up a cigarette on the street. But the vast repertoire of possible social roles, the capacities and resilience of people in accepting them, and the larger belief in the rightness of context and circumstance all contribute to making more kinds of behavior acceptable than one would imagine at the outset. Special categories for unusual behavior and personalities are conjured up when necessary—categories such as *shauk* (passion, fancy), *man kiya* (the mood struck you), *kala* (art) and *kalakar* (artist), and so on. Besides all this, the pride in urbanity, courtesy, and decorum is so strong that I consistently found myself the loser at the game of politeness. Everyone had a better idea of what to say or do in strange situations than I did. Everyone made a habit of exaggerating my qualities and purposefulness and overlooking my awkwardness. In the old city, no woman could be molested or even made to feel uncomfortable, and this is an attribute of age. There were plenty of young smart alecks roaming free and unchallenged in the newer university area, but none would be tolerated in the lanes of old Banaras.

There was another dimension to my relative success as a woman that I grew to accept gradually. People enjoyed giving me time and having a conversation with me *because* I was a woman, provided that I had a clear-cut definition and attributes (sister, outsider, writer, "public worker" of a kind). This I put down to the fact of men being relatively isolated from women's company, yet free and comfortable with them because of the sister-daughter-cousin-sister-in-law association. I have since noted how easy it is for most Indian men to get along with strange women in the role of elder brother or younger brother-in-law. I reaped the advantage of that. Because I was a woman, I could impose on strangers, draw them away from work, press them for information or guidance, or make them lead me to places and people more easily. They treated me with greater gentleness and consideration than if I were a man. I never had to exaggerate or belittle my femininity; as soon as I presented myself as a normal person, albeit with a peculiar agenda, they were willing to serve and befriend me.

There were some relationships that became more weighty. With Nagendra, my innocent use of the term "bhai" for him decided our future. I was for then and evermore his sister by *dharma* (natural law) and, as I have described, inherited a vast array of relationships in the bargain. That first experience was a jolt. I consider it a fair-sized project to adapt yourself to the families of which you are part by accident of birth and then by marriage, to grow to appreciate your actual siblings, cousins, and in-laws. If you acquire even more relatives simply because that is the way things are done in the place you work, you may start getting impatient. Since you have a choice, is this the brother you would "choose"? You may tell yourself that it is nothing but a linguistic device, that you can call him "brother" and forget about him. But in Banaras expectations run higher. Your brother has the freedom to come to you at any time, seek advice and hospitality, sit at loose ends for hours in your home, bring his children over to meet their aunt, consult with you about his job and miscellaneous affairs—and to demand that you do all of this in turn with him. My first sisterly responsibilities, because of the novelty of it all, seemed overburdening.

I became Tara Prasad's sister out of choice. He was busy, engrossed in a range of activities, often on his feet and therefore elusive. I was jealous of all the other demands on his time and wanted a special relationship with him. I knew he had no sister. After I volunteered myself as one, I discovered that he had another one or two such as me, but I was happy

My brother Markande with his most prized possessions: his
bicycle, radio, and watch

enough. I also wanted to have a claim on the progress of his
daughter, then seven or eight, quiet and intelligent, and his
illiterate, helpless wife. I wanted to come and go in his house
as I pleased, eat with his family, sleep overnight with them,
share their worries and thoughts. Maybe I could have accomplished all this without invoking the relationship of sister,
but I think it did make them more comfortable and allowed
me to reciprocate in many ways for all their help to me.

My third new brother was Markande. I do not remember
how the relationship became explicitly named, but it was a
gradual and natural development, since he *wanted* to depend
on me as an older sister. He was the oldest of four children,
and his youth and rawness were often more than his family
status allowed people to acknowledge, since he was also one
of the two working members of a large family. I think he was
also keen to get married, and typically the older sister or
sister-in-law broaches the subject and launches the search for
a wife. I did not of course. Throughout I did the barest minimum to occupy the position of sister. Again, if I had a dif-

ferent kind of personality, if I had had more experience at social roles, I could have made so much more of the opportu-
nities to learn about my new brothers and semi-brothers.

Then there was Majid bhai. I liked the idea of "father"
Shaukatullah, sister Nurunissa, and sister-in-law Habibu-
nissa, so far from me in religion, education, occupation, and
consciousness. That they should accept me so well was a
very positive sign to me in my research and promoted my
confidence about my style. It also made me feel better as a
human being, as if their simplicity and likability announced
that I must be likable too. Majid had many sisters, but he reserved a special slot for me, as I supposedly did for him,
something his family regularly made joking references to.
Sisterhood can be embarrassing because your brother must
often provide gifts and pleasures for you. As long as these
were in the form of time and research help, I was happy. But
there were too many other kinds of occasions. At Raksha-
bandhan, you tie a *rakhi* (ritual thread) on your brother's
wrist, and he in return gives you money and the promise of
protection. The last is okay; I needed it on my midnight music recording forays. But the money was a problem. How
could I not accept it, or return it, without humiliating the
giver? On most such occasions, I tried to match it with a gift,
a very obvious device, but I could hardly accept something
worth over 10 percent of the family's weekly wages without
reciprocation. For Majid bhai, there was no *rakhi* occasion,
but all my visits were treated with the high spirits that a returning daughter's or sister's visits occasion, and I was sent
home with presents each time. This could be a recently
cooked sweet, given with the severe injunction not to return
the dish it was packed in; it could be a piece of silk woven by
Majid or his other brother (it was curious how one brother
could become your brother, whereas the other, while technically your brother as well, never really did assume that relationship). I was in constant pain over the number and variety
of their gifts, and no presents I gave in return ever could
match theirs, ultimately because a sister's or daughter's
could not be permitted to.

Other choices were inadvertent, brothers acquired because of the lack of another relationship to set up. Some pricked to the end of my stay, such as that with the communal-minded Seth Govind Ram, to be whose sister seemed to place me in the same rabid Hindu category (not a necessary connection, by the way, only one in my mind; one does not inherit the qualities of one's adopted kin). But all in all, as I grew more comfortable with kin terms and categories, my appreciation for the workability of the system increased. I continued to feel that I, as woman, outsider, and researcher, benefited more from it than my newly acquired fictitious kin, but that was perhaps only unfounded apprehension. They had a capacity for deriving pleasure from the unplanned and the odd that, I suspect, outmatched mine.

17

Rapacity and Recovery

There was another incident I experienced as a woman researcher that flared with the fury of a passing meteor at the
Nakkatayya of Chaitganj. I had never seen the like before nor
have I endured it since. I have to speak in some detail about
this event.

The Nakkatayya of Chaitganj is a mouthful as a name—for
days I couldn't decide *what* people were trying to say—and a
handful as a topic of study. It is cited as one of the two largest, most important parades in Banaras, and it goes on all
night, with several hundred thousand in attendance. All this
is told to you with great glee, and the importance of the occasion is underlined with comments like, "You must get
there a few hours before because roads get totally blocked";
"You must find a place to watch it from, there is never any
space on the roadsides"; "If you don't see it, you've seen
nothing in Banaras." The Nakkatayya was to take place in
early November, and I had just started feeling comfortable
with my activities in Banaras. I could make plans to go to
places at night and was becoming bold enough to go to places
without any idea of what to expect. The Nakkatayya of Chaitganj was a prime attraction, because apart from its size, long
duration, and indisputable importance, no one could describe to me what exactly would transpire there. The parade,
I gathered, consisted of numerous floats that were taken out
in procession in the locality called Chaitganj, down the main
road called Nai Sarak and then past it into winding lanes.
The word *nakkatayya* itself meant, in Banarasi lingo, the cutting of the nose, referring to an episode in the *Ramayana* that
would be enacted that night. Very, very promising.

My husband did not think so and insisted that I arrange
for a police escort. The local police station promised a jeep,

The Nakkatayya of Chaitganj

driver, and policeman at 9 P.M. I waited till 10 P.M., then 11, then midnight, finally realizing with frustration that it was one of those times that the police had let me down. I woke my sleeping husband, informed him urgently that he *had* to come with me; we organized the rest of the night for the sleeping baby and crept out of the house.

A rickshaw took us within a half-mile of the place, joining many other rickshaws and pedestrians going in the same direction. The rest of the city was asleep, but toward Chaitganj there were lights, decorations, loudspeakers, and music. We had to abandon the rickshaw at a point and merge with the walking crowd. On Nai Sarak itself we were pleasantly surprised.

This road, like most others in Banaras, is ordinarily almost unwalkable, being full of vendors, traffic, potholes, and filth. That night, it looked like a fairyland. The road was swept and sanitized, with bamboo structures to delineate one-way lanes on either side and to separate sidewalk from street. There were huge gates every few yards, rows of pretty lights on each side, and ultra-bright floodlights to remove all shadows. There were vendors of foods—all looking delectable, although I resisted the temptation to poison myself by trying anything—and hawkers of balloons and toys, of pottery, masks, souvenirs, and all the paraphernalia of an Indian fair. No garbage, dust, flies, or other disturbing features were visible anywhere. Thousands of people were strolling up and down the road in very festive spirits. What seemed initially intolerable was the amplified music, a different kind every few yards, each clashing with the next in uncontrolled cacophony, but, surprisingly, one got used to it quickly enough. I noticed that the strollers were all men and that the women and children at the fair kept to the sides or had taken up vantage places on the verandahs and rooftops of all the surrounding houses.

It was past one at night, and the parade was supposed to start soon. We needed to find a vantage point ourselves. We thought of aiming for the balcony of the Chaitganj Police Station, where we had been promised seats, but as we headed in that direction, something happened. Suddenly we were caught in a tidal wave. Some kind of barrier had just been erected a few yards further on, and the whole crowd had been dammed and forced to turn back. People were now rushing back in the thousands, with the uncontrolled speed and indifference of a powerful elemental force. One who trips and falls on such occasions gets trampled underfoot, I thought, and I remained steady on my feet. But I was unprepared for what else could happen to me. Suddenly the only woman in the middle of the road, I was surrounded, pushed, and pulled by an anonymous crowd of thousands of rushing men. Hands were reaching out to me, touching me here and there, at random, purposefully, disgustingly, revoltingly. I would push off one, and there were a dozen more. Sombabu was only one defender, unable to surround me. He was also a victim, and he became separated from me. I was being tortured, victimized, degraded. I was at the mercy of a mad crowd.

The whole episode must have lasted but a few seconds, and it ended as abruptly as it began. Two or three men made a protective circle around me, their arms on each others' shoulders in practiced grips, and pushed me along through the crowd to the side of the street. The press of bodies was so strong that we could not stop of our own will but kept going to the very edge of the road. My saviors and torturers jointly pushed me into the safety of a urinal, together with others, including my husband. Urinals are structures on the sides of Indian roads similar to little boxes, enclosed in front and back but not on the sides, and of course terribly smelly and unsavory. I have maintained a strict distance from them always and regard them as the most disgusting appurtenances you can encounter outdoors. Here I was cowering in one for safety. The urinal was wet, and that side of the street was slimy and muddy. My legs were filthy well above my ankles, but I was so grateful to be out of the bearbaiting that nothing mattered. I even thought humorously of the fact that a despised urinal had provided shelter. I also thought gratefully of the men who had saved me, although other men of Banaras had gone crazy the moment before.

We were near the police station, so we went in and cleaned ourselves. No one there paid the slightest attention to us, being entirely preoccupied with the event that was about to begin. The barrier had been put up by the police to clear the road of people at that point and let the parade start. I am surprised, when I think about it now, at how rapidly I recovered and how my only thought was to climb up to the balcony quickly so as not to miss a single spectacle of the parade. We weren't late, as it turned out. We found seats, and I compiled a complete list of the floats that formed the Nak-katayya parade that night.

The more I think of that episode, the more unreal it seems. It was overwhelmingly sudden, a complete turnabout of the peaceful strolling, festive activity, lights, beauty, and music that we had been part of just a few seconds before. Had it really happened? Maybe there had been a rush of people turning back upon us, maybe we had been momentarily trapped in the onslaught of bodies. But had the crowd deliberately aimed at me and *my* body? At the time I had felt that it was the end of me, that I would be ripped bare, destroyed morally and psychologically if not physically. But perhaps, like the Englishwoman in Forster's *A Passage to India*, I had imagined it all or at least greatly exaggerated it? Possibly a couple of hands seemed to me hundreds? Perhaps the men were not touching me any more than they were touching one another in that pressing crowd? The last is a distinct possibility, because I admit that I am so tense about the touch of strangers in crowds, I am always ready to spot a potential offender even when there is none. An accidental touch always makes me want to scream. In very thick crowds, I walk rigidly, with my elbows out to protect my upper body. As a raw, unsuspecting youngster, I had been touched and humiliated in both likely and unlikely contexts—from dark cinema halls, where anonymous shadows developed creepily intimate hands, to the security of my own home, where silent, familiar servants and innocently trusted uncles turned into unrecognizable monsters. Those were well-repressed memories and had made me frightened of the possible touch of strangers, I suppose.

Such an incident had not happened for a long time, however, and had never happened so far in Banaras. I was far from expecting it, at least consciously. I pushed the whole thing to the back of my mind because there was nothing I could do with it, no complaint to lodge, no reform to undertake, no fresh interpretation to make. It bothered and disturbed me, but once safe, I turned eagerly to the business of the evening. Nor, interestingly, did it leave me with a distaste for the Nakkatayya or for such occasions in general. I have been to many since, wiser perhaps and more alert, and that one proved such an aberration that it simply did not affect me significantly. The fact that a urinal became my final resting place made more of an overall impression on me, and the way that I had been enclosed by linked arms and propelled to safety.

My husband lost his watch, but that apart, we agreed that we were none the worse for the outrageous experience. Perhaps he had been separated from me by too far a distance to notice what happened to me, or was too absorbed in fighting off his own attackers, or no such attack took place, just an accidental push of bodies lasting a few seconds—but whatever the case, he himself was more outraged by the Nakkatayya parade than by the previous demonstration of crowd behavior. The parade was something to exclaim about, no doubt. It was of prime carnival vintage, with sufficient absurdity, nonsense, and surprise to keep us diverted for the next three or four hours—but I have written about it at length in other places so I shall refrain from describing it here.

18

Progress and Its Limitations

January through April were exhilarating months for me. I realize as I write this that I myself am very "season oriented," quite like my Banarasis, because I give the credit for the successes of that time partly to the wonderful seasons that prevailed. To call them winter, spring, and summer seems misleading. It is necessary to understand them as the people of Banaras did, broken up into little entities of a month each: Paus, end December to end January; Magh, January–February; Phalgun, February–March; and Chaitra, March–April. Paus is somewhat windy and temperamental; at the end of it occurs Makar Sankranti, the winter equinox, which is *always* rainy and chilly. The month is forever associated in my mind with the Bengali song (of Tagore's?) "Pos tother dak diyechhe, aiyere chale aiye!" ("Paus is calling out to you: Come outside, come!"), with accompanying images of people rushing outdoors, flinging their arms out in abandon, reveling in the season.

Magh is the climax of the cold season, brilliant with sunshine and crispness, golden and beautiful, and is marked by the festival of Basant Panchami, celebration of the spring harvest, known in cities simply as the day everyone must wear something yellow. The whole of Magh is celebrated by the Magh *mela* in Ramnagar: picnics outdoors near the Durga tank, with a special menu of baked flour balls, eggplant curry, and lentils, all cooked outside. Everyone is in top spirits, it seems, because of the unbroken opportunity to sit in the sun, whether to work, talk, sleep, eat, or play. Indeed, there is little to beat the winter sun of North India.

Phalgun marks a change of season, from cold to warm, and as befits such liminality, has to be cautiously welcomed.

An ice-cream vendor at the Ramnagar fair in Magh (January)

Colds and sicknesses become more frequent; it can be chilly one day, unpleasantly warm the next—yet in consistent progression, nothing like the variability of Chicago or New England—for which it is difficult to prepare physiologically. To wash it all away is the festival of Holi, or Phagua, at the end of Phalgun, when everyone takes a dunking in water and is thus immunized against seasonal infections. The festival itself is crazy, and so is the month by association, because spring makes people restless, even demented, in inexplicable ways. Such was the power of this suggestion that I instinctively looked around for some demonstration of this spring madness in people's behavior. Thanks to both the season and its supposed effect on humans, Phalgun was a wonderful period for my research, as I shall shortly describe.

Last, but in fact first, is Chaitra, the primary month of the year according to the North Indian Hindu calendar. In Banaras both Hindus and Muslims by consensus consider it the best time of the year. One of my biggest thrills came when the staid and self-conscious Kishan Maharaj, *samrat* (em-

Tabla maestro Kishan Maharaj with the horse he keeps for racing

peror) of tabla playing, internationally famous, always dignified, aristocratic, the center of his universe, told me solemnly,
"For me the best season is that of Chaitra. The river is at a
perfect temperature: neither too hot nor too cold. You can go
out on *bajras* (large boats) and have music to your heart's
fill . . . The best *melas* were in Chaitra . . . " This was a thrill
because it followed closely upon Abdul Jabbar's disclosure:
"The month that I would consider most superior is Chaitra.
The perfect season for going out . . . You know that the largest *mela* around here, the one at Chunar, is held in Chaitra.
Then the celebration at Chandan Shahid, with music every
Thursday for the whole month . . . " This was the testimony
of Abdul Jabbar, poor, untraveled, with no self-consciousness,
no empire, than whom a starker contrast to Kishan Maharaj
could not be found. There were echoes of the same sentiment
from whomever I chose to listen to, sighs of "Ah Chaitra!"

from Tara Prasad, Mohan Lal, Matiullah, Mahadev Mishra—
just about everyone in Banaras. It was infectious, and I found
so much to observe and participate in at that time that I was
full of enjoyment, too, and decided that my informants were
extremely perspicacious people.

The weather contributed directly, of course—there was a
tangible difference between functioning in the monsoons or
in the summer heat and functioning in these near-perfect
months—but there were many other reasons for this triumphant feeling of life. The reader may have discerned a steady
development in the narrative from complaint on many
fronts, including my own personality and ignorance, the re-
serve of the people, the difficulty of access to things unknown; to an assertion of control over events, circumstances,
myself, and others. Partly this progress was simply a function of time. But most of all it was my growing knowledge: I
found my feet in the city, I grasped its functioning, I could
sense its motion, and I developed an instinct for the way its
people's minds worked. All of this may be summed up in another way: my research problem and my choice of location
showed themselves to be appropriate ones, and I developed
the talent for framing suitable questions. I remember feeling
this very powerfully one fine day in March as I cycled around
from one to another of that day's stops (I had inherited my
father-in-law's strong old English bicycle). "I used to think
that I would be doing this," I told myself, "cycling around in
Banaras, stopping to eat *pan* like a typical Banarasi, and cycling on . . . and here I am." The image derived directly from
what a friend in Chicago, returning from a year in Banaras,
had told me. "So what *did* you do in Banaras?" I had asked
him persistently. "Oh, I went around with my friends, eating
pan . . . " was the best he could do by way of answer. Now in
Banaras, I did not in the least feel strange on my bicycle,
high, gent's bike that it was, or imagine that people stared, or
experience any diffidence about my being an outsider, a
stranger, or a fool. All the thoughts that had plagued me
daily during the initial two or three months had vanished like
the monsoon clouds, and I now harbored a cheerful confi-

dence, an optimism, unshaken by the inevitable everyday disappointments, that an endless vista of rewarding discoveries were yet to be made, each in turn rolling out yet more vistas.

What exactly had become different about my system of working? It's a difficult thing to pin down. One tangible difference was that I was now a friend to many more people, *almost* in the literal sense of the word ("a person attached to another by respect or affection"), though my hidden agenda sometimes pricked my conscience. I spent many hours with people simply enjoying their company, sharing their activities, genuinely pleased at their pleasures and saddened by their sorrows, laughing at their jokes, and telling them some of my own follies. They discovered more about me than I had ever supposed they would. They came to understand me and my preferences, and we could each assert our own when necessary. "Are we going to the Maduadih shrine on Thursday?" would ask Abdul Jabbar. "Let's take a taxi. It's far, and the afternoon gets hot." "Oh no!" laughed his daughters. "Let us go the way we usually do; that's what *she* would like, she's writing this book you know!" I was accepted, bag and Chicago-proposed research baggage.

The pleasure that I received from spending my days with the people I got to know was something of a surprise to me. I had heard from everyone returning from the field what a lot of fun it had been (apart from the inevitable gastronomic problems), but I had been hard put to imagine when and how the fun would begin, aside from the occasional satisfaction of a job well done. Then slowly, like a miracle, I became part of a world I had not particularly worked toward creating or belonging to, and that world was more compatible than any I had heretofore seen. I became extremely close to some of the many friends, particularly Tara Prasad, Brij Mohan, Guru Prasad, Mohan Lal, Shaukatullah, Markande, Alimuddin, Abdul Jabbar, and their respective families. With many others I had a hearty colleague's relationship, tempered, of course, by my junior age and position, such as with the poet Shaukat Majid, the Maulana Abdus Salam, sundry priests and literati, and the great musicians Kishan Maharaj and Mahadev Mishra. I can say without romanticism that I discovered what "happiness" was. It was to reach one of their homes or places of work unannounced and to sit there without tension or worry, welcomed and loved, as long as I liked. All the little touches that came of my being a sister, daughter, and comrade added to the feeling of lightheartedness and acceptance.

An additional dimension had crept into my work: apart from accepting that I needed to exploit the resources embodied in these people, I realized that the pleasure I received from their company was unplanned and very powerful because it was reciprocated. Some spoke directly of *prem, sneh, mohabbat, lagav* (love, affection, attachment) as characterizing our relationship and thought nothing of philosophizing further on it, holding my hand, patting me on the shoulder, or looking into my eyes for a response. These unfamiliar expressions troubled and shocked me because they expressed an ease with emotions that I had never learned to communicate, and they made me dissatisfied because I did not have a similar repertoire of words and gestures to express *my* feelings in return.

Mohan Lal told me of an extraordinary adventure when, having not seen me in over a week and missing me terribly, he took a rickshaw on his own and set off, half deaf and blind that he was, to track me down. He did not have my address, only a vague notion that I lived "near Majda cinema," so of course he wasted eight rupees learning what I already knew, "No discovery without an address." This developing *need* for me, which many of my friends voiced, was an unexpected compliment, mirroring as it did my far more carefully planned need for them, and it made my throat catch with its starkness and vulnerability.

The other tangible development was the widening of my circle of acquaintances in impressively relevant directions. Guru Prasad was a friend cum comrade, friend because such was his personality and his family's, comrade because he wrote poetry and considered me, as a writer *of sorts*, in the same category. I was also a daughter because of my age, though he was one of the few poor but practical people who did not feel it necessary to stand on ceremony for that reason. Quizzing Guru Prasad about the history of his art, I was given the name of another poet in Madanpura and told in the familiar, exasperating way, "You know the grand old house of the poet Nazir Banarasi? Take the second lane going in on the opposite side, if you are coming north from Assi, and ask anyone to direct you to Jameel Sahab the poet. He is a *hafiz* (one who knows the Quran by heart). There will be no problem finding him. He usually sits in his *baithaka* morning and evening. If you go before 8 A.M. it's better." The last was a difficult suggestion for me, but our household was certainly better organized than earlier, and though to leave at unscheduled times put everyone to some trouble, it could be done. On this occasion, the sparse directions worked out, and I traced Jameel Sahab without difficulty.

Jameel Sahab was a gold mine for me. Not only was he a poet with a well-developed sense of the history of poetry in Banaras, but also he was scion of one of the older (the oldest, according to his claim) families of Madanpura and able to hold forth at length on the history of the locality. Months later, he also disclosed that a nephew had in his possession an unpublished manuscript on the history of the weavers of Banaras. Moreover, Jameel Sahab could give me introductions to *akhara* managers in Madanpura, to *madrasa* committee heads, to the Barawafat festival organizers, to silk merchants, to designers, and to civil activists. Beyond all this, I sat with him many mornings in his *baithaka*, chatting about this or that. We had a lot in common because he was a poet, I a writer—he was appreciative of the fact that I used a nom de plume, Nita *Kumar*, instead of my married name; he was full of curiosity about everything in the world, and I was obviously driven by the same curiosity; he had been a Communist in the past, and I had lived in Moscow; he had plenty of time, being semi-retired from his profession of sketching sari designs, and I had all the time in the world; he loved to play with and observe language, and I was always preoccupied with how things were said; and most of all, he loved to haunt teashops, chat idly, call upon acquaintances, gossip . . . all of which were becoming not merely research tools but special weaknesses of mine. Unlike Abdul Jabbar, he had no speech impediment, was a well-educated intellectual with few prejudices and a lot of imagination, and understood that to befriend me or help me did not mean to wrap up my research with a wave of his magic wand. Abdul Jabbar, by contrast, thought that I was simply in trouble and that with his sincerity and help, I could be gotten out of it. At every moment he was ready to believe that the end was in sight, and that prospect haunted our every movement, so that as we were preparing to meet a fresh person or look at yet another mosque, the tenor of his talk would indicate that after this one time, God willing, the case could be closed and the whole burdensome problem of describing the culture of the artisans of Banaras would be solved forever. Jameel Sahab was obviously much more sophisticated. He was not quite certain of the general direction of my research (a reflection of my own stance?), but he ascribed sufficient complexity to it to tolerate all kinds of particular inquiries and questions as valid.

What intrigued me about the whole thing was the business of poverty. Jameel Sahab, it seemed, was as poor as poor could be. He lived on the third floor of a much-partitioned and ill-maintained house, and one reached his quarters by gingerly ascending steep slabs of stone, one side of the steps exposed to a sheer drop below. After several exhilarating intellectual meetings with him downstairs in his *baithaka*, the occasion arose to climb up to his rooms. I experienced a rude shock and had to refrain from gaping at the scenes of squalor that beset me. His relatives and co-sharers of ancestral property were apparently paupers, or chose to live as such. On reaching the top, pretend as I might, I was aghast: I was confronted with two tiny rooms, a family of apparently one-dozen adults and children, no furniture, poor possessions, grime and dirt, rags and tatters, and the toothless, smiling poet (he always put on his teeth when he came downstairs) amidst it all. He certainly had sufficient money to eat, educate his children, marry off his daughters, and be hospitable to his guests. Yet "poverty" was a way of life with his family. What struck me as extraordinary and unbearable (how unbearable, I cannot say) seemed to them entirely unremarkable. Although Jameel Sahab *was* poor, he was not as poor as his life-style made out. His life-style—living poorly, as I called it—was a cultural mode common to him, with all his learning and poetic talent, and to Abdul Jabbar, who was starkly illiterate and unliterary.

To the end of my stay, and throughout my subsequent visits, there remained this invisible wall between me and my best friends in Banaras: their imperturbability in the face of filth, overcrowding, disease, even death; their disinterest in cleanliness, family planning, home maintenance, and control of the environment; and, by contrast, my own nervousness about it all. They were as tightly conditioned as was I. I *never* got used to their idea of tolerable surroundings. Even at my most comfortable with them, I worried about this aspect of their culture, conscious that no matter how happy I could feel while with them, I would *not* like to be one of them.

This was also a big wall between me, with my growing love for Banaras, and the city itself. What I saw in each home, I saw on the larger scale as well: open drains, free urination, piles of garbage, no functional separation of spaces, no comprehension of germs and sanitation, a gay disregard of very obvious problems. These were not simple attributes of poverty, though because I visited mostly poor homes, I initially believed they were. But I also visited a sufficient number of wealthy traders' and merchants' homes to confirm that, no matter how different their income from that of ordinary weavers, they shared the weavers' cultural world rather than what I naively had imagined to be a universal world of the comfortably settled, financially secure family, necessarily characterized by cleanliness and order. Nor was "living poorly" a function of illiteracy and "backwardness," as Jameel Sahab's case dramatically brought home. It wasn't class and it wasn't education; it was partly ages of being conditioned to live tightly in an overpacked city environment, where natural forces had once provided relief but where city services had not expanded proportionately to the population. Cultural proclivities—ways of dealing with refuse, techniques of cooking and washing—were no longer adaptive to the size of the population and the layout of the city. Cultural habits had a force of their own at this stage, and if the inhabitants of Banaras had been transported elsewhere, say to Siberia, they would speedily have proceeded to convert the new environment into a version of Banaras.

It should be obvious that while my world continued to expand in Banaras both qualitatively and quantitatively, there were some distances I could not bridge. There was always this one unspoken subject between my people and me. What could I have said to Jameel Sahab regarding his living arrangements? Why doesn't someone sweep and mop this room? Why let the child urinate there? Why not wash in another part rather than make this mess? I shuddered at the very idea of this impossible insult, and I suppose, at the practical risk of creating a rift that may have proved injurious to my research.

19

The Pleasures of the Body

Another approach I adopted which was fundamentally different from my previous one was to take up a topic and concentrate on it intensely for a few weeks. I was not aware that I was doing this until I had explored wrestling *akharas* for most of March and then decided I must discover what the music called *biraha* was. One evening I had a team of milksellers singing up a storm in my living room when one Mr. Bahl, a wrestler and body builder of former all-India fame, who had taken the trouble to show me around many *akharas*, dropped in to pay me a visit. As soon as he entered, he smiled, "So! You're doing music now?" And the whole picture became clear to me. I had "done" *akharas*, I would now "do" folk music, then bookshops, then Holi, then Hindu silk merchants, then Muslim ones . . . Mr. Bahl provided me with a useful handle.

To proceed in this topic-wise way became increasingly simple. *Akharas* had been a mystery as a topic, for I could find no academic work on the subject; they were also closed doors to me, doors, moreover, whose location I could not guess. On Luxa Road was a sign I had observed for many days, reading "The Health Improving Association." That seemed explicit enough. I walked in one morning, following the narrow lane that led inside until I reached another gate with the same announcement. Entering that, I found myself in a walled compound with open land on one side and a concrete space shaded by a tin roof on the other. There were exercising devices all over the place, the parallel bars and dumbbells among which I recognized in a flash, though most were unfamiliar. I tried to focus on the many men doing various things on the far side. I hesitated to approach them not only because they were all busy but also because they were practically naked. I made some sounds and movements to attract someone's attention. As soon as I had been observed, there was a visible shrinking away—how could they know that I was rather nearsighted—and even signaling for me to go away. I held my ground, and finally a fully dressed man emerged from the room adjoining the tin shed and came up to me.

"What do you want? This is a gents' *akhara!* Whom did you want to meet? Where are you from?"

All I wanted to know had already been said, that this was in fact an *akhara.* I drew him aside and explained that I wanted to write about *akharas* and had walked in because of the sign. Could he help me?

Mr. Bahl was an insurance agent, a rather typical middle-class Banaras gentleman in that he spoke in a mixture of Hindi and English to me and Bhojpuri to everyone from Banaras. He dressed in smart modern clothes, but underneath his covers, so to speak, he was also an avid wrestler and *akhara* goer. He was so enthusiastic about *akharas* that he wanted to see them publicized, and he saw me as a godsend. For the longest time he considered me a journalist who would write some eloquent articles glorifying *akharas* (illustrated with glossy photographs) in important magazines. After my repeated disclaimers that I was but a humble research student, he convinced himself that my whole book was going to be about *akharas.* This suited me fine, because it implied needing a vast amount of data, and I desisted from explaining too much. Mr. Bahl had a motorcycle, which, like a typical Banarasi, he was competent to wield through the narrowest *galis* and crossings. For the next few weeks, I was his guest in the world of Banaras *akharas.* Perched on the back of his motorcycle, clutching the seat with feigned nonchalance, I went systematically with him to the old and unused *akharas,* the new and flourishing ones, the famous ones, the unknown ones, the local neighborhood ones, the grand all-Banaras ones, until I myself was ready to declare that I had had enough.

I had been wary of the topic right from the beginning. I had taken immense pleasure as a youth in cycling, swimming, skating, riding, playing basketball, and even cross-country running. But my connection with sports was restricted to my own participation. I never read the sports pages of the newspaper, listened to cricket or any other sports commentary on the radio, talked about sports, or gave them a thought. I certainly did not intend to waste my valuable time researching sports. The importance of *akharas* had been established for me through my few months' stay in Banaras, mostly from incidental talk and stray references, and I was resigned to the prospect of "doing" them as an unavoidable part of the subject of popular culture. What I discovered almost immediately was that sports did not mean simply muscular development. There was a philosophy to the practice, in this case a very articulate, holistic philosophy, that started to excite me as much as any other part of my research. The first and most eloquent presentation of it was totally serendipitous. I was in a press owner's shop in Chauk, discussing printing and dissemination of literature. This was mid-morning. Entered his son, a man slightly more curious than his father, who asked me a few key questions about my research. He immediately exclaimed about the obvious part that *akharas* would play in such research and, being an *akhara* goer, just back from the *akhara* in fact, proceeded to expound on their philosophy. What he told me that day, sitting among the litter of paper and ink as I raced to record it all, could still serve as a treatise on the subject.

A very interesting thing happened. Here was I, professedly indifferent to sports after the age of twenty, my whole being centered on an intellectual pursuit to the exclusion of all else, listening to an account of a physical activity that was exclusively for "gents" by all accounts. I became absorbed, then mesmerized, then slowly converted into thinking that this was *it*, this was the pure philosophy, the holistic approach to life, the subtle balance between extremes that I had vaguely suspected must exist somewhere in the world. I loved every word I heard about *akharas*, and so enthusiastic did I become about them that I took extra trouble to go around and double-check all that I was told, suspecting that I had reached the point of admiration where I was capable of idealization, prejudice, and exaggeration. I was also afraid of giving proportionately greater time to *akharas* than the subject warranted in the overall scheme of things in Banaras, thanks both to my emotional satisfaction in pursuing it and to the capacity of the people of Banaras to be articulate about it.

Prem Mohan Bahl was not my only guide. There was the District Secretary of Wrestling, Banarasi Pandey, who spent many instructive hours giving me an overview of the phenomenon of wrestling. There was Rajesh Kumar Sonkar, a beautiful, perfectly proportioned man who had held the district body-building title every year from 1979 to 1981 and who showed me the clubs of his choice. But gradually almost everyone I knew became a guide to *akharas* or a source of information about them. Tara Prasad, fragile, bent, wrinkled, announced proudly that he had an *akhara* right in his home and showed me its remains. Indeed, broken, discarded *joris*, the pair of clubs used for swinging, were to be seen all around, now that I knew how to recognize them. Nazir Akbar, one of my poorest and most spineless weaver friends, immediately picked up the pair languishing in his courtyard and swung them for my benefit. Incidents such as these clinched the *akhara* argument. Then I started hearing announcements for *dangals*, the wrestling competitions put on locally, and I witnessed as many as I could. If I had still been unconvinced or indifferent, the *dangal* crowds and accompanying excitement would have certainly made a convert of me there.

Such discoveries tell you a lot about yourself. I had believed that I was very keen on music but not a sporty type after the excessive energies of adolescence wore off. Yet when it came down to time, priorities, and the sheer labor of marching around dusty, filthy *galis* in pursuit of an object, I gave far more time, less grudgingly, to *akharas* than to the music of Banaras. I gave enough to the latter, God knows, but for all my tabla lessons and singing of *chaitis* and *kajlis* in the bathroom, I could more readily visualize myself as rolling in the mud of

An enthusiastic *akhara*-goer swings his *joris* (clubs)

the *akhara*—and felt a kinship with those who did so habitually—than I could imagine doing more *riaz* (practice) at my
music lessons.

A point has to be made about the masculine aspects of the
whole business. Women never go to *akharas*, though there is
a lore about women wrestlers and those who could do hundreds of push-ups a few centuries ago. Women constitute
neither the audience of the competitions held in *akharas* nor
the patrons of them in any other form. The reason seems obvious: the overall exclusion of women from all stimulating,
self-developing public activity. For me there was also a pragmatic reason: men exercise in the barest minimum of cover-
ing, the *langot*, a string with a fig-leaf-sized cloth attached to
the front. When resting or receiving visitors, they deign to
put on their *janghias* (thin cotton underpants). Where is one
supposed to look? Not merely into their eyes, or at their impressive *gadas* (the heavy wooden clubs encountered even in
the epics), the idea being to observe the whole scene in all its
detail. I quickly adopted the stance of the approving connois-
seur of *akhara* culture, a situation, as in all those associated
with art, where the sex, age, caste, or any other attribute of
the individual is irrelevant. Whenever I entered an *akhara*,
there was a change in activity, a hush, even actual retreat by
a few into the shade of the trees. I would stay, quietly waiting
for my presence to merge with the surroundings. Gradually
people would continue with what they were doing. I would
talk to a few willing ones, some would even demonstrate favorite styles to me, others summon friends to answer particular questions. As at music gatherings, no one laughed, com-
mented on, or diverged from the conversation I initiated. All
took for granted that I was learning about a precious fact of
life. That I was a female made little difference; I was merely
one of the wiser, more awakened ones of my species.

I never felt consciously excluded from this world of male
exercise and activity, though all females by definition were. I
was no feminist then, and in retrospect, it seems, it had escaped me that there was something to worry about, complain
about, or resent. The *akhara*-goers were simply people for me,

and their craft was sufficient food for thought. When I systematized all my information back in Chicago and sat down to write my first piece on *akharas,* I found myself saying, "And if there is anything to criticize in this system, it is that women are deliberately excluded from the culture of *akhara* exercise and body building."

My inclination to think more as a "person" and less as a "woman" sprang from my personality, class background, and upbringing, of course, but it was greatly encouraged by the pragmatic demands of research and the fact that I was hardly exposed to women at all. When I selected artisans as subjects of study, I had no forewarning that those in Banaras would be exclusively male. But upon discovering that they were, and that their leisure and recreation comprised domains from which females were systematically excluded, I was not much concerned. The excitement of the work to be done was great enough, and it was supplemented by the comfort I felt in males as objects of study and as companions—as objects because I had been trained in a history and an anthropology that emphasized male worlds; and as companions again because of personality and upbringing, including education in the English "old-boy" style.

The people I spent time with, those who took me around and assisted me—all were without exception males. My sex perhaps made them more patient and generous with their time than they would have been with a man. But they did not explicitly or primarily think of me as a "woman," in the sense of becoming protective, concerned, careful, or guarded with information. They assumed that I was competent and accepted me as their equal in intellect, imagination, and even physique. Tara Prasad always made me walk miles in every season of the year, Abdul Jabbar made me take rickshaws with him for unmeasured distances, Bahl put me behind him on the bike, and all demonstrated the inner details of whatever we were inspecting without reticence. I was shown the different muscles of the body and how they would develop with this or that exercise. I was told the particular relevance of celibacy to good living, why refraining from sex was the precondition of all success, and how the control of semen equalled the storing up of virtues (*hira* they called it, diamonds). Most of the terms for these things were incomprehensible to me (since I had never had a Hindi-speaking boyfriend or husband) till a later, more thoughtful time, but I do not remember anyone lowering his eyelids or pausing for breath at these moments in the conversation. My assurance that Banaras was a totally mature society, able to take in its stride women pursuing odd inquiries, appearing in forbidden places, asking unlikely questions, was further confirmed.

20

Holi Saturnalia

I had a shock in store for me on the occasion of Holi, the spring festival of the Hindus, which is described vividly in places like *Anthropological Notes and Queries* as saturnalia, reversal, carnival, and so on. I have played Holi every year that I have lived in India, which is to say the first half of my life at least, and I know it well. You wear old clothes, equip yourself for battle, and go outside with buckets of colored water and trays of colored powder—orange, blue, yellow, purple, red, and green. You greet everyone you see with a dusting of color on the face, and if you can manage it, with a shower of colored water on the body. In earlier years *taisu* flowers were used for dyeing whole tanks of water yellow, and the unwary would be lifted up and dunked in them. For playing or fighting we used metal syringes to squirt the water, quite genteel and harmless. In later years the flowers disappeared, the tanks were condemned as too rowdy, and mugs and pots came to be considered more practical than syringes for throwing color. Those in good spirits would simply lift the bucket itself and empty it on the target. All in all, I loved Holi, and each time I started playing it, I could not stop.

While the practices of Holi were familiar to me, its purposes were hazier: inversion of social order, of course, and creation of solidarity. The policemen of the city would pour into our bungalow in pickup trucks all morning to play rough and intimate with their boss, the S.S.P. It was overwhelming as I watched from a safe distance, usually the rooftop. Daddy would be so drenched with paint that he would have to change clothes three or four times during the morning. From my child's perspective, however, I could see where the limits were. Children could act wild and grown-ups could join in, but in practiced ways. Grown-ups did atypical things: joke and laugh excessively, eat and drink *bhang*, get dirty, and embrace one another, but with self-control. Servants were embraced but continued to be on duty and to maintain the whole thing as a merry garden party through necessary service and obsequiousness. Structure girded the occasion; lines of separation marked genders, age groups, and classes, the outside/unknown and the inside/permissible.

"It's unfortunate that I know Holi so well," I told my husband on the morning of Holi 1982. "Now if I were an American researcher, I would have taken so much care to look into all the details of it, but me? What should I look into?" I felt guilty about not bothering to investigate something because I supposedly knew it already. But, as I said above, I was due for a shock.

I had heard Mr. Tripathi of Adampur *thana* mention a Holi *julus* (procession), or as he called it, *dulha julus* (bridegroom's procession). This had alerted my senses a little, for I had never heard of a *julus* at Holi before. It sounded like the Western phenomena of charivaris and reversal at carnival from the little that I knew of them from European history. I immediately begged Mr. Tripathi to be allowed to witness this procession in his ward. "Begged" is the right word. Whereas otherwise I led and the inspector followed, on this occasion he seemed bemused and doubtful, and I had to plead with him that of course it would be all right. No matter what it was in fact like—I had vague images of rowdy, uncontrolled crowds, a combination of the Nakkatayya and spring madness—I had to observe it for my research. Tripathi acceded, and on Holi day I was present in his police station bright and early, before people were out on the streets with their buckets of color, or whatever they used in this part of the world.

In time we went in his jeep to a point where the procession could be observed, and there it was. About twenty men, unrecognizable in their identical colored clothes, all of them well washed with Holi colors, were dancing and singing. The song was rhythmic and musical, though I couldn't catch the words. "What are they singing?" I asked my escort tactlessly. "You can't hear them?" he asked half-suspiciously; "Well, *I* can't tell you." Then he added more kindly, "They are only joking." I strained and strained, because I wanted to have just a *tiny* idea of the particular form their obscenities took, but I couldn't catch a damn thing. The dance itself was pretty easy to follow. It was centered in the pelvic region, a vigorous shaking of the belly, not side to side as Hawaiian hula dancers favor but rather back to front. A few minutes of watching served to clarify that it was a mimetic version of copulation, with many parts in slow motion, exaggerated for effect, and dramatized. I had to watch the whole thing because once I was there, I had no way of leaving. In the middle of it all was a donkey with a rider sitting front to back, wearing a bridegroom's headdress, and waving a gigantic penis made of rags and paper. This spectacle required no questions and no explanations. I looked on with a semblance of academic interest, but I would have preferred a small glimpse to extended observation.

The party came up to us and put color on the inspector's face. I pressed back into the shadows. No one took any notice of me or approached me. The men went on, and we followed them in the jeep for the rest of the route, till I had the song, the dance, the donkey, and the whole scene well etched in my mind. I was ready to admit that I was shocked, that on this occasion I had been bested by the people of Banaras.

My next plan that Holi day was to zoom into Chauk, the heart of the city, and from a safe vantage point in the *thana*, observe the proceedings there. Because Chauk is far more densely populated than Adampura, more full of tortuous lanes and attached houses, and thus of "danger," I took little Irfana along with me as a protective shield. Surely no one would dare to play rough with a young mother (my head was covered with my sari, in the manner of a sober woman) holding her baby. No one did, though in our very progress to the center of Chauk, we became as brightly colored as everyone else. Color, paint, and water were thrown liberally all around at no particular target.

What I saw in Chauk was another surprise, though a pleasant one. In the middle of the empty space that constitutes the center of Chauk stood a singing group, its leader elevated on a wooden stand. They sang song after Holi song, each lyrical, hearty, full of throaty abandon. People gathered around, came and went, played color, and embraced in the particular way that is customary at Holi, joined the singing, or listened, without any order or planning. The air was thick with powder being thrown by several hands, and all around was a sea of colored faces. It was a special scene in itself, but of particular beauty to me because it was Holi as I would have *liked* it to be played. It made me happy. It made me feel, "Where have I been?"

The difference between Chauk and Adampura disappeared at a point. At my insistence, the inspectors of both *thanas* unwillingly and guardedly presented me with some of the obscene publications that mark Holi, looking very unsure of themselves as they did so. I was triumphant, even if embarrassed that the literature actually had to pass hands in this "Pssst . . . ! Care for some . . . ?" style. The pamphlets were pure pornography, graphically illustrating as well as mentioning by name all the well-known citizens of each ward and some better-known citizens as well, such as Indira Gandhi.

What happened at Holi was that I finally resigned myself to the fact that popular culture could be "crude," "obscene," and distasteful to my genteel middle-class sensibilities as readily as it could be beautiful, aesthetic, and refined. I had found it relatively easy so far to separate these sets of characteristics, to shut out, for example, evidence of drinking and drugs, sexuality and obscenity, in my field of study. At Holi this became impossible. Although the Chauk experience was there for me to rejoice over, the procession was really much more central and powerful, impossible to block out. There were hundreds of such processions all over the city, and everyone knew about them. The distance between middle-class and popular culture was also brought home to me somewhat forcefully, because when I had left home in the morning I had thought I knew Holi from my own childhood experiences of it. In a matter of hours, I was rid of any such illusion and was back in my old familiar situation, confronted with a problem. I was lucky to be able to spend one full year more in Banaras and to leave only after the following Holi. This was an ideal situation: having observed Holi from the outside the first year, I went to informants the next and followed their activities with them. Again, holding on tight to my little daughter—she never showed any aversion to Holi activities—I played color in different homes. I had a Holi feast in Mohan Lal's house, and with a newer metalworker friend, Chayen babu, went to Chausathi ghat for the Holi evening festivities. The relativity of noise and peace, of ugliness and beauty, of crudeness and refinement, the shifting definitions of each category, slowly fell into place.

PART FOUR

In which various kinds of introspection and retrospection are indulged in: we see what Banaras feels like from a distance rather than from the inside; what the different archives in Lucknow and Banaras yielded as experiences; and most of all, we judge the many kinds of selectivity that exercise influence on what comes to seem singularly successful and impressive research.

21

A Break from Banaras

In May, according to plan, I packed up and went to Lucknow. My husband, who had been in Chicago since March, was going to be absent another two months. I was not so much afraid of the heat as aware that, no matter how immune to it I attempted to be, work was impossible half the day. For most of April I had followed the schedule of leaving home early in the morning, say at eight, perforce to return at noon or as close to that as possible. One to three o'clock in the afternoon were by common consensus the hottest hours of the day, when everyone stayed indoors. Even at three or four, it would be difficult to find people moving about. Although I could go to well-targeted places, that part of my work which still consisted of nabbing the unwary and jumping on my prey from behind the bushes suffered. I had more than enough work to do in the archives of Lucknow, and it had been my long-term plan to see out the worst of the summer in the shaded retreat of the U.P. Archives.

When I made the transition from Banaras to Lucknow, I first of all took many steps backwards in mental image making. After all those days of building intimacy with Banaras, the pictures conjured up by the city's name were definitely not the stock tourist ones of giant umbrellas at Dasashwamedh ghat, beggars lining filthy lanes, Kachauri *gali* with its treasures of deep-fried foods and pilgrims gorging on them . . . It is not difficult to understand why: I had never had much to do with these things. But I do acknowledge their reality as suggestive images. I was far more unjust to Lucknow and even consciously permitted myself to wallow in once-upon-a-time dreams and unfounded characterizations. For instance, the term *"nawabi"* always attached itself to the name of the city for me, together with images of wizened Muslims in their long *sherwani* coats wagging their beards and flourishing their arms to say *"Pahle aap!"* ("After you!"), the compliment that supposedly indicates the peak of culture and civilization—in one version the train steams out of the station leaving two Lucknowites thus demonstrating their refinement on the platform. The images are pure legend and feed into one another: dolls in emporia, programs on television, anecdotes and reminiscences. I have known Lucknow all my life, and I have never met a pseudo-*nawab* there such as my imagination insisted on associating with it. I had partly reached a point where I could only do justice to a place upon studying it. Lucknow is still an unknown entity for me and will remain so until I incorporate it into a future research project.

My purpose in Lucknow was to use the archives, but the city began to attract me in many other unforeseen ways. After my first few days there in the summer of 1982, I almost felt as if I could never go back to Banaras. I had not realized how much the *galis*, the overbearing traffic, and the intolerable filth had affected me. Suddenly, outside them, I felt free. Every feature of Banaras was reversed: no loudspeakers, no cow dung, no bumpy rickshaws, no same old people with the same old ideas—that is, no same old investigator with the same old queries. Although I came to Lucknow to work, I was in fact on holiday—from Banaras. As I discovered the differences between the two places in more detail, the feeling of freedom became more pronounced, and I guarded it jealously. There were restaurants in Lucknow, a marketplace in which to stroll and window shop, a zoo to which to take children, movies to see, wide roads on which to drive, people with whom to exchange visits, and the comfort of knowing that you could enjoy things without straining all the time to understand. Lucknow became such an escape for me from Banaras that I actively refrained from trying to understand it.

Banaras had been a prison in many ways. For a long time we had wondered where we could ever go out to eat. I am a fan of the South Indian *dosa*, a lightly cooked lentil pancake with a potato and onion stuffing. *Dosas* can be had in the smallest and most backward parts of North India nowadays. But in Banaras even the *dosa* was transformed, including in name; it was called not *"masala dosa"* (spicy *dosa*) but *"mashal dosa"* (the fiery torch *dosa*—?!). It had dozens of variations— with stuffings of cheese and minced meat among the more extreme ones—but none close to the simple original version. There were two or three comparatively respectable establishments labeled "Coffee House of South India," "of Kerala," and so on, and I could have my fill of Banarasified *dosas* there. My husband sought more exotic fare: European, Chinese, or simply Mughlai. There was nowhere to go. European food was nonexistent save at the so-called five-star hotels, where we did splurge once in a while, but even there the interpretation of dishes was too Banarasi for our taste. We once complained of a fish platter being oversalted and overspiced, at which the chef himself arrived, apologized, and offered to make us a fresh one immediately. We awaited the new dish expectantly, only to find it equally oversalted and overspiced. We should have known: the people of Banaras would never subject guests to bland food. As for Chinese food, there were a couple of famed places that served as our last recourse for celebrations and outings, but if we ever made the mistake of ordering a Chinese dish in any other place (Chinese dishes figured on almost every menu), we could be sure of being rewarded with a heartily spiced, oversalted, and dripping with grease local version of chop suey, egg foo yung, or whatever.

Banaras had many obvious shortcomings, and I tried to ignore them for a long time, developing, as I was, a defensive and protective attitude toward the city. But the question of food was difficult to overlook even for one with simple tastes. My very favorite going-out food was *chat*, that inimitable concoction relying heavily on flour, lentils, yogurt, and tamarind. Even in this, I had to confess, Banaras floundered. What you could get on every street corner in Lucknow you had to search out in Banaras and then wait your turn at the sole source, "Kashi Chat Bhandar" (The Banaras Storehouse of Chat).

We never went out for pleasure to a market or a park in Banaras, because every place was simply too dirty and too crowded with people. Temples were wonderful places, especially those with gardens and open spaces, but they were also overcrowded during all the important occasions. A zoo was unnecessary in Banaras, since the whole place was like a living zoo, with at least ten different species of animals visible on the streets at any given time. What *was* special there was the boating on the river. I found sufficient excuse to round up the family for an early morning boat trip every second or third day, and no one ever protested.

The difficulty of developing a circle of friends was also a sore point with us. After a year there, it was still characteristic for us to drop in on people without their ever returning the visit. We thought we had found a fair number of like-minded or potentially compatible people—writers, journalists, lecturers at the university, musicians, and professionals—but they apparently did not think the same about us. It was pathetic sometimes how we hung on to them when we did meet them, how we organized dinners and sought their presence, how we made repeated trips to their homes, leaving messages when they were out, none of which were ever acknowledged or responded to. We naturally started feeling that we were doomed to be outsiders no matter how long our stay or how friendly our feelings toward the denizens of the city. There is no doubt in my mind that the people whose friendship we attempted to cultivate, middle-class, educated, professional, were—in spite of their excellence in their fields—very closed in their outlook and suspicious and intolerant of anyone from outside. They preferred to keep to their own tight circles and were not particularly well versed in common courtesies.

My own special "friends," my artisans, were not like that at all. They shamed us with their sincere affection and hospitality, and I had never any reason to blame them for anything but an excess of warmth. But people stick to their classes. When work was over, when my family and I relaxed and lived for ourselves, we sought other middle-class people. There was no question of seeking the company of a Tara Prasad or a Mohan Lal, or of their seeking ours. Our social life therefore was a total disappointment. However I may succeed in understanding it sociologically from my privileged insight into the functioning of Banaras, it was no fun.

When I praise Lucknow on this and other scores, the reader must understand how hard this praise comes to me. It would have been difficult for me to acknowledge the superiority of any place over Banaras in those days. Yet to go and live in Lucknow after exactly ten months in Banaras was to submit to a luxurious rest-cure.

22

Ethnography in the Archives

After a week in Lucknow divided among "resting," nursing a cold and cough, and getting Irfana settled into a new environment, I resolved to plunge into work at last. That there would be no letting up once I started I knew, and I felt oddly reluctant to begin. Another aftereffect of Banaras was the need to reduce the pace and lower the intensity of work.

Once at the archives, however, I realized that my reluctance had been justified. The building was new and spacious, but the rooms, including the reading room where I sat with several others, were bare and dusty, a tribute to poor design and insulation. The furniture was of uncomfortable dimensions. I was constantly compromising between leaning forward in an elbow-grazing position on a table a trifle too high for comfort and sitting back in a too-large chair, my book balanced on the edge of my desk.

Nor did the archives seem any less reluctant to take me on. I sat on the edge of my seat in the assistant director's office as he scrutinized my papers. Then he scrutinized me and decided that I was lacking. "We need your passport," was what he finally hit upon, followed by, "You need to get permission from the government." I vacillated between two smart ideas I had: one, that as an Indian citizen my passport was quite unnecessary in my country and I could engage in whatever research I wished; and two, that as a student from Chicago, I had, of course, obtained a clearance from the government along with my grant. The contradictoriness of these two arguments did me in, and I was dismissed with the direction to get a fresh letter from the University of Chicago certifying that I was myself and no other, that my research project was thus and no other (in my conversation I had made the major error of phrasing it somewhat differently from the way it was described in my papers), and that my funding was from x but my citizenship was y, so help me God.

I got heated up, having come equipped, as I thought, with all requisite proofs of identity. I demanded to see the director and was politely escorted to him. I was not allowed to hold my papers in my hand as I covered the distance from the one office to the other, in case I tampered with them, I suppose. As I entered the director's office, his phone was ringing, and I thought, "They've beaten me to it!" I was right. It was the assistant director on the phone, setting the director up to date about me. The latter was looking amused—as he would continue to look all through his subsequent conversation with me. "So what was *your* decision?" he was asking with fond paternalism on the phone, looking into the distance, not too concerned. "If you are going by *that*, what do I need to do here?" I thought angrily and desperately. Sure enough, it was a close battle. I ended up writing an application asking for special permission to use the archives till my "proper" documents arrived, for the absence of which I professed abject sorrow. My notes, in turn, were going to be held in the archives as I made them. When I began to protest about this, I was subjected to the avoidance of eye contact and vigorous shaking of the head that signify unalterable rules in government offices and that I find more infuriating than any arguments.

Well, work began. Sometimes I gave my notes to the officials and sometimes I did not; they never remembered, it seemed, though I always half expected them to jump up and nab me when I left without offering the papers to the officer in charge of the reading room. My file got thicker and thicker. As with research in general and archives in particular, plots and subplots began unfolding as I kept at it, till I wanted to go on and on. This was fortunate for me, since the physical discomforts of the place had been heightened by the arrival of the rains in June, when the place turned into a virtual steam bath.

I used to wonder why Indians expressed distaste for, even fear of, government offices. In my own limited experience, as with "Eve teasing," I had always been either lucky or right. After my experiences with the Lucknow archives, I no longer needed convincing that distaste and fear were the appropriate feelings for all government institutions. Many trifling events brought me to that conviction.

After several weeks of close scribbling, I left some pages for photocopying at the archives, a service provided there, unlike the Nagari Pracharini Sabha of Banaras. Having given my request to the facility, I went home and boasted in a letter to Sombabu, "I don't need a typist here. I'm having things Xeroxed. I just give them the page numbers and the file, and I get them back in one day. It's all very easy." Where I developed that conviction it's difficult to say, apart from my innate optimism and tendency to first accept everything at face value—that is to say, from my inexperience.

The next day I was asked to write a "proper" application, addressed with proper dignity to the director of the archives. I did so. The application was returned to me after two days for lack of the crucial words, "I agree to pay the requisite amount." I added the words. The next few days saw no further problem reported with my application, and I was certain that I would see my bundle of photocopies any moment. Confident in that hope, I continued noting down progressively less and marking off more, making, as I cheerfully thought, faster progress. The course of my photocopies proved the worst torture I have ever been subjected to. For months, the machine was out of order, the operator sick, the paper supply used up, even the record room burgled; as a last desperate stroke, even the visit of Indira Gandhi to Lucknow was cited as an excuse for delay. I could have sworn that I saw other people's photocopies being handed over. As befits a conspiracy, everyone was polite and reassuring whenever I pursued the matter. The key question was, when was I finally leaving the country? Only a few months later? Oh, they would certainly be done before that.

All that remains to be said is that the photocopies were done literally at the last moment, and I had to come to the archives after I had finished packing for my departure to the

United States just to pick them up. By that time I had become so nervous that I had ceased requesting any copying and had resorted to taking down in longhand the notes I wanted and skipping over the data that I could possibly do without.

With regard to the Lucknow archives, I felt the delays, the obstacles, and the humiliation of smiling excuses so strongly partly because my expectations were inordinately high. Something about the businesslike building, the amused director, the vast holdings, and the good-naturedness of Lucknow in general, after the eccentricity of Banaras, had fooled me. In Banaras, I had visited a half-dozen archives apart from the Nagari Pracharini Sabha and had neither expected anything nor been disappointed. They had acted, one to all, as excellent ethnographic sites for me, providing data not only in the written records but also in the goings-on of the places themselves.

Very early on I had made a visit to the Banaras Collectorate, the center from which the collector, alias the district magistrate, rules. The Collectorate is a kind of courthouse for civil disputes and revenue hearings. As is appropriate for the seat of the highest civil authority in the district, all the servants are exquisitely uniformed in long coats, sashes, and turbans, holding scepter-like poles. Those were the epic days of generous police help, and since the Collectorate was in the far north of the city, an inconvenient distance from where we lived, I reached there in the police "VIP" car. The driver bounded in ahead of me and whispered my introduction to the collector's decorated doorman, so that when I entered, everyone in the office was ready for me and on his feet.

I had gone partly because I had been curious to see how the king of the land, the civil magistrate and arbiter of individuals' destiny in my place of research, functioned. As it turned out, I spent the day in his office, ostensibly poring over books and manuscripts but really keeping a close watch on everything he did. However, my story is not about that, and I must move on to the description of the archives. To call them "archives" is a fond exaggeration. They *were* variously called archives and library by the people in the office, but

they are better labeled a storeroom. The large room had cupboards all along the walls, and bookshelves in parallel lines
along its length, all of which were laden with papers. Even
the books had become papers, having lost their bindings and
many pages. There was no discoverable system to these piles,
chronological, thematic, or otherwise. The librarian or archi-
vist—I forget what he was called—who came in with me had
an even vaguer notion than I of what could be there or how
it could be stacked, and he refrained from comment. He
stood to one side and coughed as I raised dust. I thought it
probable that the drafts from Banaras toward the ten-year
census reports would be placed together. With the help of my
sharp wits and roving eyes, I found a pile of materials that I
could use.

Meanwhile there was a small whirlwind as the honorable
collector himself breezed in with three men in tow. He had
arrived on an "inspection." He walked around, looked up
and down, and shouted, "Humph, humph, what is this,
what is this? This place must be all cleaned up and organized, you hear me, librarian?" He departed, and the materials returned to their repose, to be undisturbed, I can vouch-
safe, for the next decade or longer. Clearly the collector had
been awakened by my arrival to the fact that this storeroom
was also part of his jurisdiction and responsibility and that, if
he did not create at least a semblance of careful supervision of
it, I might be capable of anything, such as writing about it for
the public to read.

I *knew* there were wonderful things to be found at the Nagar Mahapalika (the City Municipality). I went to obtain permission to use the records from the administrator, as he was
called, the government officer in charge of city affairs while
the elected municipal committee was suspended, which it
had been in Banaras for many years. This officer also had a
grand office, though no bedecked doormen, and was also
busy with petitioners when I entered, though his work I was
not much interested in. I had my own notions of what municipal work consisted of, and in my mind were images of
drains, taps, and streetlights that did not function. This time

I had come on my bicycle, my letter of purpose from Chicago in hand. One might suppose that the treatment I would receive would be very different from that at the collector's. In one way it was—no one rose to greet me—but not in any substantial way. When I saw the sizable crowd outside the administrator's office, each man trying to be the next to go in, and threaded my way through it to the door, my heart sank for a minute. But as soon as I said, "May I see the administrator?" and the doorman raised the *chik* (split bamboo) curtains for me to pass in, I realized that my fear had been unjustified. I had been privileged before the thirty or forty people waiting simply because of the way I looked and, more remarkable still, aroused no comment or criticism from them for the same reason.

No woman comes to the Nagar Mahapalika as a rule, just as she does not go to a police station, unless she is destitute of all brothers, brothers-in-law, and sons. I was there, and I must be someone special, since I did not look destitute of anything. My clothes, coolness, and confidence in going up to the doorman immediately marked me as someone from the top rather than from the bottom classes, and everyone in such circumstances is judged by these things. I thought, as I entered, of how far I actually was from my artisans. They would have had trouble in any office they went to, and they could barely have approached the concerned officer, leave aside be understood or sympathized with. I would have had no trouble whatsoever; I could use my face, my clothes, my manner, my confidence, even if I never resorted to my family connections, to approach whomever I wanted. As with fasting in order to experience hunger, I could never approximate the helplessness of poor people in India because I always had a past and a future different from theirs.

The record room I worked in in the municipal office had two windows that faced the bicycle parking and refreshment cum socializing area under a generous banyan tree. The window screens were opaque with age and dust, but I could hear a great deal of what was going on outside, particularly the *pan* sellers. Every *panwalla* has as part of his establishment bright little pots of brass for his condiments, which he spreads on the betel leaves with little brass spatulas. As he replaced each, there was a tinkle of pure metal striking metal, very sonorous and soothing. This sound came in from the outside every few seconds and made my hours in the record room very pleasant.

It was an interesting time for me otherwise as well. While I pored over scores of administration reports, thirstily absorbing facts of the budgets for sanitation, water supply, and drainage over the preceding century, I also observed the workings of the municipality at close quarters. The record room was not meant for researchers like me. It was the repository of all the records of the city, and its main business was giving out information about ownership and location of houses to those interested in selling, buying, and construction. This information did not come free. Sometimes the record seeker was charged two rupees, sometimes, four, sometimes six: the decision was made on the basis of what he was considered capable of parting with. The payment was openly demanded and made, and it was divided among the officer in charge of the records and the clerk who brought out the files from the huge hall in which they were stored. I had always wanted to observe CORRUPTION at close quarters, and that is what I could now do for many days. I must say it was a big achievement for me, for so far I had been unsuccessful in actually putting my finger on it. The closest I had come was when, after being judged a completely crazy researcher for whom all information was invaluable, I had requested Inspector Tripathi with as good a semblance of naivete as I could muster, "Could you actually show me how you take bribes?" He was too taken aback to even deny that he took bribes, and simply asked, "How can I show you that?" I pointed to the empty space behind his desk in the police station, "Well, if we hang a curtain here, I could hide behind it the next time someone comes . . . " We both refrained from actually trying it. I mentioned earlier that his motives in being ever ready to help me in my research were suspect, and I should explain and perhaps qualify that. I knew right away that he indulged in various dealings far more profitable than an inspector's pay; there was an easy proof of this in his very way of handling money. He was also "corrupt" in the sense that he immediately wanted a payoff from me, asking me to get him a particular transfer order from Lucknow. I realized slowly that he was unexceptional on all these scores and that everyone functioned on a quid pro quo basis in Banaras. Almost every police officer of middling rank wanted a transfer or a stay of transfer. While that sounded harmless enough, what irked were the gifts of grapes and mangoes—always the more expensive fruits—that came to our home. We were annoyed not with them but with us, that we did not quite realize what was going on and innocently accepted and *ate up* the mangoes. Then, in a fit of compensation, we toyed with the idea of hanging a sign on the path leading to our house: *"Yahan ghoos, rishwat, ityadi liya jata hai"* ("We accept bribes, under-the-table payments, et cetera, here").

The Banaras archives, already mentioned in my accounts earlier, were a source of both pleasure and dismay. They were hopeless in that their holdings had little relevance to my topic. After days of battling with information on land and property transfers in Banaras, I simply gave up. I was glad to do so, because the archives consisted of three small rooms, the electricity was frequently out, the windows provided no cross ventilation, and the director, who had to authorize the use of records, was absent, while the other workers were such a gang of cronies that they chattered incessantly. In all fairness I should add that I got my photocopying done very expeditiously here; the moral is only that there is little method to government functioning. If you expect the worst, you will be pleasantly surprised half the time.

I used three other archival-type places in Banaras which need to be described briefly. One was the office of *Aj*, the local Hindi daily, of venerable age and circulation. It was convenient to go there for specific old issues of the newspaper, rather than to Nagari Pracharini Sabha, which had the issues too but where they were unnumbered and where a request for one volume necessitated the displacement of a dozen more. In the *Aj* office, I was the only researcher, and I had a room and a person all to myself. All went well for me there except for two passing experiences. Because of a fire or some such mishap, there was a *hole* in the middle of the *Aj* building. Climbing up to the top floor, as I had to, I would suddenly come across a sheer unprotected drop to the floor below; a whole chunk of the building in the middle had totally disappeared. I almost fell to the bottom at the sheer fright of it. Then, for lunch, I would climb to the roof of the building, which was very high and offered a splendid panorama of the city. While I was busy piecing together the different parts of it from my acquaintance with them on the ground, a monkey would sneak up behind me, neatly grab my sandwich or tidbit from my very hand, and slouch away. This was not as frightening as the hole, but it did leave me hungry with nowhere to go but teashops.

Another place I discovered was the private library of one Mr. Morarilal Kedia. An old-time resident of Banaras and a cultural patron, Mr. Kedia had collected all the periodicals of the city and even of other parts of U. P. for the twentieth century. He had set aside a hall and a room for them and had appointed a smart young graduate as librarian. Mr. Kedia was too proud and self-sufficient to be approached, but his library was truly impressive. I only visited it about five times, however. I felt overwhelmed and decided that to go through all that literature would take the rest of my life.

Last of all, in terms of both chronology and the benefits I derived from it, was the Kala Bhawan, the Museum of Art, at the university. This had choice periodicals from the past, including some not available elsewhere, such as the magazines edited by the famous Hindi literateur Bharatendu Harishchandra. I cycled to the university dozens of time to use them, but I got stuck at a certain stage and never progressed beyond it. The keeper of the literature section was a sickly man with many family responsibilities. He was often on leave and chose particularly those days that I went there. Since I would go at random, I don't know how he found out which

days these would be, but he was eminently successful in timing his absences. Three directors of the Kala Bhawan came
and went. I sat in their office and wept my tale of woe. How
could I go back to Chicago without studying these precious
magazines? Each promised to "look into the matter," and
each undoubtedly did so, but how can you fight sickness and
the demands of family? And of bureaucracy and bad organization, I should add, because I repeatedly requested that
someone else be given the responsibility of administering the
periodicals when the main keeper was away, but, no, only he
could do it, and no one else could touch the volumes. Although the best-located of all the archives and libraries, the
easiest and pleasantest to reach, and in the top category of
importance, the university literature holdings remained the
most inaccessible to the end of my stay. My book consequently has only very limited references from Bharatendu
Harishchandra's magazines.

23

Patterns of Selectivity

When I returned to Banaras from Lucknow in July, I found it in flood. The monsoon that year was the "best" in years. The river had risen above the danger point, and all the riverside areas of the city, as well as other low-lying areas, were under water. Boats had replaced rickshaws as the mode of transport, people habitually folded up their garments to their knees, ready for wading at every step, and a minor exodus had begun from less safe to safer localities.

I realized very quickly that here was another chapter for my book. The floods were an entertainment, a pleasure for the people of Banaras, not simply a hardship. Everyone knew the best places from which to observe the swirling waters, and I went to check them out. Young men and children and women of all ages came to these places to "see the floods." Adventurous young men dived from the balconies of submerged homes and swam endlessly in the sheltered pools provided by the buildings under water. To reach the Sankatmochan temple was a particular sport, for it was separated from dry land by several hundred yards of water. But topmost on the list of entertainments was an excursion to the Malaviya Bridge, where one could see the whole vista of the river extending beyond either bank for miles, a field of water in between, seemingly still, but in fact rushing on with fury, carrying trees, huts, animals, and unidentified objects along with it. I even succumbed to the Faustian temptation to know everything to the fullest, taking a motorboat tour around the swollen river—a dangerous activity that I did not enjoy too much.

Our house itself was separated from the main road by an expanse of water several feet wide and equally deep. Although also referred to as "flood," it had not been caused by the overflowing river but by the accumulation of rainwater every time it rained for over half an hour, which it did several times a day. Nothing could be planned, for we were not people to wade through water of unmeasured depths. I myself regarded the floods around our house as impassable, though when they were absent or I crossed them on a rickshaw that had already been brought across to our side, I did so only to go and observe more flood waters!

This was the lighter side of things. More serious was that, now that it was July, I was completing one year of research. There could be no more "excuses." Nor did I need any: all my earlier problems of where to go, how to meet people, what to say or do, and what sense to make of it all in the process were in the past. I knew the annual cycle of events in the city, which meant that I could gatecrash all those I had already seen or heard about the first time around and could discover all those I had been forced to miss the first time for various reasons. In the former category were the major Hindu festivals—Diwali, Dassehra, Holi, Vishwakarma Puja, Durga Puja, Ganesh Puja, and so on. In the latter category were the major Muslim ones. In 1981 I had known that Moharram was celebrated in October, but I had had an actual fear, apart from simple timidity and uncertainty, about observing it. Some interesting activities took place around the *taziya* on certain Moharram nights, but could I have just walked into an unknown neighborhood at night and mingled with the males gathered there to become part of their celebration? I could not. I needed familiarity with lanes and *mohalla* patterns, and I needed friends, preferably a family, on whom I could press myself as a guest. As long as you are sturdily allied with at least one person in the course of such proceedings, you are all right. If you are an *utter* stranger, the event remains strange for you, and you for the people taking part in it. I have spoken at length here only of Shaukatullah, Jameel Sahab, and Abdul Jabbar, among my developing relationships with Muslim artisans, and but mentioned Alimuddin and Nazir Akbar, but in my second year there were dozens more besides from different *mohallas* with whom I could hang around.

Sometimes it was not so much a question of people to help me out as a general broadening of the capacity to assimilate. Many events in Banaras, as I have said somewhere, sounded peculiar to my ears when I first heard of them. The Ramlila, yes, but something called the Nakkatayya (the cutting of the nose)? Nati Imli ka Bharat Milap (the reunion with Bharat at the dwarfed tamarind tree), Nagnathayya (the churning of the serpent), Katahriya Mela (the fair of the jackfruit)—all seemed bizarre by virtue of their very nomenclature. The best example was something called Duldul ka Ghora (the horse of Duldul). My husband and I laughed at the images it suggested, and no matter how serious I became, I could not imagine what the thing represented by such a name could be. Nor did I find out in the first year. The procession of the Duldul horse passes through most of the city, in a journey taking over twenty hours, but the most dramatic episodes occur in Chauk. So much I had been told. I repaired to Chauk on the evening that the Duldul horse would pass through there and inquired politely about its whereabouts. People gestured to a neighborhood called Dalmandi, saying, "There." Dalmandi is a tortuous lane with many tributaries. Because it is a market, it is relatively dark and forbidding at night. Somewhere within it was this procession—how large? Going in which direction? Doing what? I could not have plunged into the darkness, armed only with my camera and notebook, to track down this incomprehensible procession somewhere in the maze of lanes; I simply knew too little about it. Was the horse tame or wild? Bound or loose? The people sane or drunk? Peaceful or in a frenzy of shouting? How did women figure in it; what would be the men's attitude toward me? Once in, could I get out? Where would be "out"? Dalmandi was an especially tricky proposition because, apart from being a maze and a marketplace, it was the traditional home of courtesans. With flowered curtains in upstairs windows from which emanated the sounds of tabla and singing, this was a stage where different rules prevailed from the rest of Banaras, and I for one certainly did not know what my lines should be or how to enact them. On the Duldul night my first year, therefore, I quietly put my tail between my legs and went home to sleep.

It haunted me, though, as did Moharram, Barawafat, Akhiri Budh, and Shoberaat. To detail how I was able to participate in them all the second year would be too much, but I will give the idea in brief. By September 1982, when it was Duldul time again, I had visited Dalmandi many times and been inside homes and shops. I knew, in fact, the most important grandee of the place, Hakim Mohammad Kazim. I had met with two courtesans through mutual "brothers" and knew what the inside of those curtained upstairs rooms looked like. I had interviewed musicians who made their living by accompanying these courtesans, and I had discovered a *guru bhai* among them, that is, a brother by virtue of sharing the same guru, Mahadev Mishra. Most of all, I knew to a reassuring extent what the layout of the region was. I had a rough map of the whole of Chauk and could sense where one *mohalla* connected with another. To get a grasp of the geography of a place is really the first step to feeling comfortable in it.

All this fed into my participation in Duldul, as did also the fact that I had a fair number of Muslim informants by then and was attuned to their domestic arrangements, their lifestyle and practices, and even their conversation and colloquialisms. The main characteristic of my second year in Banaras was that everything I did fed into everything else. So, at Duldul time, I walked right next to the horse for a large part of its journey (I even thought of petting the beautiful white creature a few times but didn't, because on that occasion petting was also a ritual—one I was not that up on); entered homes and courtyards along with the horse; scribbled down, without embarrassment, the words of the *marsiyahs* being sung; and made new acquaintances left and right. Duldul was in my pocket.

Most of Banaras was in my pocket, it felt. On this note I shall end the narration of my exploits because a litany of successes is not particularly edifying. Nor am I sure how to measure "success," since I for one firmly believe that the proof is in the pudding, that is, in my book *The Artisans of Banaras: Popular Culture and Identity* (1988). Logically, also, my diary became thinner and thinner as frustrations turned into fulfillment. I would like to use my penultimate chapter to describe rather the shortcomings in my fieldwork procedures that troubled me much of the time and that will probably ring a familiar note to other researchers.

The main limitation was that no matter how I strained, in however many directions, my effort remained a selective one. Even as I widened my circle of informants and interviewees, I functioned within a small universe: a dozen each, say, of weavers, metalworkers, woodworkers, milksellers, and *pan* sellers; even fewer potters, painters, goldsmiths, with one blacksmith, silversmith, and jeweler thrown in for good measure; and copper wiredrawers and motor parts repairers on the fringes. Was it not likely, I constantly asked myself, that I was getting only a part of the story, given the limited number of people I talked to?

My defense in the face of this damning evidence of numbers came from my *growing confidence* that what I was constructing, even from the tales of a few artisans, was a correct picture. There were many other discoveries that lay behind the in-depth conversations: observation and participation in activities as part of a crowd, familiarity with details of the urban landscape, random exchanges with people all the time, and of course my archival work. I felt part of my surroundings; I was like a finely tuned instrument from which a complex sound could emerge and all the resonant strings vibrate—in analogy with the sitar—when the correct note was plucked. Reports confirmed one another, facts were buttressed by more facts, interpretations rallied to one another's defense . . . I was interacting with only a few informants— on *one* level—but on many other levels I was interacting with other components of the city. I felt beyond the shadow of a doubt that I was interacting with the city itself.

More of the time I worried not so much about the methodology that called for intimate contact with only a few people, but about my own limitations as a fieldworker, limitations of gender, domestic situation, and personality. I continued to feel guilty about living comfortably in a proper house, devoting my after-work hours to family relations, even of *having* after-work hours, rather than living in an artisan neighborhood and spending day and night only with my informants. I did spend thousands of hours with them, enough to claim that I was drained and incapable of any more, but the selectivity of the procedure remained—selectivity of day over night, as I call it. My knowledge of what went on in daylight hours was far superior to that regarding nighttime. I traveled to many music sittings and temple celebrations, all in the dead of night, but these were *events*. What happened quietly on an everyday basis, I never did seek to discover. I place the blame for this wholly on my infant daughter and commonsensical husband; neither would have seen the rationale of my sacrificing a normal domestic routine for an undisturbed immersion in my subject of study. In this context, I think of Baidyanath Saraswati, resident anthropologist-in-chief of Banaras. When I first went to visit him in his monkey-infested apartment, I was told by his wife that he was out. "When will he return?" She didn't know. "Where has he gone?" She had no idea. "What time should I try tomorrow?" She couldn't be sure, even of whether he would be back. With each answer, the apparently rural, non-English-speaking lady added, *"Woh 'field' men gaye hain"* ("He is in *the field*"). I left with a sense of envy and vague dissatisfaction with myself for not being able thus to disappear into "the field," to become so totally lost there that no one would know my whereabouts, time of return, or anything.

As it was, I had a difficult time with my husband. Although he would have preferred to know where I was at any given moment, he did not because I did not. However, he served to launch me into the first round of organization of my rapidly accumulating materials by advising me to have an index card for everyone I met or interviewed, with the person's basic description and the dates of my interviews. Every morning, as I left, I was supposed to put in the front of the index card file the card(s) with the name(s) and address(es) of those I would be seeing that day. I couldn't keep to this demanding plan, but the basic idea, I felt, always remained the opposite of Baidyanath Saraswati's: circumscribe yourself and keep to the domestic routines as far as possible.

The selectivity of day over night was related to another kind of selectivity that was the product of my interests and preferences—that of public over private. One of the few things I had always found distasteful about the discipline of anthropology was its concentration on kinship. I simply failed to get aroused by the subjects of marriage, family, kinship, and domestic ritual. Something about the four walls of a house stifled me. One reason I kept happy in Banaras was that even where four walls circumscribed one, the number of people within them was so large that it was like being outside. I began to feel that the Banarasis and I shared the same set of preferences. They preferred to do everything in the open, from drying their yarn to pounding their grain to displaying their wares to relaxation and entertainment. But perhaps I thought this partly because I both looked for and saw only activities of this nature. I noted down very little that went on inside the house, unless it was a work activity or *puja* that was possible only within or it was there for some interesting historical reason. When people got together in large groups unrelated by blood or marriage ties, that was great, that was fascinating. *Mushairas* (poetry reading), music sittings, handicraft work itself, women's gossip sessions were all like that. These were for me "public" because they included many people. On one level this selection was justified because I had defined my topic as popular cultural activities, and popular culture is supposedly the culture of "the people," not of small groups within them. But I had prejudged the issue. In my book I emphasized that the public cultural life of Banaras is an especially rich one; this is partly because I looked selectively at it and never cared for the private.

Even within popular or public culture, I found certain themes much more compatible than others. Another person could write a wholly different book on the popular culture of Banaras, emphasizing the "dirty" aspects: the liquor, drugs, prostitution, gambling, politicking, thuggery, deceit, cheating, and other fully entertaining activities. I didn't write such a book because I preferred to close my eyes to these aspects of life; I was like that, and the people I drifted toward, Tara Prasad and his family, Markande and his family, were like that as well. I heard indistinct references to many kinds of sleazy goings-on but refused to pursue any of them with the vigor I employed for topics that fascinated me, like seasonality and body building.

One day as I was sitting doing nothing in Tara Prasad's home, his wife Lilavati brought me his latest wood carving to show. Giggling, she uncovered it. It was a miniature of a large four-poster bed in which a couple was making love. Everything was quite graphic, and Tara Prasad's genius had succeeded in depicting the couple as both entranced and enthusiastic. Interesting and appealing touches included a plate of *laddus* (round sweets) by the side of the bed, for when they took a minute off, I suppose, and a hand fan, for when they got heated up.

I was deeply curious and quizzed Lilavati. She had always been shy and noncommunicative with me, and moreover spoke Bhojpuri at a terrifying speed. I gathered that such wooden toys were among the presents to the bride and groom at a wedding, an old Banaras custom no longer very conscientiously observed. I realized, and I know for a fact, that there is in Banaras a whole system of attitudes toward sex, I mean as part of public belief and entertainment, not the domesticated aspect that I find boring; that they are expressed in crafts, in the performing arts, in speech and celebration; and that these attitudes are very alive, clearly articulated, and close to the people. I was sometimes very well placed to observe them, as at the Holi procession and again at an event called the Mahamurkh Sammelan, the Great Fools' Conference. At the latter, the poems and jokes were what would be called cheap and dirty in another context but were artistic and intellectual on that occasion. The main style of dancing in Banaras, which I had also witnessed at Holi, was used everywhere all the time, in wedding processions, at parties, and on happy occasions, and it was suggestive in a way that few popular dances are. Banaras was a crude, hearty, earthy place, its males very aware of physicality and sexuality and not reticent about depicting their interest in these things on every occasion and through all the media. The females were very likely the same; I never found out, though the giggling Lilavati gave me a clue. When I met the courtesans in Dalmandi, both they and I emphasized the performative aspects of their craft, preferring to pretend that that was all there was to it. I didn't ask them about their relations with men, only about their song and dance, and they didn't volunteer the information. Not clear or comfortable about sexuality, my own or anyone else's, I barely made a note of this Banarasi feature and wrote nothing about it at all. Similarly, I had no idea what to do with drunkenness or drug use, finding the subjects distasteful and myself ignorant. Nevertheless, I don't want to overplay the selectivity at work in all this, for every researcher categorizes subjects as appropriate or inappropriate in all contexts, and I did so in Banaras with relation to myself, excluding everything I regarded as "sleazy" or "dirty."

There were two other kinds of selective processes I was aware of that I would like to mention. One was that of Hindus over Muslims, and the other of the poor over the rich. The Hindu preference arose from the fact that I was a born Hindu, though not a practicing one, and knew a great deal more about the religion than about Islam. With Hinduism, right from the beginning I could pick up clues and follow innuendoes in a way that is essential for research, but only in my second year did I even begin to do so with Islam. One of the signs of my developing maturity in research was how much more time I gave to Muslims than to Hindus in my second year, in inverse proportion to the first, achieving a final balance of sorts. My earliest notes with weavers are quite garbled and are punctuated with desperate comments: "Who's *he?*" "What does *that* mean?" *"Huzur ki miraj?"* "Did she say *that?*" All these were sorted out and deciphered quite promptly, but meanwhile they created an undeniable bias in favor of working with Hindus, who were familiar, comprehensible, and as easy as *a, b, c.* My language abilities in Hindi also far exceeded those in Urdu, particularly in reading and writing. I would tire very quickly of an Urdu paper or document and set it aside to read later in consultation with an Urdu-speaking friend—which sometimes happened and sometimes did not—but I needed no special patience or motivation to read Hindi language materials.

I worked so hard to overcome these shortcomings that I was largely successful in doing so. Toward the very end of my stay I was rewarded by repeatedly being taken for a Muslim in Muslim *mohallas*, often as a lady from Pakistan. I did not plan the deception but did not try hard to undeceive the deceived either, simply taking even greater care with my Urdu vocabulary and pronunciation. This greater ease in Muslim contexts was relevant not merely to my personal satisfaction and sense of balance but also to the materials I could pick up—apart from the oral data that I could record—which increased many times over. Muslims would pull out old books and papers, calendars and wall hangings, diaries and manuscripts because they thought that I was capable of perusing them, and, as a good Muslim, cared to do so and could be trusted not to defile the name of Allah, which was everywhere. They would say as much and look inquiringly into my eyes, and I would look back at them with a steadfast, clear, honest gaze that neither denied nor affirmed, because I did not feel I was lying about being a Muslim; *of course* I would not defile the name of Allah.

The poor were naturally to be privileged because I had written my research proposal like that. I do not mean to say that I was at fault for deciding on a research focus, because that everyone has to do. I am saying I was biased toward poor people in ways that can only be called emotional or sentimental, and that bias served my research ill. I had developed the method of asking a large cross-section of people about the same thing, to surround and attack it, as it were, on all fronts. Thus, on the question of temple going, I learned all about my artisans' ideas; then I looked up the information on all these temples in my various written sources; I had Na-gendra Sharma scouting around temples collecting a random set of interviews with temple-goers; and finally I went to each and every *mahant* (temple head), chief priest, and assorted minor priests. In such cases, if the people I wished to inter-view were rich, as undoubtedly most *mahants* were, that was fine, because they belonged to my arena of activity. But in any other context, rich people seemed like rude interruptions to be shrugged off as distracting. I sensed that they were valuable sources of information and that I should not harbor such strong prejudices against them. I did so out of sheer im-maturity, naivete, and rebelliousness. Maybe it paid off in some unsensed, unobvious way, such as making me think only of the poor or seeing life only from their point of view, but I am not sure. I know that toward the end of my stay, I suddenly got knots in my stomach thinking of all the gaping holes in my information, and made quick trips, among others, to some of the wealthiest businessmen and traders of the city. But these were again people to "use," so that was all right.

Since I was myself so clearly "wealthy," that is to say, not suffering from the shortage of any necessity, or even of most comforts, of life, I had to struggle very actively to keep other well-off people away and the poor close to me. To have dressed differently would not have been the solution, be-cause I actually wore rather cheap saris and sandals, usually old, sometimes even torn. Raja Ram, our King Canute, scorned them in his inimitable way. "If you wore these in our village," he told me once, overseeing my check of laundered saris, "even the dogs would bark." But other things marked me as well-to-do: the shine of my hair, the well-creamed look of my skin, the well-fed and well-watered look of me alto-gether, the matching blouses, the watch, bag, sunglasses, the lack of reluctance to pay *rickshawallas* certain amounts . . . I could have taken care of one or two of these characteristics, but not all. It would have taken years for my face to develop the thin, pinched, worried look that marks many of the poor. Nor do I consider such physical alignment necessary. It

comes up because I was constantly accosted by well-off people with invitations to join them and their kind rather than to
hang around, as I was seen to be doing, with the poor and
the backward. One of my favorite places in Banaras was the
teashop of Lallan Yadav. It was not deeply recessed in the
building, so it lacked the dark, cavernous quality of all those
other teashops that remained closed to me. It had rows of
photographs of wrestlers on the wall, benches and tables
with fresh newspapers, and a clientele that by its look
seemed to consist of artisans and laborers, but included in
fact writers, poets, philosophers (I mean professional ones—
everyone was a philosopher in his own right), and priests. I
went to this teashop many times a week and sat many hours,
talking to Lallan Yadav and whoever else was willing. It was
always rewarding and also relaxing, and the only thorn in my
side was the special tea that Lallan *sardar* kept pressing on
me, the kind that has a dollop of cream floating on top.

Opposite this teashop in Brahmanal was a silk trader's, a
business run by many brothers. Unknown to me, they had
kept a watch on my activities, and one day they finally signaled me over. I was made comfortable on the white sheets
and bolsters of the *gaddi* and given some tea. "Why don't you
sit here and do your work?" they asked me solicitously. "It
doesn't look seemly for you to sit around in that teashop." I
was in agony and didn't know how to get away, short of being rude. Now if I had been calmer, I could have talked about
the silk industry with them, the *mohalla* of Brahmanal, the
subject of teashops and tea drinking from *their* perspective,
and a host of other things. But my ire had been aroused by
their class, their protectiveness, their assumption that they
were superior, because they had money and education, to
those like Lallan Yadav, who had little of both, and by all
those other qualities that I lumped together as "middle-class"
conservatism and puritanism. So, not only did I suffer need-
lessly, but I also failed to seize an opportunity and aroused
their hostility by my obvious discomfort in their company.

Similarly, Tara Prasad often passed on to me the requests
of his rich neighbor, an oil presser's family, that I visit them.

They were prosperous, with a large house and actual furniture; all the members dressed smartly in expensive, modern clothes. The whole idea was unappealing, and I resisted it for days. When I finally had to succumb, I gave an object lesson in how to be an awkward guest. Now these people were patrons of the Khojwa Ramlila, and I doubtlessly could have learned a lot from them about the Ramlila, about the oil-pressing business, and about Khojwa in general. But happiness for me was Tara Prasad's house, and this comfortable furnished place with its well-dressed inhabitants was close to a torture.

If I could do the whole thing again, I would be open, I *think*, to people on the basis of their merit as providers of information and not have blinders on my eyes to everyone who appeared affluent or successful. But then, as I also think, I might be subject to the danger of having a more mixed reportage on what the lives of the poor are like, and that deficiency might reflect the distance of the rich from the poor.

24

Departure

It was only the poor who came to see us off as we left Banaras in early 1983. We were taking the overnight train to Lucknow; our luggage had been sent on ahead, and we carried only sleeping bags and hand baggage. Abdul Jabbar cycled over to the station, Tara Prasad came with his daughter, Nagendra, who had been helping us, came to the station with us, and Markande stood shyly on one side. No one had any farewell speeches to make, nor had I a word to say. All I could think of was how to give each a little cash in parting without disrupting the mood, for sisters *may* give money, even to elder brothers—anything at all is possible. But it had to be done in the correct way and with the properly selected words. I finally chose the easier way of giving my *niece*, Tara Prasad's daughter, a doll and a few rupees, to her consternation. With Markande, it was easier, for he was much younger anyway and did not yet have the veneer of courtesy that characterized older adults in Banaras. Abdul Jabbar had once had his son-in-law, a tailor, stitch some pajamas for us, so I could squeeze a fifty-rupee note into his fist with a mumbled injunction to pass it on to his son-in-law. As for Nagendra, he was also a younger brother, but my research assistant as well, and I had learned the importance of keeping the two roles distinct. It would never do to have given him money because he was a poor brother. He would have simply returned it with a flourish, saying something like, "I may be poor, but I am proud; I do not accept money from my sisters." But I could press a hundred rupees into his hand, saying, rather, "For your transport this last week, for your going up and down by rickshaw all over the place . . . "

They all stood quietly and waited—still no farewell speeches. Finally Tara Prasad gave a toothless grin, "Be sure to write!" I pointed to ten-year-old Mangra by his side, now in class 4 in school. "I'll write to *her*. Make sure she writes back." That made the others wake up a little. "Alright, jijji, come back soon!" said both Nagendra and Markande, using the familiar, affectionate term for older sister that was so loaded with intimacy for me—my brother Sunil used it all the time—that it made tears come to my eyes. Abdul Jabbar wagged his beard with a weak smile.

I looked at my informants-brothers-friends, realizing that I had at some point, without having planned it, erased the dividing lines between these categories. That may be called the first lesson of my fieldwork for me: an informant, no matter what *my* plans, could strain at my restrictions and alter my efforts, and in all honesty I had to acknowledge the person's right to do so. Once I realized an informant's equal power to influence the relationship, I came to a second realization: equality could tolerate difference, and this was not a matter for guilt or regret. By freeing myself from the limitations of my inherited world and broadening my definitions of self, I saw that I could both consider others my equal and hold on to my preferences and beliefs without apology. Those values I chose to retain were now tested and conscious ones and not simply the identification marks of a class or a period. I was less of a cog in the machine of history.

Closely following on this was a third realization: being the person I was, I *had* to interfere in my subjects' lives, as they had indeed expected. But although my ethnography had to be influenced by this recognition, the activist project was necessarily separate from the anthropological one. It required, as did any well-conducted activity, proper training, planning, and fund raising, not merely a general feeling of goodwill toward humanity.

I also came to realize that ethnosociology, as commonly understood, is a dubious proposition. It was feasible and desirable—in fact, essential—to understand and represent with empathy people's own versions of their actions. But this empathy disappeared rather dramatically when an issue directly affected the anthropologist's work, comfort, or family—particularly baby. There were as likely to be two distinct versions, yours and theirs, and if you continued to write of theirs while maintaining silence on your own, it was at best a very mechanical anthropology, at worst blatantly hypocritical.

The last lesson of my fieldwork then was to shun passivity with conviction. Of course, as I have made clear, I consider scholarship a form of activism too if an informant is seen as a person, not just a provider of information, which means actually widening the horizons of academia in ways every scholar has to discover individually. For me the people of Banaras had become more than informants, not so much through any effort of mine but rather through the strength of their personalities, the power of their generosity and love, and the possibilities inherent in the methods of ethnographic fieldwork.

All these thoughts jelled slowly, with time and many influences, including that of my husband to whom this book is rightly dedicated. On that April evening at the train station, I thought rather of how I had come with vague purposes, then become proud of my swelling notebooks, believing that I would capture these people of Banaras and take them away with me, but how in reality they had captured *me* and forced me to leave much of myself behind. The sweetness of accomplishment was accompanied by a stab of pain: one more place to belong to, to think about nostalgically, to plan returns to; one more set of people to ache for.

Glossary

Key terms are defined in the glossary and their proper spelling indicated. Diacritic marks are omitted in the text to preserve its accessibility to non-Hindi-speaking readers.

aghor panth	a sect of Hindu renouncers
Ahīr	a Hindu caste, usually milksellers; same as Yadav
akhāṛā	a gymnasium or club for wrestling, music, poetry, and so on
annaprāsana	the first solid food ceremony of a Hindu infant
Ansārī	the name used by Muslim weavers, denoting lineage
āyāh	a maidservant
bābā	old man, father; usually a form of address
bābu	a term of respect, often used as a suffix for Bengalis
bahan; bahanjī	a sister; respected sister (direct address)
bahrī alang	the outside
baiṭhaka	a sitting place, a room
bajṛā	a large boat, specifically for groups and gatherings
Bārāwafāt	a Muslim festival celebrating the Prophet's birth
beṭā	child; usually a form of address

bhābhī; bhābhījī	a brother's wife; respected brother's wife (direct address)
bhāī;bhāī (sāhab)	a brother; respected brother (direct address)
bhāng	*cannabis sativa indica*
Bhojpurī	the language of eastern U.P. and western Bihar
birahā	a genre of folk music
bīṛī	a "cigarette" rolled in a leaf
buā	father's sister; usually a form of address
chabutarā	raised delineated space for sitting outdoors
chāchā; chāchājī	a father's brother; respected father's brother (direct address)
chāchī	father's brother's wife; usually a form of address
chaitī	a genre of music typical of the month of Chaitra
Chaitra	the first month of the U.P. Hindu calendar, season for *chaitī*
chāiwāllā	a teashop keeper
chanā	dried chickpeas or lentils
chāṭ	a savory snack food
Chauk	the center of a neighborhood or city
chaurāhā	a crossing of four roads
chhēnā	a kind of cottage cheese
chhoṭē log	the lower classes; literally, the small people
dāl	a lentil dish, commonly eaten once a day in Northern India
dangal	a wrestling match
darshan	an auspicious sight for Hindus

Dassehrā	a Hindu festival when the Rāmlīlā is staged
desī	indigenous, old-fashioned
dharma	the law of nature
ḍholak	a two-sided drum, used mostly in folk music
dhotī	a traditional garment worn by men on the lower body and consisting of one long stretch of white cotton wrapped around the waist and between the legs
Dīwālī	a major Hindu festival, with worship of Lakshmi
Ḍom	a caste, mostly cremation ground workers
dosā	a South Indian snack
Duldul	a Muslim procession at Moharram
dulhā	a bridegroom
dupaṭṭā	a scarf worn by women in different styles over the chest
Durgā	a major form of the goddess in Hinduism
Durgā Pujā	the festival of Durga's worship, coinciding with the last days of Rāmlīlā
gadā	a long tapering weight used for body building
gaddī	a seat of business, marked by white sheets and bolsters
galī	a narrow lane
gamchhā	an all-purpose cotton scarf traditionally carried by men
Ganesh	a Hindu god, for whose public worship a procession is taken out

Gangā	the Hindi term for the Ganges river; also a Hindu goddess
garīb	poor, used only in the literal sense
gaunhārin	a professional female singer at life-cycle ceremonies
ghāṭ	a riverbank
ghī	clarified butter (the real thing); also a vegetable oil product
guru	a teacher; also a form of direct address
Hanumān	a Hindu deity, in form like a langur monkey
Harijan	a name used for some untouchable castes
hīrā	diamond
Holī	a major Hindu festival in the spring; also (lowercased) a genre of folk music
Īshwar	God, for Hindus
jānghiā	underpants
jhulā	a swing
jijjī	an older sister; an affectionate form of address
joṛī	a pair of clubs that are swung, used for body building
Julāhā	a traditional name for weavers, regarded as derogatory and not used in Banaras now
julus	a procession, such as at Durgā Pujā, Moharram, Vishwakarmā Puja
kachchā	consisting of clay and thatch
kachoṛī	a deep-fried, lentil- and spice-filled savory; also the name of a famous lane in Banaras where these delicacies are sold
kajlī	a musical genre of the monsoons

kalā	art
kalākār	an artist
Kālī	a Hindu goddess
kārigar	an artisan, a craftsman
kārkhānā	a workshop or factory; a loom
karmakāṇḍī	a specialist on Hindu rituals
Kasērā	a Hindu caste, usually metalworkers
Kāyastha	a Hindu caste, traditionally scribes and bureaucrats
khamsā	a form of folk music
koṭhari	a small, closed room, usually used as a storeroom
kotwāl	historically, the chief police officer in a city
kshetra	an area of operation, a field
kuṇḍ	a tank, an artificial reservoir of water used in Banaras for bathing and rituals
kurtā	an upper shirt-like garment, usually worn by men over a *dhotī*, or pajamas
laḍḍu	a round sweet, commonly seen at festivities
Lakshmana	the brother of Rama in the epic *Ramayana*
Lakshmī	the goddess of wealth and prosperity in Hinduism
langoṭ	a small string and cloth contraption worn by men underneath the *janghia* when exercising, somewhat like the U.S. jock strap
lāṭhī	a bamboo pole, often carried by policemen
lekhikā	a woman writer

loṭā	a round brass or copper vessel used for washing up
madrasā (also *Madrasāh*)	a Muslim school, usually for higher studies
Mahādev	the great god, a name for Shiva
mahant	the chief priest of a temple
majār (also *mazār*)	a Muslim shrine
mandir	a Hindu temple
manoranjan	entertainment
marsiyā (also *marsiyah*)	music composed and sung at Moharram
maṭh	a Hindu monastery
maulānā	a Muslim wise man, a religious leader
maulvi	a learned and religious man, an interpreter of Islamic law
mausā	mother's sister's husband; usually a form of address
melā	a fair
memsāhib	a lady, a "ma'am" sahab
mohallā	a formally delineated neighborhood in a city
Moharram	a Muslim mourning period with a festival of the same name, differently celebrated, but always with a *tāziyā*
moksha	release from rebirth, in the Hindu system
muṇḍan	the ritual shaving of a child's hair
mushairā	a public reading of Urdu poetry
nahānā-nipaṭanā	defecation and bathing
nakkās	a repoussé worker
namaste	a greeting of respect with two hands joined
nawāb	an aristocrat, a lord, typically Muslim

nawābī	aristocratic
nīch qaum	the lower classes or castes
nīm	*margosa indica*
pakkā	literally, of masonry; figuratively, solid, correct
pān	a betel leaf wrapped around some condiments
paṇḍā	a Hindu priest, usually a pilgrim priest
paṇḍit	a Hindu priest, usually a domestic or temple priest
pankhā	a ceiling fan, once of cloth, operated manually by pulling a rope
pānwāllā	a seller of *pan*
pāpaṛ	a paper-thin savory made of dried lentils
parāṭhā	bread toasted in *ghī*
pardāh	curtain, the predominantly Muslim custom of keeping secluded from the public
Pārsī	a religious community based in Western India
Paṭhān	one of the upper classes, or lineages, of Muslims
paṭṭīdār	a co-sharer of property
piṇḍa	a Hindu ritual performed in memory of the deceased; literally, a ball, symbolizing a body
prasād	the leavings of God or of someone special, for Hindus
pujā	a ritual of worship
puṛī	deep-fried bread
raīs	the landed gentry, traditionally patrons of culture

rākhī	a ritual thread tied by a Hindu woman or girl on her brother's wrist
Rāma	a major deity of the Hindus, hero of the *Rāmāyānā*
Rāmāyānā	the epic of Rama, written 1,700 to 2,300 years ago
Rāmcharitmānas	a seventeenth-century rendering of Rama's story
Rāmlīlā	the annual performance of excerpts from the *Rāmāyānā* and *Rāmacharitmānas*
Rāvana	the antagonist of Rama in the epic
riāz	a disciplined practice
roṭī	dry home-baked bread
sādhu	a Hindu monk, an ascetic
salwār kamīz	the Punjabi pant- and shirt-suit, in U.P. usually worn by young women and considered fashionable
samrāṭ	an emperor
sardār	a head, a leader
saṭṭī	a wholesale market
Sāwan	a monsoon month on the Hindu calendar, season for *kajlī*
shauk	fondness, passion
shaukīn	one of good taste
shāyarā	a woman poet
sherwānī	a formal knee-length coat, part of Islamic culture
Shiva	a major Hindu deity, the presiding deity of Banaras
Shobe-raat	a Muslim festival with all-night activity at shrines
sīdhā pallā	an old-fashioned style of wearing the sari

sindur	the vermilion powder used by married Hindu women in the part in their hair
Sitalā	the Hindu smallpox goddess
solah	sixteen
sringār	an annual celebration at Hindu temples and shrines
Srivāstava	a last name used by Kāyasthas
taujī	a father's oldest brother
thānā	a police station
Upanishads	Hindu sacred literature dealing with abstract philosophy
Vaishya	a caste cluster, usually traders
Vedas	Hindu sacred literature in Sanskrit, meant to be chanted
vidāī	a ritual farewell to a daughter leaving the natal home
Vishwakarmā	a Hindu deity, supreme craftsman, crafter of the universe
Yādav	a Hindu caste, usually milksellers; same as Ahir
zarī	the gold and silver thread used in Banarasi sari weaving and for embroidery

Index

Adampura, 29, 156; Holi in, 204–5, 207; *thana*, 148–54, 204, 206; weavers in, 67, 99
Aj (Hindi newspaper), 84, 146, 223–24
Akbar, Nazir, 198, 227–28
Akharas, 49, 89, 124, 195–201
Alimuddin, 168, 189, 227–28
American Institute of Indian Studies, 28
Animals, 165, 214; cows and bulls in roads, 37, 55, 107; monkeys in living areas, 32–33, 65, 224, 231
Annaprasana, 133–34, 138
Ansari, Kamruddin, 96–97
Ansaris, 96–97, 99–105
Anthropological Notes and Queries, 203
Apana Swasthya (Our Health), 79
Archives, 10; of Banaras Hindu University, 125; of Collectorate, 219–20; in Lucknow, 211, 216–19; of Morarilal Kedia, 224; of Nagari Pracharini Sabha, 40, 46, 48–53, 119, 146–47, 218–19, 223–24; of Nagar Mahapalika, 220–23; of Uttar Pradesh, 124, 211
Artisans of Banaras: Popular Culture and Identity (Kumar), 229–30
Aryan Kashtha Kala Mandir (Aryan Temple of Wooden Art), 84
Ayah. See Servants

Bahl, Prem Mohan, 195–96, 198, 201
Bahri alang. See Picnics
Banaras, 27, 36–40, 188–89; beggars in, 36–37, 211; Collectorate,

219–20; filth in roads of, 31, 55, 90, 171, 212; hospitality of, 19, 165–66; map of, 29; newspaper of, 52–53, 73, 146; as prison, 212–13; public behavior in, 174; speech impediment in, 161–63; traveling within, 41–46, 111–12, 181. *See also* Chauk
Banaras Hindu University, 29, 125, 134, 224–25
Banaras Silk Corporation (BSC), 67–68
Beggars, 36–37, 211
Bhang, 81–83
Bharat Jiwan (Banaras newspaper), 52–53, 73, 146
Bharat Sewa Sangh *sadhus*, 118, 130
Bhelupura, 27, 29; *thana*, 30, 96, 118–19, 121
Bhojpuri language, 95, 233; as language of Banarasi, 16, 100, 103–4, 196; and resistance to other languages, 87–88
Bismillah, Abdul, *Jhini Jhini Bini Chadariya*, 11–12
Boating, 37, 187
Body-building, 195–202
Bribes, 222–23
Bureaucracy, 14–15; and archival materials, 223–25; and Indian distrust of officials, 117–18, 217–19; and police officials, 30, 117

Calcutta, 127, 133, 138, 141
Cantonments, 12, 14, 38–39
Carpenters, 45, 111
Castes, 15–16, 51; of traders, 89; of weavers, 102; of woodworkers, 84, 87. *See also* Classes

253

Compositor: BookMasters, Inc.
       Text: 10/12 Palatino
    Display: Palatino
     Printer: Haddon Craftsmen
      Binder: Haddon Craftsmen